PAUL

CAPTAIN

CUFFEE

1812.

ENGRAVED FOR ABM. L. PENNOCK, BY MASON & MASS.

PHOTOGRAPH REPRODUCED WITH PERMISSION
OF THE WHALING MUSEUM, NEW BEDFORD, MASS.

Paul Cuffe

BLACK AMERICA AND THE AFRICAN RETURN

Sheldon H. Harris

SIMON AND SCHUSTER
NEW YORK

ACKNOWLEDGMENTS

In the course of writing this book I received help and encouragement from many friends, teachers and librarians. Their unstinting willingness to share their knowledge and institutional resources with me was a constant reminder of the generosity of the academic profession to one of its own. It also demonstrated to me the need for scholarly humility, because genuine scholarship is truly a cooperative venture.

My foremost obligation is to my friend Herbert Hill. His patient understanding of the many problems I encountered in completing my work, his quiet encouragement and his timely and perceptive analytical suggestions materially improved this study.

The following friends read the manuscript in its various stages and by raising thoughtful questions and offering honest and provocative criticism helped me to avoid many pitfalls and errors of fact and judgment: Professor Norman Holmes Pearson, of Yale University; Professor John Hope Franklin, of the University of Chicago; Professor Earl J. Dias, of Southeastern Massachusetts University; Professors Paul Koistinen, Reba Soffer and Rena Vassar, of the San Fernando Valley State College History Department; Mr. Maynard Robinson, of the California State Colleges Chancellor's office; and Mr. Allen Block, of the University of California at Los Angeles.

The Trustees of the New Bedford, Massachusetts, Free Public Library own the copyrights to the Paul Cuffe papers. I am grateful to them for permission to publish freely from the collection. I also want to thank the library staff for their help.

Miss Rita Steele and her able staff at the Millicent Library, Fairhaven, Massachusetts, rendered me frequent and efficient assistance. The staffs of the Library of Congress, Boston Public Library, National Archives, New Bedford Whaling Museum, Rhode Island Historical Society, New York Public Library, New-York Historical Society, and the superb librarians of the San Fernando Valley State College Library made my research a pleasurable experience.

Providential grants from the American Council of Learned Societies and the San Fernando Valley State College Research Foundation enabled me to complete my field research.

Mesdames Margaret Ball, Selma Rosenfeld, Nancy Meadows, Christy Robinson and Rosemary Buttera with good humor and great skill typed countless drafts of this manuscript.

Finally, a special thanks to my children Robin and David, two lively youngsters who patiently accepted a father who was all too often preoccupied with things as they were in the uncomplicated life style of one hundred and fifty years ago rather than in their complex contemporary world.

S.H.H.

Granada Hills, California
July, 1971

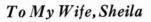

To My Wife, Sheila

Contents

I advance it, therefore, as a suspicion only, that the blacks, whether originally a distinct race, or made distinct by time and circumstance, are inferior to the whites in the endowment both of body and of mind.—THOMAS JEFFERSON, *1784*

[Negro] amalgamation with the other color produces a degradation to which no lover of his country, no lover of excellence in the human character can innocently consent.—THOMAS JEFFERSON, *1814*

The plan of converting the blacks into Serfs would certainly be better than keeping them in their present condition, but I consider that of expatriation to the governments of . . . their own colour as entirely practicable, and greatly preferable to the mixture of colour here. To this I have great aversion.—THOMAS JEFFERSON, *1816*

Political, social and industrial America will never become so converted as to be willing to share up equitably between black and white. . . . If you cannot live alongside the white man in peace; if you cannot get the same chance and opportunity alongside the white man, even though you are his fellow citizen; if he claims that you are not entitled to this chance or opportunity because the country is his by force of numbers—then find a country of your own and rise to the highest position within that country.—MARCUS GARVEY

Everything that comes out of Europe, every blue-eyed thing, is already an American. And as long as you and I have been over here, we aren't Americans yet. They don't have to pass civil rights legislation to make a Polack an American.—MALCOLM X

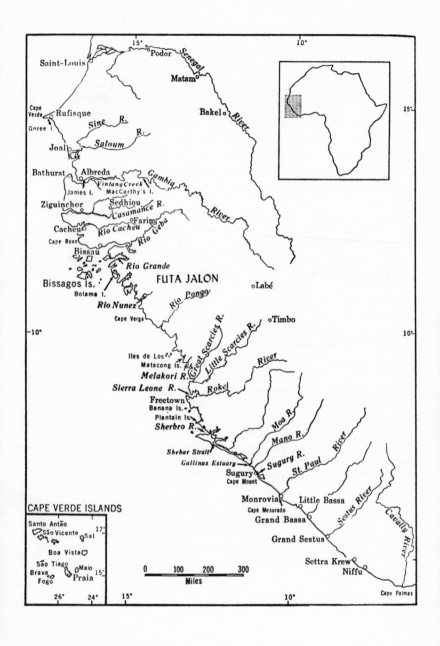

I

"A well-known man of color"

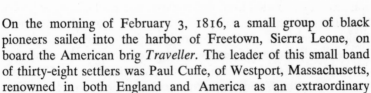

On the morning of February 3, 1816, a small group of black pioneers sailed into the harbor of Freetown, Sierra Leone, on board the American brig *Traveller*. The leader of this small band of thirty-eight settlers was Paul Cuffe, of Westport, Massachusetts, renowned in both England and America as an extraordinary phenomenon—a black who was a wealthy man of property, a petitioner for equal rights for blacks, owner of a fleet of vessels, an able sea captain, founder of a public school, a devout Quaker, friend of President James Madison—and now sponsor of the first black nationalist movement in America to attempt the African return.

In America other movements that had attempted to colonize Africa with American free Negroes met with little success, prior to Paul Cuffe. These other colonizing efforts had all been the work of white men who were eager for solutions to the embarrassing presence of black Americans. For, whatever their differences on other issues, the settlers who came to America from England and Europe were in agreement on one thing: that this land was predestined to become a white man's country, and therefore, the Negro, free or slave, was not accepted as part of the American community. Article I, Section 2 of the Constitution of the new United States fortified the nonperson status assigned to the Negro by decreeing that a black slave was the equivalent of three fifths of a person.

To most white men, blacks were members of a despised and

innately inferior race, and consequently it was widely believed that when in close and constant contact the two races of necessity created a "mutual antipathy." Although slavery long continued to be accepted both in the North and in the South, by the eighteenth century, an ambivalence such as that expressed by Jefferson in reconciling slavery with the spirit of the Declaration of Independence required a new solution. The idea of colonization seemed at first a reasonable and logical one. Given the racist attitudes of white Americans, this argument maintained, the only realistic long-term remedy was to colonize Negroes in another part of the world. It did not matter where the despised population chose to settle so long as they departed from this country. Gradually, however, most colonizers fastened on Africa as the promised land for America's émigrés, since an African return promised many dividends: it would rid the nation of an unwanted people, and at the same time it would return to Africa her own people, now properly Christianized and civilized, and prepared to convert the native population. These black missionary, civilizing and relocation projects occupied the thoughts of many humanitarians in the eighteenth century, but inadequate finances and simplistic thinking about the obstacles involved in any mass relocation scheme contributed finally to their failure. Most importantly, perhaps, was another factor the eager colonizers had not counted on: the reluctance of Negroes to cooperate. Despite their difficult conditions here, few free Negroes were willing to abandon this country permanently for any white man's utopian promises.

It was not until more than a century after the first white-sponsored colonization project was proposed that Paul Cuffe's group of black nationalists ventured to settle on the Dark Continent. In each generation since, Negro Americans have debated anew this crucial question of their relationship to Africa. In our own time, the intransigence of American racism and the power of black nationalism as an idea have again posed the difficult question of the African return. Whatever the merits of that complex argument today, it is evident that Paul Cuffe in his life and career was the first to demonstrate the significance of this idea in the lives of Negro Americans.

The presence of Paul Cuffe's family in Massachusetts at an early date can be easily documented. Paul Cuffe's father, Cuffe Slocum, emigrated involuntarily from the west coast of Africa to the Bay State in 1728; he was ten or eleven years old when he disembarked at Buzzards Bay, the entryway to mainland southeastern Massachusetts. Cuffe Slocum's birthplace is unknown, but "Kofi," "Koffe," et cetera, are common surnames in Ghana, and it is assumed that he was of Ghanaian origin.[1] The young man was a slave of Captain Ebenezer Slocum, of the town of Dartmouth, Bristol County, Massachusetts. Some fifteen years later, on February 16, 1742, Captain Slocum sold "a certain negro man of about twenty-five years of age named 'Cuffe' " to John Slocum for £150 current money or payable bills of exchange.[2]

There is a family story, apocryphal perhaps, that John Slocum worked out an agreement with Cuffe whereby the slave in a few years' time could acquire his freedom. By securing employment at odd jobs here and there after attending to his master's daily assigned tasks, Cuffe Slocum was able to save enough money to procure his liberty.[3] Whatever the case, less than three years after John Slocum purchased his slave from Captain Ebenezer Slocum, Cuffe Slocum was a free man.

Shortly after achieving his freedom, Cuffe Slocum's engagement to Ruth Moses, a Gayhead Indian descended from the once powerful Wampanoag tribe, the Indian confederation that under their mighty leader King Philip terrorized eastern Massachusetts during the mid-1670's, was announced publicly on January 3, 1745. Cuffe Slocum and Ruth Moses were married by the Reverend Philip Taber on July 7, 1746.[4]

[1] Christopher Fyfe to the author, Bristol, England, August 8, 1962. Professor Fyfe, without question, is the leading Occidental authority on West African history in the eighteenth and nineteenth centuries. His monumental *History of Sierra Leone* is *the* definitive history of Sierra Leone.

[2] Original bill of sale dated February 16, 1742, Paul Cuffe papers, New Bedford Free Public Library.

[3] "Ms. Memorandum of Ruth Cuffe," Fall River, Massachusetts, February 12, 1851, Cuffe papers. See Appendix A for the text of Ruth Cuffe's statement.

[4] Ms. memorandum of family marriages, Cuffe papers.

Little more is known about the Cuffe Slocums. However, from the scanty evidence scattered among the manuscripts of Cuffe Slocum's son, it can be reasonably inferred that the newlyweds settled among the Indians living in Cuttyhunk, one of a chain of sixteen diminutive islands midway between the Massachusetts mainland and Martha's Vineyard. These tiny specks of land were called collectively the Elizabeth Islands; and Cuttyhunk, its 516 acres blessed with fertile soil and dense woods, was the largest and most populous of the islands.[5] Here Cuffe Slocum engaged in farming and in fishing.[6] Apparently all ten of the Slocum children, four boys and six girls, were born in Cuttyhunk. Here too Cuffe Slocum prospered. Later on, the Slocums moved to Martha's Vineyard, settling near the little town of Chilmark. Good fortune continued to attend Cuffe Slocum, and on December 15, 1766, he purchased from one David Brownell a 120 acre farm in Westport, a fishing and farming community on the mainland. Located some nine or ten miles from the soon-to-be-thriving whaling port of New Bedford, the farm cost its new owner the substantial sum of six hundred and fifty Spanish milled dollars.[7]

By the time Cuffe Slocum relocated in Westport, the village and its environs had taken on the appearance of a long-established and reasonably prosperous community. Not many blacks—either slave or free—resided in Westport. Like Cuffe Slocum during his bond-man's days, a few were employed there as household servants, while several free blacks tried their hand at farming for a living. The community, of course, discriminated against the free Negroes and tended to regard all blacks as inferior beings. On the other hand, masters did not treat their slaves with the cruelty so common in the South, nor were the slaves worked as hard. But life in Westport was not exactly paradisical for the black man.

In general, Negroes were scarce in southeastern Massachusetts. There were only thirty-four blacks in all of Dartmouth Township

---

[5] Daniel Ricketson, *The History of New Bedford,* p. 130.

[6] Many Wampanoag Indians still live on Cuttyhunk and the other Elizabeth Islands today. They eke out a living by commercial fishing and by farming.

[7] Ms. bill of sale, "Cuffe Scrapbook," Cuffe papers.

in 1754.[8] In 1776 Bristol County, Dartmouth's home county, counted a total of five hundred eighty-three Negroes. This broke down to 2.1 percent of the county's 27,241 residents.[9] Thus, their impact on the region was slight indeed.

Cuffe Slocum died in Westport in March, 1772. His wife, Ruth, endured a lonely widowhood on the family farm for fifteen years, until—as John Cuffe Slocum recorded it—"Our honored good old Mother . . . deceased the sixth day of January 1787, at eight O'Clock in the morning."[10]

Paul Cuffe, the youngest boy in the family, was born on January 17, 1759.[11] Not much is known of his youth except that it was spent principally in hard work on the family farm. There was little leisure time available for the Cuffes. As a result, Paul's formal education was brief and limited. He was largely self-taught, and even at maturity he was only semiliterate. Nevertheless, Paul Cuffe's native intelligence more than compensated for his literary imperfections and inadequate education. Although his spelling and punctuation were unique, even for a society blessed by the efforts of the great lexicographer Noah Webster to create simplified and Americanized spelling, he did not find these deficiencies a great hindrance to personal success in his later life.[12]

Cuffe Slocum evidently had considerable confidence in his young son's abilities, since he bequeathed the family farm jointly to Paul and his older brother John.[13] Consequently, at the tender age of thirteen, Paul Cuffe had to shoulder a large part of the responsibility of providing support for his widowed mother and his three younger sisters. The dedicated manner in which he took up his new obligations amply evidenced a profound concern for his

8 Lorenzo J. Greene, *The Negro in Colonial New England, 1620–1776,* Appendix A, p. 239.

9 *Ibid.,* Appendix C, p. 342.

10 John Cuffe Slocum Ms. memorandum, n.d., Cuffe papers.

11 Sometime in the 1770's the family dropped the cognomen Slocum, replacing it with Cuffe Slocum's Christian name as their surname.

12 For the convenience of the reader I have altered Cuffe's spelling and included the appropriate punctuation in all the Cuffe passages quoted in this Introduction.

13 Ms. Deed of Indenture, March 26, 1785, Cuffe papers.

family's well-being—a concern that was to be one of his strongest characteristics.

Although the Cuffe farm seemingly produced enough food to supply the family's needs, Paul soon became dissatisfied with the scant income the New England land could provide him. Like many of his white Yankee contemporaries, young Cuffe looked to the sea to brighten his prospects. He was never to turn his back completely on farming—even after amassing a considerable fortune from maritime activities—but by the age of sixteen Cuffe had entered upon the career that he was to pursue for the remainder of his days. As he put it in his journal in later years, Paul Cuffe became a "Marineer." That this black Yankee succeeded in his chosen profession is all the more remarkable, given the ever-present racial prejudices of the late eighteenth century.

At first he sailed as an ordinary seaman. He made voyages aboard whalers as well as on regular commercial vessels. In fact, Cuffe's initial passage was on a whaling bark that hunted the great leviathans in the Gulf of Mexico. Following this trip, he signed as a common hand on board a general cargo vessel bound for the West Indies. His third cruise was brief but eventful. The young mariner's ship was captured by the British in 1776, and Cuffe and his crewmates were imprisoned in New York. After detaining him there for three months, the British permitted him to return home to Westport. Here he remained in premature retirement for more than a year, reflecting on his recent adventures. By 1778, however, he resumed his maritime career, embarking on still another voyage to the Caribbean.[14]

Cuffe's horizons as well as his knowledge of seamanship expanded enormously because of these youthful experiences. He not only became familiar with the navigational hazards normally encountered in the Gulf of Mexico, in the Caribbean, among the West Indies, off South America, and the like, but also was intro-

---

[14] Information concerning Cuffe's seagoing activities as a young man is singularly scarce. All secondary accounts, including this one, rely substantially on a two-part biographical sketch of Paul Cuffe published in the Liverpool *Mercury,* October 4 and 11, 1811. Since Cuffe was in Liverpool at the time, it is reasonable to assume that he furnished the data the newspaper printed.

duced to different societies and their mores. These early voyages served as a kind of apprenticeship period for Paul Cuffe. He was learning his trade under the watchful eye of professionals; he was also acquiring knowledge concerning the white man's prejudice as it related to the black-skinned inhabitants of the Western Hemisphere.

In 1779, Cuffe and his brother David decided to go into business for themselves. The time seemingly was propitious for new ventures in the coastal trade. Old patterns of commerce and old business relationships had foundered in the wake of the American Revolution. Two hard-working, enterprising, adventurous, frugal, honest young men could by dint of their industry make their way as a result of the new opportunities that were opening. The Cuffe brothers built a small boat adequate to carry on trading with the little fishing and farming communities in Buzzards Bay, Narragansett Bay off the Massachusetts–Rhode Island border, and in Long Island Sound.

Paul and David Cuffe may also have engaged in blockade running as well as in legitimate commercial activities. At this time the British stationed a sizable naval force off the New England coast. A successful blockade runner not only received a premium for whatever goods he managed to sneak through the barrier of enemy ships, but also was considered to have rendered great service to the patriot cause. Still, although the coastwise trade offered promise of success, this type of enterprise was not without its hazards. In addition to the ever-present threat of interference or seizure by British patrol vessels, the bays and inlets of the area were infested with pirates. Not overly concerned with considerations of loyalty or patriotism, these cutthroat freebooters pounced on any boat that offered prospect for plunder.

The Cuffes' small boat was attacked by some bold brigands a few months after it had entered the coastal trade. This initial brush with the seagoing criminal class so impressed David Cuffe that he abandoned his partnership with Paul and retreated permanently to the family farm. Paul Cuffe was made of sterner fiber, and he resolved to return to maritime ventures at an auspicious time.[15] Some months later Paul did, indeed, resume his activities in local

[15] Liverpool *Mercury,* October 4, 1811.

waters only to suffer further humiliations at the hands of local
buccaneers. Still, he persisted, and by the mid-1780's Paul Cuffe
was on his way to becoming a successful mariner.

Each year, seemingly, Cuffe invested the profits of a previous
voyage into building a still bigger vessel. He began with an open
boat and then expanded to a 14 or 15 ton closed-deck boat called
Box Iron, which was succeeded by a small schooner of some 18 or
20 tons. In the late 1780's Cuffe's flagship became the 25 ton
schooner *Sun Fish,* named because the first fish caught from her
deck was a sunfish. *Sun Fish* was followed by the 40 ton schooner
Mary. Then *Mary* yielded to *Ranger* in 1795, a 69 ton schooner.[16]
By 1800 Cuffe's fortunes had advanced to such a degree that he
arranged for the construction of the bark *Hero,* some 162 tons. By
comparison with *Box Iron,* the 268-ton sloop *Alpha,* launched in
1806, was a leviathan. Also built in 1806 was the 109 ton brig
Traveller, the ship that ultimately became Cuffe's favorite vessel.[17]

By the turn of the century this black man from Westport was
well on his way to fulfilling the American Dream. Some thirty
years before the birth of Horatio Alger, Cuffe became the arche-
typal hero of the Alger story: the man who progresses from rags to
riches. Here was a man who—in the tradition of Benjamin Franklin and the other sages of the Protestant ethic—early in life
acknowledged that he was nothing but an insignificant person,
born with the "wrong" skin color, yet determined to make something of himself. His rapid rise (in spite of his blackness) and the
manner in which he achieved his station were in keeping with the
most persistent and powerful theme in nineteenth-century
America: the success story of the self-made man.

Cuffe sailed in whatever direction business prospects suggested.
He engaged in whaling; he carried lumber, animals, foodstuffs and
general cargo between New Bedford, Martha's Vineyard and
Nantucket. His vessels were to be found off St. Georges Banks

[16] The Westport sea captain did not keep all the boats he built. Some of
the smaller craft were sold when their larger successors were completed. On
occasion Cuffe would sell a boat to raise cash. Nevertheless, in his later
years he maintained either part or full interest in a fleet of ships: *Hero,
Alpha* and *Traveller* formed the nucleus of the Cuffe flotilla of merchant-
men. See various entries in the Cuffe Journal.

[17] Ms. memorandum of John Wainer, n.d., Cuffe papers.

employed in commercial competition with his Yankee compatriots. He hauled miscellaneous cargo to Philadelphia, to Wilmington, Delaware, and to Baltimore, Maryland. He transported cargo to the Baltic and to the Caribbean.

Energetic, bold, determined and inventive, Cuffe made ample use of these qualities and others during his voyages. An illustration of these virtues occurred during an incident that took place in 1793. Sometime that summer Cuffe embarked on a whaling expedition to the Strait of Belle Isle off the northwest coast of Newfoundland. There he discovered four rival vessels, fully equipped with boats and harpoons to hunt the whales. Paul discovered also that "he had not made proper preparations for the business, having only ten hands on board and two boats, one of which was old and almost useless." As soon as "the masters of the other vessels found his situation, they withdrew from the customary practice of such voyages and refused to mate with his crew."[18] Turning the other cheek against this slight, as he was required to do so often in order to survive,

> in this emergency Paul resolved to prosecute his undertaking alone, till at length the other vessels thought it most prudent to accede to the usual practice: as they apprehended, his crew by their ignorance, might alarm and drive the whales from their reach, and thus defeat their voyages.

But the victory remained with the black sea captain, since

> during the season, they [the combined fleet] took seven whales. The circumstances which had taken place roused the ambition of Paul and his crew. They were diligent and enterprising, and had the honor of killing six of the seven whales; two of these fell by Paul's own hands. He returned home in due season, heavily freighted with oil and bone. . . .[19]

Sailing for the most part with a crew that consisted solely of Negroes and Indians, the intrepid sea captain ventured into ports

[18] This statement reflects Cuffe's reluctance to attribute openly base motives to those who were unkind to him. Obviously, racial prejudice was a contributing, if not the major, factor in the initial aloofness displayed by the other masters and crews.

[19] All quotations are taken from the Liverpool *Mercury,* October 11, 1811.

in the American South. No doubt he and his men at times caused consternation there among the local citizenry. And, of course, Cuffe was sensitive to the ever-present racism of his contemporaries, both Northern and Southern.

Customarily he endeavored to overlook surliness and rudeness whenever he encountered it. He preferred to use the soft-sell approach, as with the whaling episode off Belle Isle. For much of his career he employed the tactic of quietly demonstrating to skeptics and detractors that black men possess the talents and skills necessary for achieving success. This course of action frequently won for him and his men acceptance even in Southern communities, where fear of and hostility to "men of color" was the rule.

Cuffe was too proud a man, however, to make compromises with his integrity. No matter what the goal or the opportunity open for personal gain, he would never lower himself to play the role of Sambo, the slobbering, fawning, clownish near-idiot that white America customarily associated with Negroes. But like other black men he realized that he was required to play-act, too. To get ahead, he had to fool the white man by playing the white man's game. Thus, he once advised a nephew who was about to sail on a voyage as a mate under a white captain

> thou art not insensible how much this captain has suffered in his feelings before he could consent to receive thee, a person of color, to be his Mate, to sit at his table, and to have a share in the government of the ship. . . . Now I advise thee, as a part of thy duty, to be so much the more modest, respectful and condescending in thy deportment towards him, as to counterbalance this sacrifice of private feeling.[20]

Another case in point occurred in the winter of 1795–96. Alerted to the possibility of securing a schooner load of corn at a favorable price, the Westport captain navigated *Ranger* up the Nanticoke River to the tiny community of Vienna, Maryland. His arrival filled the local populace with "astonishment and alarm." A vessel owned and commanded by a black man and "manned with a

[20] Boston *Weekly Recorder,* November 4, 1817, p. 186.

crew of the same complexion, was unprecedented and surprising." Local leaders feared that Cuffe and his men were there to stir up mischief. Many suspected that he was planning to lead a slave revolt. Some urged Customs officials to deny his vessel a landing permit. Since his papers were in order, however, Customs reluctantly authorized *Ranger's* entry.

Aware of local apprehensions, Cuffe combined "prudence with resolution," conducting himself with "candor, modesty and firmness." His men behaved "not only inoffensively, but with a conciliating propriety." In a few days' time Vienna's nervousness was replaced with "respect and kindness." The most prominent member of its aristocracy entertained Cuffe in his home. Others visited *Ranger,* and returned from their adventure shaken by the experience of having fraternized with intelligent, articulate, skilled Negroes and Indians.

In three weeks' time, Cuffe successfully completed his transactions in Vienna. He sailed for Westport with a cargo of three thousand bushels of corn, which ultimately yielded him a net profit of more than one thousand dollars.[21] Despite the initial frosty greeting in Vienna, Cuffe and his crew in most instances received remarkably cordial receptions in most communities, North and South, when one considers the prejudices of the time.[22]

Over the years Cuffe succeeded so completely in deceiving white folk concerning his sensitivity to racial slurs that after his death a reporter, unconsciously revealing his own racism, complimented the decedent for "his great civility." The writer observed, moreover, that "the marks of attention which he received did not render him vain and arrogant. He knew the place which propriety required him to occupy, and he could yield to a popular, or even unreasonable prejudice without resentment."[23] This was the behavior white America expected of even outstanding black men.

[21] *Ibid.*

[22] In 1806, for example, *Traveller* delivered some 300 bushels of apples to Savannah, Georgia. *Traveller's* captain and crew were so delighted with the welcome Savannah offered them that they remained there more than three months. Sheldon H. Harris, "Paul Cuffe's White Apprentice," *American Neptune,* XXIII (July, 1963), pp. 192–96.

[23] Boston *Weekly Recorder,* November 4, 1817, p. 186.

As his business enterprises increased, so too did Cuffe's contacts with the business elite of southeastern New England. Many of these business associations ultimately blossomed into warm personal friendships. Prominent among those who considered it a mark of distinction to be Cuffe's friend was William Rotch, Jr., scion of one of New Bedford's most important whaling-banking-manufacturing families. Rotch was fascinated with Cuffe's struggle for success and acceptance. He took an inordinate interest in Cuffe's affairs, always with a concern for Cuffe's well-being.

Rotch frequently employed Cuffe to transport lumber, food supplies, general merchandise, et cetera, from New Bedford on the mainland to Martha's Vineyard and to Nantucket. Occasionally, the two men engaged in joint commercial enterprises. Their mutual affection and trust was so great that Cuffe usually consulted with this friend first before commencing any major venture. Because of his encouragement and advocacy, William Rotch, Jr., must be ranked as the sea captain's leading companion, counselor and protector.[24]

Still, despite their close relationship, Cuffe could never forget that he was a black man dealing with a white man. An incident, slight in itself, illustrates clearly how Cuffe behaved with his benefactors. Rotch, his father, and some visiting English Quakers attended church services in Westport one day in 1810. After services Cuffe invited these distinguished gentlemen to dine at his home. "After the dinner was laid upon the table in a neat and bountiful manner," William Rotch, Sr., "observed that Paul and his wife had no chairs set for themselves, and were modestly preparing to retire or remain until their guests had dined." Rotch would hear nothing of the kind. He "arose, and, in a firm but kind manner, addressing his host and hostess, said that he could not consent to such an arrangement, and that he should not take his seat at the table unless Paul and his wife presided." Moreover, "with all his

---

[24] The Cuffe papers contain a substantial number of Rotch business letters, bills of lading, and other commercial documents. In addition, there are several revealing letters of a personal nature. See also Augustine Jones, "William Rotch of Nantucket," *American Friend*, VIII (May, 1901), pp. 413–16, 440–43; Ricketson, *History of New Bedford*, pp. 253–62.

gentleness and humanity, no man was more unflinching where a matter of conscience was concerned than Friend Rotch, and Paul was too well acquainted with this trait in his friend's character to demur. The company was soon seated, and an agreeable as well as bountiful dinner partaken of."[25]

Next to the Rotches, Moses Brown and other members of this notable Providence, Rhode Island, family[26] were the most important and influential of Cuffe's white supporters. The Brown family showed Cuffe their affection in myriad ways over the years. Merchant capitalists, bankers, sponsors of Samuel Slater's cotton textile mill in nearby Pawtucket (the first to be established successfully in the United States), the Browns of Providence were also noted for their philanthropic activities, particularly in the field of education, and for their dedication to the abolition of slavery in America. What with their concern for Negro emancipation and their close business connections with leading New Bedford commercial interests, it was inevitable that Cuffe should be drawn into the Brown family's orbit. Cuffe's journal entries for late April, 1812, offer eloquent testimony to the unyielding confidence and unquenchable loyalty Moses Brown and his son Obediah manifested for him in his hour of greatest need.[27]

Ultimately, Cuffe was to number among his friends prominent attorneys, government officials and community leaders. In short, the Establishment welcomed him as an associate member, but perhaps more as a curiosity than as a social equal.

And to the white man, Cuffe was, indeed, a curiosity, a freak of nature. He seemed so "untypical" of the white community's conception of a black man. Cuffe was sober, industrious and civic-minded. Yet, Negroes were assumed to be licentious, lazy and mentally incapable of governing themselves. In a society in which financial holdings were an important determinant of one's social standing, Cuffe was America's first wealthy Negro. Blacks, how-

[25] Ricketson, *History of New Bedford,* p. 255.

[26] See Mack Thompson, *Moses Brown, Reluctant Reformer, passim.*

[27] Surprisingly, the Cuffe papers are barren of Brown family correspondence, both business and personal. However, it is obvious from the April 25 and 26, 1812, journal entries that Paul Cuffe was a close friend and associate.

ever, were not supposed to have money! No wonder humanitarians never ceased to marvel at his activities, or to hope piously and to cluck patronizingly that it would be so wonderful if other members of the African race would follow Paul Cuffe's example.

Aside from profiting in his business activities from his contacts with important members of the white community, Cuffe gained from them something of even greater value: a new outlook on life. Pre-Irish eighteenth and early nineteenth century Massachusetts was overwhelmingly Congregationalist in its religious affiliation. However, the southeastern section of the state and parts of adjoining Rhode Island harbored a large colony of Quakers. In fact, many of the early settlers of Dartmouth Township were members of the Society of Friends. Quakers selected a six-acre tract in the center of the town and, as far back as 1699, built a Meeting House. The first church erected in the region's metropolis, New Bedford, was the 1785 Friends' Meeting House. Quaker influence was widespread in southern New England throughout the eighteenth century. But membership in the Society began to drop off after 1810 as Quakers split into wrangling factions over doctrinal questions.[28]

In its heyday the Society of Friends proved particularly attractive to the area's business leaders, and one can state with a degree of assurance that most members of the business community were of the Quaker faith. Certainly, the vast majority of Cuffe's white associates were Quakers, and no doubt their religious practices impressed him profoundly.

Little is known of Cuffe's youthful religious beliefs. His parents were Christians,[29] and the children most probably received some religious instruction. However, it is doubtful whether the elder

[28] Still, with all their quarreling, Quakers continued to play an important role in southern Massachusetts in the antebellum period. As late as 1858 they were able to support fourteen Meeting Houses scattered throughout the limits of the old town of Dartmouth. (Ricketson, *History of New Bedford*, pp. 24–40.)

[29] A specialist in Quaker history asserts that Paul Cuffe's parents "had been attenders of the Friends' Meetings." (Henry J. Cadbury, "Negro Membership in the Society of Friends," *The Journal of Negro History*, XXI [April, 1936], p. 197.) It is highly unlikely, however, that either Cuffe or Ruth Slocum ever made application for membership in the Society. No record exists of their having been admitted to the Society of Friends in Westport.

Cuffes attempted to convince their children that one sect or another was the true religion of God. In middle age, Paul Cuffe, as his journal clearly reveals, received spiritual comfort from many religious sources. Just being in God's House afforded Cuffe great solace.

Nevertheless, the Society of Friends had particular appeal for him. Aside from the fact that so many of his well-wishers were believers, the Quaker emphasis on the spiritual equality of all men, Quaker concern for the plight of the American Negro, and increasing Quaker involvement in abolitionist activities tended to draw Cuffe into the Society's orbit. He formally joined the Westport Monthly Meeting of Friends in 1808.[30]

Cuffe's admission to the Society of Friends is, ironically, still another testimony to his unique standing in American life. Few Negroes in the eighteenth and early nineteenth centuries belonged to the Society, for the simple reason that Quakers did not welcome a black presence in their midst. They wanted little formal social contact with black Americans.[31]

Yet, there is no reason to doubt that Quaker commitment to the antislavery movement was genuine and strongly felt. They were among the first to join the antislavery cause. In New England, for example, Quakers as early as their 1773 yearly Meeting banned members from owning slaves, and by 1782 they could proudly note that no Friend in their part of the country owned slaves. Still, despite their antislavery stance, white Quakers were part of a racist society and displayed as much anti-Negro bias as their fellow white Americans. White Quakers failed to recognize any contradiction between their abolitionist commitment and their disdain for the black man.

Thus, many local Meetings refused to admit blacks as members. Other, more tolerant, Meetings permitted Negroes to join their organization, but insisted they attend services on a segregated basis. Many of these Meetings established separate "Negro benches" for their black associates.[32] That Cuffe encountered

---

[30] Ms. memorandum of John Macomber, Westport, January 6, 1851, Cuffe papers.
[31] Thomas E. Drake, *Quakers and Slavery in America,* pp. 70–80.
[32] *Ibid.,* pp. 120–22.

little or no discrimination in his Meeting is sufficient evidence of
the awe with which his Westport neighbors regarded him.

Never content to be just a nominal participant in any venture,
Cuffe brought to this new affiliation the intense dedication and
enthusiasm[33] that he demonstrated for every project he undertook. Cuffe was forty-nine years old at the time of his conversion.
Accepting the basic tenets of the Quaker faith completely, and
acting as if he had been forewarned that his remaining stint in this
world would be brief, the new recruit appeared determined to
prove to himself and to his neighbors that he was, indeed, a
humble but sincere servant of Christ. Consequently, every enterprise, every activity of his co-religionists commanded his vigorous
participation. He plunged into the affairs of the Westport Friends
with a fervor that must have astonished the older and more staid
members of the Meeting. Occasionally, he appeared in the local
ministry, conveying to his fellow communcants a "deep religious
feeling in the meeting."[34]

Other Quaker Meetings soon learned of the Negro sea captain's
piety and religious zeal, and during the course of Cuffe's travels he
was invited frequently to lead these Friends in their devotions. He
once preached such a remarkably powerful sermon in Philadelphia's Arch Street Meeting House—the Westminster Abbey of
Quakerdom—that at its conclusion one of the leading members of
the congregation, "moved [from] his place, and touched his
[Cuffe's] arm, directing him to a seat beside himself, but Paul
Cuffe made a gesture of dissent and walked back down the aisle to
his place among his own people."[35]

Of Cuffe's many services to the Westport Friends, one undertaking is particularly noteworthy. As we have seen, the Quakers had
come to southeastern Massachusetts in the late seventeenth cen-

[33] Although Cuffe's commitment to the Society of Friends was absolute,
evidently his enthusiasm was not duplicated by other members of his family.
Professor Cadbury speculates that "probably few of his family were
officially Friends, though they had Quaker associations" (Cadbury, "Negro
Membership in the Society of Friends," p. 198 fn.)
[34] Horatio P. Howard, *A Self-Made Man, Capt. Paul Cuffee* [sic], p. 27.
[35] Frances Tatum Rhoads, "The Social Life of Yearly Meeting Week—
Past and Present," *The Friends' Meeting-House, Fourth and Arch Streets,
Philadelphia, A Centennial Celebration,* pp. 93–94.

tury. In due course, a Meeting was established in Westport at the beginning of the eighteenth century. Its first Meeting House was dedicated in 1716 in Central Village (also known by its Indian name as Acoaxet), Westport. Quakers were still using the Acoaxet Meeting House a century later, when Cuffe joined the Society. It soon became clear, however, that the old Meeting House would have to be replaced with a larger structure, since the Society of Friends had increased its membership considerably over the years. By 1812 the need for a more commodious Meeting House was critical.

It was at this juncture that Cuffe volunteered to underwrite a substantial share of the cost for a new Meeting House. The pious Quaker, with considerable justification, could have limited his contribution, since his finances were none too secure in 1812–13. It must be remembered, too, that the War of 1812 was raging and, as a consequence, Cuffe's maritime activities were severely restricted. Also, he had suffered reverses from his epochal 1811 voyage to Sierra Leone. That he did not make just a small or token offering is in its own way eloquent confirmation of his consistent adherence to a code of conduct that was forged in early life: personal sacrifice for the well-being of mankind returns an infinitely greater reward than the intrinsic cost of the offering.

Thanks to Cuffe's splendid gift, in 1813 the Westport Friends erected a new Meeting House. The cost of this simple but handsome structure came to not quite twelve hundred dollars.[36] Cuffe contributed almost six hundred dollars in cash and supplies to the building fund.[37]

Although he was a man of such outward humility and self-effacement that at times his modesty appeared carefully studied, Cuffe's commitment and benefactions to the Society of Friends did

[36] Westport Friends still use Cuffe's Meeting House for their religious observances. The building now enjoys most modern conveniences, such as indoor plumbing and electricity, but its exterior has not been altered. The Meeting House was the site for elaborate ceremonies in 1961 celebrating the sesquicentennial anniversary of Paul Cuffe's first voyage to Sierra Leone. See the Boston *Sunday Herald,* October 29, 1961, Sec. IV, p. 3; New Bedford (Mass.) *Standard-Times,* November 6, 1961, p. 1.

[37] Ms. tally sheet of Paul Cuffe's contributions to the Westport Meeting Building Fund, Cuffe papers.

not go unnoticed. Quaker appreciation for his activities found expression in simple but practical ways. Many of Cuffe's business deals after 1808 were developed through his Quaker contacts. Moreover, in the course of his travels, Friends extended to him their warm hospitality and, when necessary, their protection.[38] Prominent Quakers supplied him with letters of recommendation whenever he embarked on ventures to potentially hostile territories.[39] The Westport Meeting furnished the sea captain with "special certificates . . . to faraway places" in at least four instances.[40] In addition, Westport Quakers appointed a large committee in 1810 and again in 1815 to advise their illustrious colleague in the formulation of his plans for Africa. These committees also provided him with letters of endorsement.[41]

Cuffe demonstrated his concern and devotion to community needs and interests in many other ways. One area of special note was his concern with education. As with so many other Americans, Paul Cuffe placed great faith in the ability of the school to provide the wherewithal for subsequent material achievement.

Like his father before him, Cuffe selected an Indian girl for his bride. Paul Cuffe and Alice Pequit, a member of the Wampanoag tribe, were married on February 25, 1783.[42] The marriage was an extremely happy one, despite Cuffe's periodic and prolonged absences from home in the course of his maritime career. Over the years seven children—two sons and five daughters—were born.[43]

Resolved that his children should receive more formal education than he had, Cuffe was distressed and shocked to learn that Westport lacked any school facilities whatsoever. Characteristically, the

[38] See various Cuffe Journal entries in April, May, June, 1812.

[39] Letter of Benjamin Rush, M.D., addressed "to whom it may concern," Philadelphia, December 27, 1810, is a typical example. See p. 49 for the complete text.

[40] Howard, *A Self-Made Man*, p. 27.

[41] Ms. memorandum of John Macomber, Westport, January 6, 1815; Ms. copy of memorandum of Ebenezer Baker, Westport, November 16, 1815, Cuffe papers.

[42] Ms. marriage certificate, Cuffe papers.

[43] Ms. Vital Records of Westport, Mass., to the year 1850, Westport, Mass., Town Clerk's Office. Birth dates of Cuffe's children are: Naomi, March 8, 1783; Mary, Oct. 5, 1785; Ruth, Aug. 10, 1788; Alice, Sept. 10, 1790; Paul, Jr., Dec. 20, 1792; Rhoda, March 29, 1795; William, June 19, 1799.

semi-literate sea captain promptly began a drive to provide the town with a school. In typical Yankee town meeting fashion, Cuffe called his neighbors together, outlined the problem and urged immediate action.

However, his fellow townsmen refused to go along with the plan. Some expressed reservations about the necessity for a school, and others declared their firm opposition to the proposed undertaking because of the potential costs involved. The real reason for their opposition was never expressed, but no doubt everyone was cognizant of its presence. In the 1790's the barriers of racial prejudice in the United States were too great to overcome even for the simple farmers of Westport, Massachusetts. They were as yet unprepared for a black man to take the lead in pointing out the need for civic improvements.[44] And they were equally unprepared, no doubt, to offer the children of the community a non-segregated educational experience.

Undeterred by this rebuff, Cuffe resolutely and courageously decided to go ahead on his own. Setting aside some land on his own farm,[45] and using his own funds, he proceeded to have a schoolhouse constructed. He then offered the people of Westport the free use of the school. Their Yankee penury overcoming their racism, and recognizing a good bargain when it came along, Westporters accepted the black man's generous proposal with alacrity. Paul Cuffe's school, erected in 1797, remained the town's sole educational institution for many years.[46] It was, of course, one of the first integrated schools established in the United States.[47]

[44] Peter Williams, Jr., *A Discourse, delivered on The Death of Capt. Paul Cuffe, before the New York African Institution, in the African Methodist Episcopal Zion Church, October 21, 1817,* p. 9.

[45] In 1797 Cuffe purchased a large farm in Westport for $3,500. His property faced the Westport River, thus providing an outlet to Buzzards Bay and the ocean. After building a wharf and a warehouse, he was able to oversee his shipbuilding, trading and farming ventures. Liverpool *Mercury,* October 11, 1811.

[46] Westport ultimately built a larger school to care for the increased needs of the community, and Cuffe's school was then converted into a Quaker Sunday school. The Sunday school continued to function for many years after his death. Boston *Weekly Recorder,* October 28, 1817, p. 182.

[47] Howard, *A Self-Made Man,* p. 15; William C. Nell, *The Colored Patriots of the American Revolution,* p. 80; see also *The History of Prince Lee Boo, to Which Is Added the Life of Paul Cuffee, A Man of Colour*

Most men, looking back upon their lives, can single out some one year or some one incident that proved to be a turning point for them. Generally such an event was likely to have occurred at the onset of their careers. For a few, however, their hour of decision or moment of truth comes toward the middle or the end of their life's work.

Paul Cuffe clearly belongs to this latter group. He was fifty-one years of age in 1810. Obviously, he had reached the stage in life where normally he should have begun to consider the prospect of easing up, of shucking off a few of his responsibilities and obligations.

Of medium height, stocky and tending toward portliness, fashionably dressed (for a Quaker), he looked every inch the country squire—except for his skin color. Although he was not a truly handsome man, his features were fair and pleasant to the eye. His skin tone was that of a soft-hued copper color, while his facial characteristics were more Negroid than Indian. Most observers noted that he was soft-spoken and courtly in manner. In conversation he was essentially the sober Quaker with *thee*'s and *thou*'s heavily interlacing his every sentence. But interspersed with Cuffe's Quaker simplicity was the elegant but stylized and carefully developed speech pattern of the self-taught.

Cuffe was happily married. His finances can be described as placing him in the comfortable-to-rich category.[48] He was well liked by his neighbors. Most assuredly, he had achieved recognition and status in the community. Indeed, Paul Cuffe had come a long way from his humble beginnings. Still, it was at this very moment that Cuffe commenced the undertaking that was to become his principal concern for the remainder of his life, that was to command most of his energies and resources, and that elevates

(Dublin, 1818), *passim*. For a general survey of Negro educational opportunities in the North in the antebellum period, see Leon F. Litwack, *North of Slavery: The Negro in the Free States, 1790–1860* (Chicago, 1961), pp. 113–52; John Hope Franklin, *From Slavery to Freedom,* 3rd ed., pp. 160–61, 228–32.

[48] Cuffe's estate in 1810 by conservative estimate would have exceeded $25,000.

his experience from a local, albeit astonishing, success story to one of considerable historical significance.

As a "man of color," Cuffe early in life became acquainted with the disability such a distinction carried. He and other members of his family owned property in the Bay State that was subject to taxation. Property holding was, of course, the very foundation stone of the American system. Long before the English philosopher John Locke declared in 1690 that property, along with life and liberty, were unalienable natural rights,[49] Americans had connected citizenship with the possession of property. The proposition that only men of property held an interest in the political community was almost universally accepted. From this it followed logically that the right to vote and to hold public office rested on property holdings. Nevertheless, the Cuffes and other propertied "men of color" were denied numerous citizenship rights in post-Revolutionary Massachusetts.

Unwilling to accept this rebuff to the sacred concepts inherent in property, the black men protested this blatant discrimination against them. As men of property, they wished to be treated with the respect such title ordinarily conferred on the owner. They reasoned that if racism was to transcend proprietary interests, then those so beset by this injustice were entitled to some other compensatory gratification. Consequently, beginning in February, 1780, Paul Cuffe and his brother John, and others similarly affected, bombarded the Commonwealth's General Court (legislature) and authorities in Bristol County and the Town of Dartmouth with petitions requesting exemption from property and poll taxes. Although they offered an assortment of arguments, their principal contention paralleled the pre-Revolutionary slogan of the Colonial patriots: no taxation without representation. Since neither Negroes nor Indians were admitted to the election rolls in Massachusetts, the petitioners reasoned that these same groups should have their names removed from the tax ledgers.

Their initial petition,[50] a moving and at times heartbreaking

[49] John Locke, *Two Treatises of Government* (London, 1698), p. 341.
[50] Ms. copy of "A petition for tax relief," Dartmouth, February 10, 1780, Cuffe papers.

and painfully eloquent document, was submitted to "The Honorable Council and House of Representatives, in General Court
Assembled, for the State of the Massachusetts Bay in New England" on February 10, 1780. The petitioners noted that they were
"several poor Negroes and Mulattos who are inhabitants of the
town of Dartmouth," and that

> we being chiefly of the African extraction, and by reason of long
> bondage and hard slavery we have been deprived of enjoying the
> profits of our labor or the advantage of inheriting estates from
> our parents as our neighbors the white people, and having some
> of us not long enjoyed our own freedom, yet of late, contrary to
> the invariable custom and practices of the country, we have been
> and now are taxed both in our polls[51] and that small pittance of
> estate which through much hard labor and industry we have got
> together to sustain ourselves and families withall.

To continue to impose property taxes upon them would be
"hard usage," and would reduce "us to a state of beggary whereby
we shall become burdensome to others . . ." Compounding this
injustice was the fact that,

> while we are not allowed the privilege of freemen of the state,
> having no vote or influence in the election with those that tax us,
> yet many of our own color, as is well known, have cheerfully
> entered the field of battle in the defence of the common cause,
> and that as we conceive against a similar exertion of power in
> regard to taxation.

Proceeding to the crux of the problem, the appellants with some
bitterness pointed to the fact that "in these difficult times . . .
there is not to exceed more than five or six that hath a care in this
town [for their distress]." Negroes and mulattoes were not "allowed in voting in the town meetings . . . nor to choose an
officer." No Negro had ever been "heard in the active court of the
general assembly." Therefore, "we poor despised miserable black
people have not an equal chance with white people, neither by sea
nor by land."

They drew attention to their pathetic condition by observing

---

[51] Massachusetts continued to impose a poll (head) tax on all adult males
until 1963, when the legislature finally repealed this ancient excise.

that some of the petitioners were "poor old Negroes" who had been "in bondage some thirty, some forty, and some fifty years and now just got their liberty—some by going into the service and some by going to sea, and others by good fortune." Other petitioners were "poor distressed mongrels which have no learning and no land and also no stock; neither where to put their head." Some "shelter themselves into an old rotten hut which thy dogs would not lay in."

The Dartmouth Negroes concluded their appeal by praying that "those who have the rule in their hands may be merciful unto the poor and needy, give unto those who ask of thee; and he that would borrow of thee, turn not away empty." Unmoved by this powerful and impassioned plea, the legislature did turn them away empty. John Cuffe ruefully recorded on one of the duplicate petitions in the Cuffe papers: "This is the copy of the petitions which we did deliver unto the honorable council and house for relief from taxation in the days of our distress. But we received none."[52]

Despite the legislative setback, the Cuffe brothers persisted in their struggle for equal rights. As a part of their protest, they had refused to pay their county property taxes and poll taxes during the years 1778, 1779, and 1780. By late 1780 their delinquent tax bills exceeded £155. The law in all its awful majesty prepared to swing into action. The brothers, in a last-ditch attempt to head off prosecution, submitted a petition to the Court of General Sessions of Bristol County in December, 1780. Their brief requested relief from taxation since the petitioners were

> Indian men and by law not the subjects of taxation for any estate, real or personal, and humbly pray your Honors that, as they are assessed jointly a double poll tax and the said Paul is a minor for whom the said John is not by law answerable or chargeable, that the said poll taxes aforesaid on their and each of their real and personal estate aforesaid, may be abated to them and they allowed their reasonable costs.[53]

On December 15, 1780, the authorities issued a warrant for the arrest of John and Paul Cuffe; the brothers had failed to convince

[52] Ms. "note," n.d. [late June, 1782], Cuffe Scrapbook, Cuffe papers.
[53] Quoted by Henry Noble Sherwood, "Paul Cuffe," *The Journal of Negro History*, VIII (April, 1923), p. 163.

the court of the merits of their complaints. John and Paul were arrested on December 19 and were hauled off to the county seat's common jail in Taunton, "there to remain until they . . . shall pay and satisfy the above sum [their delinquent taxes] with all necessary charges." However, their confinement lasted only a few hours. That afternoon the Taunton jailkeeper was served with a writ of habeas corpus in the "Name of the Commonwealth of Massachusetts to have the bodies of John and Paul Cuffe said to be Indian men whom you have now in keeping [released from prison]."[54]

Trial was set for March, 1781, but delays and postponements prevented disposition of the case until spring. Then, conceding defeat, the dissenters paid the county on June 11 "eight pound 12 shillings silver money in full for all John Cuffe's and Paul Cuffe's rates until this date, also for all . . . court charges."[55] On June 12, the Court of General Sessions ordered that "the petition of Paul Cuffe and John Cuffe and the proceedings thereon be dismissed."[56]

An account of the Cuffes' protracted struggle to secure tax relief would not be complete without taking notice of their efforts with still another governmental agency. The brothers, quite literally, worked their way down the hierarchy of government in Massachusetts. First, they tried the state legislature and failed. Then, they turned to the county courts. As prospects for success grew dim on this level, they approached town government for deliverance. On April 24, 1781, John and Paul submitted to the Selectmen of the Town of Dartmouth "A Request."[57] A brief document (by Cuffe standards), this latest petition urged the Selectmen to

> put a stroke in your next warrant for calling a town meeting so that it may legally be laid before the town by way of vote to know the mine [sic] of said town whether all free Negroes and Mulattos shall have the same privileges in this said town of Dartmouth as

[54] *Ibid.,* p. 164.
[55] Ms. paid receipt, Dartmouth, June 11, 1781, Cuffe papers.
[56] Quoted by Sherwood, "Paul Cuffe," p. 166.
[57] Ms. copy of "A Request to the Selectmen of Dartmouth," April 24, 1781, Cuffe papers.

the white people have respecting places of profit, choosing of officers and the like, together with all other privileges in all cases that shall or may happen or be brought in this said town of Dartmouth, or that we have relief granted us jointly from taxation whilst under our present depressed circumstances. . . .

The Selectmen refused to comply with the request.

Paul's and John's defeat was now complete. Appeals, petitions, even outright defiance of authority, had failed to yield concessions to the protesters. Equal political rights for Negroes and other non-Caucasians in Massachusetts would have to await a later date.

The story of the Cuffe brothers' fight for equal treatment in Massachusetts is significant for a number of reasons. Although the struggle terminated in failure, the fact that such a battle was waged at all suggests much concerning their character, courage and determination. Further, a careful examination of their numerous petitions reveals a basic confusion on the part of the Cuffes as to their status in society. Several documents observed that John and Paul Cuffe were "Indian men and by law not the subjects of taxation for any estate real or personal."[58] Still others—particularly their appeal to the Bay State's legislature in 1780—stressed their Negro ancestry.

As offspring of a racially mixed marriage, the brothers' evident racial perplexity is both natural and understandable. Then, too, it was not uncommon in southeastern Massachusetts for Negroes to marry Indians. Captain Paul Cuffe ultimately selected his wife from his mother's tribe. Other members of the family as well were destined to find their mates among the local Indians. Until his religious conversion in 1808, the sea captain vacillated between his Negro and his Indian origins. His racial ambiguity was genuine and was not based on expediency and the need to bow to shifting community attitudes. Thus at times he would refer to his Indian ancestry; on other occasions, however, he would stress his Negro paternity.

Cuffe's admission to membership in the Westport Meeting of the Society of Friends appears to have brought his racial dilemma to a

---

[58] Quoted by Sherwood, "Paul Cuffe," p. 163.

climax. Quaker groups in Massachusetts, in Pennsylvania, and in scattered communities throughout the country were beginning to devote increasing attention to the plight of the American Negro slave. Based in part on their religious convictions, a number of small Quaker-oriented abolitionist societies began to spring up here and there.

Undoubtedly, the heavy emphasis that the Quakers placed upon personal sacrifice and upon serving mankind, their growing involvement in abolitionist activities, their interest in the general condition of the Negro, and their sense of obligation to spread the faith to the heathen, all combined to turn the attention of the recent Quaker convert to those whom now he called his "unfortunate brethren in our own nation and in Africa." Cuffe's newly found religious convictions seemingly resolved his racial predicament. His correspondence after 1808 scarcely mentions his Indian legacy. On the other hand, Africa and the Negro absorbed his interest.

Significantly, Cuffe's concern with Africa exceeded for some time his solicitude for the plight of the American Negro slave.[59] For him, the "redemption" of Africa was of paramount importance. Keenly aware of the horrors of Negro slavery, touched by the suffering of those trapped within the slave system, Cuffe still believed that Negroes in Africa required assistance more urgently than their American counterparts. Cuffe's feeling was that Negroes in the United States might be in chains, but because of their forced contact with Western culture and their equally involuntary conversion to something resembling Christianity, they were infinitely better off than their African comrades.

With an emphasis that intensified with each passing day, Cuffe began to identify totally with Africa and his African heritage. He would refer to his African origins and his desire to assist his fellow Africans at every opportunity. To friends he wrote typically: "As I am of the African race, I feel myself interested for them, and, if I

---

[59] A careful search of the Cuffe manuscripts failed to disclose any record of Paul Cuffe's involvement with Negro emancipation schemes—evolutionary or revolutionary—prior to 1816. On the other hand, plans for African development occupy much space in Cuffe's correspondence from 1808 until his death in 1817.

am favored with a talent, I think I am willing that they should be benefited thereby."[60] And,

> as to poor me, I feel very feeble and almost worn out in hard service and unable of doing much for my brethren the African race. But blessed be God, I am what I am, and all that I can conceive that God please to lay upon me to make an instrument of me for that service, I desire ever to be submissive that His will may be done. . . .[61]

These statements are representative of many others that Cuffe made during this period.

For Paul Cuffe, then, the redemption of Africa began to take on the aura of a personal crusade. And it was from a Western cultural perspective that the thoroughly Westernized Cuffe viewed that redemption. He felt that Africa was destined to remain in a state of savagery and ignorance until its tremendous energies could be liberated by the introduction of Western culture, Western techniques, and above all, Western Christianity. He was convinced that the African's acceptance of Christianity would bring him salvation and happiness. He was equally certain that the African's adoption of Western habits and techniques would occasion a tremendous improvement in his economic well-being.

Westernization, Cuffe believed, could ultimately free Africans from a dependence on profits from the slave trade—that hated institution perpetuated by the Africans' need for Western goods. He was keenly aware of how vital a part of the African economy the traffic in human beings had become. To this black American the fact that Africans engaged in the infamous slave trade for centuries, that they willingly participated in a commerce whereby fellow black men were bartered and condemned to the barbarities of New World slavery, was more reprehensible than chattel slavery itself.[62]

The inhumanity of the business was, of course, most distressing to him. But more important, the slave trade was, according to

[60] Ms. copy, Paul Cuffe to John James and Alexander Wilson, Westport, June 10, 1809, Cuffe papers.

[61] Ms. copy, Paul Cuffe to James Pemberton, Westport, September 14, 1808, Cuffe papers.

[62] See for example pp. 80, 82, 131, 194, 224.

Cuffe, at the very heart of the institution of slavery. Somewhat simplistically he appeared to conclude, therefore, that once the traffic was eliminated, it need be only a matter of time before slavery would begin to disappear. By drying up the source of fresh supplies for the institution, chattel bondage gradually but inexorably must wither away. Thus, to Cuffe the elimination of the slave trade could serve a dual function: it would lead to the eventual abolition of slavery in the United States and elsewhere, and at the same time it would end the corruption and brutalization of those many Africans who participated in the activity.

Cuffe might have been correct in his forecast had he lived in the seventeenth century. But by the beginning of the nineteenth century such expectations were hopelessly unrealistic. In 1809 more than one million black slaves labored in Southern fields. This native population was an adequate demographic base to assure for the immediate future a reasonably sufficient and continuous supply of chattel bondsmen. Moreover, in the event of a prospective shortage, slave-breeding farms, already a feature of Southern culture, could always have increased their production. Even more important, perhaps, was the fact that racism was so deeply ingrained into the American fabric by the Age of Jefferson that the abolition of the international slave trade would not have affected most Americans in their attitude toward perpetuating black slavery in the United States.[63]

The evils of the slave trade preyed constantly on Cuffe's mind. After 1808 the subject became for him quite literally a monomania. His journal entries and his correspondence dwell on the topic. In almost any general conversation with friends, both whites and blacks, he was certain at some time to allude to the topic.

Although black men were not supposed to speak out on political or social questions, Cuffe's public opposition to the slave trade did not endanger his standing with the white community. If anything, his position enhanced his stature with the white power structure. While white Americans still disagreed over the immorality of slavery, there was no such division concerning the peddling of human flesh. In fact, most people (in Europe and in the

---

[63] See Winthrop Jordan's brilliant discussion of America's racial attitudes in his *White Over Black, passim.*

Americas) long considered the international slave trade to be an outrage against humanity. It was *too* dirty an occupation. In the United States, Congress outlawed the business at the earliest date the Constitution permitted, and other countries also vigorously condemned the trade.

Still, as the traffic diminished after 1809, Cuffe became increasingly concerned with the task of finding a humane substitute that would sustain black Africa's economy. He was certain that Africans were not about to abandon their desire and need for Western goods. And he feared, with good reason, that unless some new industry was developed rapidly, Africans would engage in large-scale illicit slave commerce to satisfy their cravings. But, ever hopeful when it came to Africa, he expected that ultimately some new type of triangular trade between the Dark Continent, the United States and Europe, one that relied on native African products, could be put together as a replacement for the discredited slave trade.[64]

As Cuffe's thoughts became increasingly concerned with Africa, he began to formulate tentative plans that in practical terms would lead ultimately to the fulfillment of his messianic vision for African emancipation. Although always careful to temper utopianism with a degree of pragmatism, Cuffe never set down in elaborate detail a precise timetable or method of operation to achieve his goal. Nevertheless, from the sea captain's subsequent activities, and from his surviving correspondence, one can reconstruct a general outline of his scheme.

He planned to sail to Africa for an on-the-spot investigation of the possibilities for inaugurating his project. Hopefully, he would find an area and a community that would welcome his attentions and that would agree to cooperate by becoming a pilot project for the rehabilitation of the entire continent. He would then proceed to assist these people to improve their economic conditions; moreover, he would introduce to them the blessings of Western Christian civilization. Once prosperity and Christianity established firm roots there, the recently enlightened natives would be expected to act as missionaries, advancing Western civilization and Christian truth among their less fortunate African brothers.

[64] See pp. 95–96, 105, 183–85, 190–96.

The residents of the pilot colony were to be helped by what twentieth century Americans would label a privately sponsored black Peace Corps. Cuffe did not envision a Marcus Garvey type of back-to-Africa mass black migration.[65] Nor did he at first think in terms of even a medium-sized emigration scheme comparable to the proposals of desperation made by Bishop Henry M. Turner and other black nationalists during the dark decades at the turn of the nineteenth century.[66] Rather, Cuffe believed that he could induce a small number of skilled free Negro Americans to settle somewhere along the west coast of Africa. With the help and cooperation of these newcomers, and with the opening up of trade in native products between Africa, the United States and Europe, and the support of interested American and English philanthropists, he was confident that his prototype enclave would shortly become a shining beacon for all of Africa to follow. In Tennyson's words, these newly inspired Africans would "follow the gleam."

Cuffe's African plans were not original. As we have seen, a number of American and British humanitarians had advanced similar missionary and civilizing projects in the past.[67] But of even greater significance in assisting Cuffe in the formulation and development of his ideas were the recent African experiences of certain British Quaker philanthropists. The work of several of these meliorators received wide publicity in the American religious press, and Cuffe, no doubt, became familiar with their activities.[68]

At the close of the American Revolution, the British found that they had on their hands a few thousand newly freed American slaves. These former slaves had heeded British proclamations that

[65] E. David Cronon, *Black Moses: The Story of Marcus Garvey and the Universal Negro Improvement Association* (Madison, Wis., 1969), *passim*.

[66] Edwin S. Redkey, *Black Exodus*, pp. 24–72.

[67] See above, pp. 13–14.

[68] The following account of the early history of Sierra Leone under British rule is based in large part on Christopher Fyfe, *A History of Sierra Leone*, pp. 1–112; A. P. Kup, *A History of Sierra Leone 1400–1787*, *passim*; Michael Bainton, *West African City, A Study of Tribal Life in Freetown*, pp. 5–10; Philip D. Curtin, *The Image of Africa: British Ideas and Action, 1780–1850*, pp. 88–176.

offered them their freedom on condition they desert their masters and serve His Majesty's cause. Now, British authorities did not know what to do with the blacks. They could not, in good conscience, send them back to their previous owners. Nor could they abandon them to the tender mercies of the Southern-oriented new American government. In despair, the British evacuated many of the liberated blacks to Canada. And a short time later some of these transplanted American Negroes made their way to London. Here they swelled the capital's vast population of the friendless and the destitute. A smaller number of black sailors, stranded in England after their voyages, joined this nucleus of American Negro émigrés in their poverty and squalor.

At the beginning of 1786, a number of London businessmen, moved by the suffering of this alien black population, formed a committee to collect funds to help provide these strangers with food and medicine, and with jobs for those wishing to return to sea. Shortly after this Quaker-dominated Committee for the Black Poor commenced operations, it was contacted by the amateur botanist Henry Smeathman. The "Flycatcher" (as Smeathman liked to call himself) offered to remove all of London's black poor to Africa and to establish them in a colony near the Sierra Leone River. Anticipating that relocation expenses would not exceed £4 per head, Smeathman assured the Committee that commercial opportunities in Africa were so great that the Committee's initial outlay would be returned many times over within a few years.

Impressed with his arguments, several of the Committee's more influential members prevailed upon the British Treasury to secure Treasury's agreement to subsidize the scheme. Anxious to rid London of its dependent black population, Treasury readily consented to finance the project, leaving the Committee with the responsibility for making arrangements for the exodus and for managing the colony after its establishment. Smeathman, whose motives for promoting African colonization were somewhat suspect, because of his contradictory and often untruthful statements to the Committee, died of a "putrid fever" before the expedition got underway. Granville Sharp, the great humanitarian reformer and champion of Negro rights, now succeeded the Flycatcher as the prime organizer of Negro emigration.

Sharp's motives cannot be challenged. He was genuinely concerned for the welfare of all oppressed peoples, and he looked forward to the establishment of a democratic, self-governing, prosperous African Negro state. Still, the character of subsequent British involvement in Sierra Leone colonizing ventures was to be patterned along the lines Smeathman had developed. The majority of British humanitarians supported the Sierra Leone development for its money-making potential as well as for more altruistic reasons. These philanthropists were willing to devote much time, energy, and a little sterling to Africa; however, they anticipated that heavy expenditures, of necessity, would be the responsibility of the British Treasury, and that their modest personal investments would return considerable profits from trade and other business and commercial opportunities in the Dark Continent.

Sierra Leone colonization got under way during the spring of 1787, the Royal Navy providing transportation for the prospective emigrants. The Committee for the Black Poor, unable to persuade Negroes in large numbers to volunteer for Africa, secured the cooperation of London authorities in rounding up for deportation any Negro indigent found in the streets. As an added fillip, approximately seventy white prostitutes became members of the expedition. In search of a more secure future, the promise of husbands proved to be an irresistible lure to these women. Their profession had evidently conditioned them against racism—seemingly the only profession with the ability to transcend the color line—and they raised no objection to the forthcoming amalgamation of the races. The presence of the prostitutes on board ship and later in Sierra Leone no doubt added a touch of cosmopolitanism to the colony. Ultimately, on April 8, 1787, some four hundred souls departed England and headed for Sierra Leone.

The colony was plagued with serious problems from the outset and proved to be a severe disappointment to its London sponsors. Quarrels among the settlers, large-scale desertions, tropical fevers, and an unfriendly welcome from the natives, all contributed to the enterprise's failure. Granville Sharp's dream of a self-governing black commonwealth was ended in 1791, when the Sierra Leone Company, a commercial company chartered by Parliament, assumed control of the colony.

This new organization did not represent, however, a repudiation by either the philanthropists or the British government of the earlier colonizing efforts. The original sponsors never abandoned hope for the ultimate success of the Sierra Leone enterprise. During the colony's many vicissitudes and changes in constitutional structure they clung doggedly to the dream that this steamy, tropical territory with limited natural resources would become a great Negro refuge. Consequently, they made certain that the aims of the Sierra Leone Company would remain the same as the Granville Sharp undertaking. Moreover, a number of the directors of the new company came from the original group of humanitarian sponsors of colonization. Still sublimely confident, they now anticipated that a well-organized trading company would offer the colony a more stable basis for development than it had previously enjoyed. They anticipated that under this revised setup the colony soon would become more attractive to potential emigrants, and that some profits could be extracted once the colony began to thrive.

Starting off with the usual great expectations so characteristic of all utopian colonizing attempts, the fledgling company expended considerable sums of money in its dominion. The Crown, too, demonstrated its faith in the undertaking by continuing to extend a subsidy to the colony. Settlers were lured to Sierra Leone from the big colony of Negroes—refugees from the American Revolution—who were living on the brink of starvation in Nova Scotia. In all, approximately twelve hundred black Nova Scotians came to the colony in 1792. Other pioneers migrated to Sierra Leone from Jamaica by way of Nova Scotia. In 1800 more than five hundred so-called Jamaican Maroons arrived in the colony's capital, Freetown.

Despite the optimism of the new company, the colony failed to prosper. The immense sums of money invested by both the Crown and the Sierra Leone Company descended into a bottomless pit. The newcomers quarreled with the earlier settlers and among themselves. Trade with the natives was slight; agriculture languished; disease took a heavy toll of settlers; native assaults on new settlements caused much damage to property and some loss of life. A squadron of French naval vessels disguised as British men-of-war delivered a near-fatal blow to the colony in September, 1794, by looting, pillaging, and destroying everything they could find. By 1806 the Sierra Leone Company was on the verge of bankruptcy. Parliament was induced to intervene, and legislation was passed in August, 1807, converting Sierra Leone into a Crown Colony. The company's dream of combining philanthropy with commercial profit once more proved to be illusory.

Although the directors of the defunct company were delighted to be relieved of their financial responsibility for the colony, they continued to maintain considerable interest in Sierra Leone's future. William Wilberforce, Zachary Macaulay, William Allen and other former company directors were genuinely motivated by religious and humanitarian concern for the African. Anxious to put an end to the slave trade, ever on the alert to introduce Christianity and Western culture to Africa, these philanthropists did not intend to relax their efforts now that the company was dead. They were quite willing to have the British government shoulder the burden and expense of governing and maintaining Sierra Leone. However, they were not prepared to abandon their moral obligation for the welfare of its inhabitants.

The African Institution, a private, nonprofit charitable organization, was created in 1807 to promote the objectives of the philanthropists. Boasting a most prestigious Board of Directors, and having as its nominal head the King's nephew, the Duke of Gloucester, the African Institution wielded considerable power over Sierra Leone's affairs for two decades. Royal officials normally were appointed to positions in Sierra Leone only upon the recommendation of the Institution. Much of the colony's trade and, for a short period of time, the colony's finances were administered under the watchful and beneficent eye of the African Institution.

Paul Cuffe was well acquainted with the early, unhappy history of the Sierra Leone experiment.[69] As his plans for African de-

---

[69] James Pemberton to Paul Cuffe, Philadelphia, June 8, 1808; James Pemberton to Paul Cuffe, Philadelphia, October 27, 1808; Ms. copy, Paul Cuffe to John James and Alexander Wilson, Westport, June 10, 1809; Ms. copy, John James and Alexander Wilson to William Dillwyn, Philadelphia, June 21, 1809. All in Cuffe papers.

liverance and self-help germinated, the failures of the English philanthropists must have caused him moments of anguished doubt. If a comparatively well-organized and well-financed undertaking ended in disaster, the prospects of success for his proposed enterprise were slim indeed. Still, however bleak the outlook for Sierra Leone's future, no other territory in Africa offered a better opportunity to introduce his scheme.[70]

Despite all the agonies inflicted upon the colony during its early history and its continuing economic and governmental instability, Sierra Leone's cultural development was of a higher order than what obtained in the rest of black Africa. "Having been informed

[70] The most recent historian of antebellum African colonization schemes misunderstands completely, and therefore wholly misrepresents, Cuffe's motives for going to Sierra Leone. According to Professor P. J. Staudenraus, Cuffe "attempted to penetrate the British market at Sierra Leone with an offer to bring free Negro emigrants from the United States. . . . In 1808 he began looking to Africa for markets. . . . He volunteered to carry Negro farmers, artisans, and mechanics from the United States in return for trading privileges at the colony." (*The African Colonization Movement 1816–1865*, pp. 9–10.)

The following is one example of many that could be offered in rebuttal to Staudenraus' portrait of Cuffe's venality: Two Philadelphia Quakers in 1809 observed that Cuffe was a

man of property and in whole and in part is concerned in several vessels . . . therefore if way should open in his and their minds to move, their business will of consequence be removed with them. Therefore, they wish to know whether in this case they could have secured to them all the rights and privileges that British subjects enjoy in their trade and business. This precaution we fully approve of, and could not encourage them in the undertaking without their having a reasonable prospect before them of making a comfortable support for themselves and families and something more.

Yet it is our belief that Paul's concern reaches beyond this, and that he has more at heart the improvement of the natives in civilization, so as gradually to open and prepare their minds for the introduction of the principle of Truth, and that they may in time be made partakers of the many privileges and benefits that a subjection to its holy influence bestows, and that freedom which it alone gives.

Nevertheless, in this first voyage it will be necessary, if the African Institution approve of and encourage the undertaking, to afford him some pecuniary assistance, either by engaging to defray the expenses that may be incurred or give him a freight from this country, or some other way whereby he may be remunerated.

Ms. copy, John James and Alexander Wilson to William Dillwyn, Philadelphia, June 21, 1809, Cuffe papers.

that there was a settlement of people of colour at Sierra Leone under the immediate guardianship of a civilized power," Cuffe later wrote, "I have for these many years past felt a lively interest in their behalf, wishing that the inhabitants of the colony might become established in the truth, and thereby be instrumental in its promotion amongst our African brethren." If he was to be an instrument of Divine Providence, as Cuffe truly believed he was, then with God's help perhaps he would succeed in fulfilling this divinely ordained mission where others had faltered. "It was these sentiments that first influenced me to visit my friends in this colony."[71]

The Westport Quaker received encouragement from many sources. A Philadelphian wrote:

> Now if thy concern for the good of the poor untutored people continues and finds thy mind impressed with a sense that any portion of the work is allotted for thee to perform, I hope and trust thou wilt give it thy most serious consideration, and should it open to such a degree as to bring thee under an apprehension of religious duty to perform it in such a way as that wisdom which is superior to human may point out, a consultation with thy friends on the occasion may be reasonably useful, tending to thy strength and encouragement.[72]

Sympathizers in New York, Baltimore and Boston urged Cuffe to go forward resolutely with his project.

Most important, influential members of the African Institution reacted with keen interest to Cuffe's proposal. Zachary Macaulay assured him that the Institution would make every effort to insure the success of his contemplated voyage.[73] William Allen, a prominent businessman and a dedicated member of the African Institution, exchanged countless letters with Cuffe on African affairs. Allen, too, welcomed the promise of American interest in Sierra

[71] Paul Cuffe, *A Brief Account of the Settlement and Present Situation of The Colony of Sierra Leone in Africa as communicated by Paul Cuffee* [sic] (*A Man of Colour*) *to His Friend in New York*, p. 3.
[72] James Pemberton to Paul Cuffe, Philadelphia, September 27, 1808, Cuffe papers.
[73] James Pemberton to Paul Cuffe, Philadelphia, June 8, 1808, Cuffe papers.

Leone. He constantly reassured Cuffe that the possibilities for success were good, and no doubt Allen's enthusiasm helped to embolden the sea captain.

Cuffe had wrestled with the question for nearly three years, discussing with friends the hazards involved, the opportunities for establishing "the true light of Christianity" in Africa, and the possible consequences of moving his family and business there. By June, 1809, still cautious, he made up his mind to take the chance, "if times should be so settled between this and next fall so as to be advisable to undertake such a voyage, it looks pretty clear to be put in execution in case there should be encouragement."[74] Finally, in September, 1810, Cuffe called a meeting of the Westport Friends to discuss his plans and to secure the Society's endorsement. This was readily granted, along with a formal letter of recommendation from the group.[75]

The missionary astutely fortified his cause also with letters of testimony from a number of notable Americans. Benjamin Rush wrote:[76]

I have had the pleasure of a personal knowledge of Capt. Paul Cuffe for several years and from his conduct and conversation, as well as from the character I have uniformly heard of him from all who know him, I have been led to entertain a high opinion of his integrity and other moral virtues. He visits Sierra Leone in order to aid the benevolent views of the London African Institution towards the African nations. He is hereby recommended to the notice and protection of the friends of liberty, humanity and Religion in every part of the world by

Philadelphia
December 27, 1810

BENJM. RUSH, MD.
President of the Society for abolishing the commerce in slaves, and for extending liberty to them, established in Philadelphia.

[74] Ms. copy, Paul Cuffe to John James and Alexander Wilson, Westport, June 10, 1809, Cuffe papers.
[75] Ms. memorandum of John Macomber, Westport, January 9, 1851, Cuffe papers.
[76] Ms. copy, Cuffe papers.

Rush's declaration was typical of a number of letters that Cuffe carried with him to Africa. Their worth was established frequently during the course of Cuffe's travels.

Cuffe inaugurated his exploratory expedition on January 2, 1811. Employing his favorite brig, *Traveller,* Cuffe sailed with a cargo of general merchandise from Philadelphia for Africa and arrived in Freetown, Sierra Leone, on March 1, 1811, after fifty-eight days at sea. The Freetown populace as well as the white British authorities in Sierra Leone greeted the explorer and his crew cordially, if somewhat stiffly. Cuffe was allowed to dispose of some of the cargo he had brought from America and was permitted to roam freely throughout the colony. He traveled everywhere, carefully observing social and economic conditions. On balance, he was favorably impressed with the colony's possibilities.

Sierra Leone officials sympathized with the Westport sea captain's over-all plans, but they did not welcome his efforts to introduce American goods into the colony. Furthermore, they lacked the power to grant the American permission to bring his fellow countrymen to Freetown as colonists.

Some of the colony's white officials, however, resented Cuffe's presence in Freetown. They were afraid that the Bay State sea captain, with his plans for black Africa's rejuvenation, might upset the applecart and somehow affect adversely their exploitative money-making activities. A few of these public servants made enormous profits in dealings with their gullible charges, and now an upstart from the other side of the world threatened to end this cozy affair.

Consequently, Cuffe was harassed by officious authority, by red tape, and by subtle sabotage. One official went to the extreme of writing a leading member of the African Institution in London a poison-pen letter concerning the newcomer. Horrified, Zachary Macaulay showed the letter to another member, William Allen, since "he thought it only candid to show me," Allen later wrote, "a paragraph in a letter which he had received from Smith, the judge advocate (or some such title) at Sierra Leone, and that said Smith was a *most respectable* person." Allen read "with astonishment that he [Smith] wished Macaulay to be on his guard against any representations that Captain Cuffe might make, as no credit whatever should be attached to anything he might say, that he [Smith] had treated Cuffe with great kindness on his arrival and had rendered him most essential service, but the result was, that he had never known a more mercenary or unprincipled man, except perhaps a slave-trader."[77]

The African Institution almost immediately discounted the charges, but Cuffe lived under a cloud of slander for two and one-half years. It was not until January 6, 1814, that one of the Institution's leading members noted in his diary, "On the 6th of First Month we examined J.C. and are to meet on the 14th to hear the remainder of his evidence. I think we shall be able to prove that the principal thing attended to by the white people of Sierra Leone, at least by many of them, has been getting money, and that in the shortest way. The mystery of poor Paul Cuffe's ill usage is now unravelled."[78]

Because of his previous contacts with the African Institution Cuffe had powerful friends in London whom he expected to help him obtain the needed licenses, permits, et cetera, to carry on his operations in Sierra Leone. Determined to effect the success of his project, no matter what the obstacles, Cuffe decided to go to London to seek help. He sailed from Freetown on May 11, 1811, and landed at Liverpool some sixty-two days later, on July 12, 1811.

His visit to England caused a sensation there. The English had never seen an American Negro sea captain and an all-Negro crew. Liverpool outdid itself in extending a cordial welcome to the visitor. Cuffe undoubtedly must have sensed the irony in his reception there, since he was well aware of Liverpool's notorious one-time role in the slave trade. It was from this gloomy English port that slavers in the short space of a generation, from 1783 to 1804, carried more than 625,000 Africans to the slave plantations of the Americas.[79] Now, a scant seven years later, an observer noted, "During the time I have been at Liverpool, Paul Cuffe, a black man, owner and master of a vessel has come into port. . . . He is

[77] Anon. ed., *Life of William Allen with Selections from His Correspondence,* 2 vols., I, pp. 101–2.
[78] *Ibid.,* p. 138.
[79] Elizabeth Donnen, ed., *Documents Illustrative of the History of the Slave Trade in America,* Vol. II, p. 567.

a member of our Society [of Friends] and resides in New England. The whole of his crew are black also. This, together with the cleanliness of his vessel, and the excellent order prevailing on board, has excited very general attention." Moreover, "It has, I believe, opened the minds of many in tender feelings towards the poor suffering Africans, who, they see, are men like themselves, capable of becoming, like Paul Cuffe, valuable and useful members both of civil and religious society."[80]

Cuffe and his men were lionized wherever they visited. *The Times* of London, *The Edinburgh Review* and various provincial newspapers covered Cuffe's activities extensively. So much interest was generated by this black man's presence in England that an enterprising author hastily compiled and printed a 29-page pamphlet, *Memoir of Captain Paul Cuffee, A Man of Colour: To Which Is Subjoined the Epistle of the Society of Sierra Leone, in Africa, &c.* The pamphlet sold out within days of its publication, and a second printing in 1812 did almost as well.[81]

The Times provided its readers with a reasonably accurate biographical sketch of Cuffe, observing that he and his crew were "negroes, or the immediate descendants of negroes," and noting that "when Mr. Clarkson's *History of the Abolition of The Slave Trade* fell into his [Cuffe's] hands, it awakened all the powers of his mind to a consideration of his origin, and the duties he owed to his people." It found the black American to be of "an agreeable countenance, and his physiognomy truly interesting; he is both tall and stout, speaks English well, dresses in the Quaker style, in a drab-coloured suit, and wears a large flapped white hat."[82]

Having learned from the newspapers and from private correspondence of Cuffe's arrival in Liverpool, *The Edinburgh Review* loftily decreed that this historic event "should be commemorated in some less perishable record." The *Review* reported that the recent arrival was "said to be very skilled both in trade and navigation, as well as to be of a very pious and moral character."

---

[80] Benjamin Seebohm, ed., *Memoirs of the Life and Gospel Labours of Stephen Grellet*, 2 vols. (Philadelphia, 1874), Vol. I, p. 171.

[81] William Alexander, *Memoir of Captain Paul Cuffee* [sic], *A Man of Colour, to which is subjoined The Epistle of the Society of Sierra Leone, In Africa, &c.*

[82] *The Times*, August 2, 1811, p. 3.

Pointedly recalling that Liverpool had formerly been the principal English depot for the slave trade, the periodical commented wryly that "It must have been a strange and animating spectacle to see this free and enlightened African entering, as an independent trader, with his black crew, into that port which was so lately the *nidus* of the Slave trade."[83]

The modest sea captain was entertained by leading abolitionists during his stay in England. The depth of his mind, his quick grasp of things, and his simplicity of manner pleased them beyond their wildest expectations. To some, he appeared to be a heaven-sent messenger of deliverance. William Allen joyfully recorded in his diary that "[Thomas] Clarkson and I are both of the mind that the present opportunity for promoting the civilization of Africa, through the means of Paul Cuffe, should not be lost; he seems like a man made on purpose for the business; he has great experience as well as integrity."[84]

The African Institution, in recess for the summer vacation period, hastily reconvened to meet with Cuffe. His Royal Highness the Duke of Gloucester dashed into London from his country retreat to preside over this conference with their "dark-coloured but civilized ally."[85] Cuffe gave the Duke a present of an African robe, a letter box, and a dagger. The gifts were intended to impress Gloucester with the native intelligence and skills most Africans possessed.[86] And while Gloucester and the other Institution members were indeed impressed with the samples of African craftsmanship, they were even more delighted with their articulate black American associate. He responded to their questions with "very sensible and satisfactory answers, and his simplicity and strong natural good sense, made a great impression upon all parties." The Duke was so moved, that "after Paul Cuffe had withdrawn, a vote of thanks was passed to him, and a committee appointed to see what use might be made of him."[87]

---

[83] "Report of The African Institution," *The Edinburgh Review,* XVIII (August, 1811), p. 321.

[84] *Life of William Allen,* I, p. 103.

[85] "Seventh Report of The African Institution," *The Edinburgh Review,* XLII (July, 1813), p. 473.

[86] Cuffe Journal entry, August 27, 1811.

[87] *Life of William Allen,* I, p. 104.

As with any other tourist, his English hosts were determined that Cuffe not leave England without viewing their country's landmarks and monuments. When not occupied with Sierra Leone matters, Cuffe was taken in tow to explore the historic sights of London: the Tower, the national mint, the Houses of Parliament, et cetera. About the only items he seemed to have overlooked in the capital were the changing of the guard at Buckingham Palace and an audience with King George III.[88]

Cuffe even found the time somehow to journey to Manchester, and this brawling, booming cotton-textile town both delighted and astonished the American. Affluent cotton manufacturers personally escorted him on inspection tours through their factories. Their machines and the "ideal" working conditions in the factories captivated the Yankee visitor. Thus, while others sputtered that "The town is abominably filthy, the Steam Engine is pestiferous, the Dyehouses noisesome and offensive, and the water of the river as black as ink or the Stygian Lake,"[89] Cuffe saw only Manchester's "newness," its hustle and bustle, its advanced technology, and its manufactured affluence.

Eventually, the rubbernecking part of his journey came to a conclusion. Thanks to the intervention of the African Institution, Cuffe in August received permission from the government to continue with his mission to Sierra Leone. The way was now clear to get on with the African project. Still, Cuffe's impending departure from England was for many of his newfound friends a sad event. They had become very fond of him during his all too brief stay, and, as his friend William Allen noted with a touch of the morose, "I was very busy in getting seeds and various articles together for him, and presented him with a telescope. We had an affecting parting, as it is not very probable we shall see him any more."[90] Cuffe sailed from Liverpool on September 20, 1811, and landed in Freetown on November 12. The relatively tranquil voyage took him fifty-four days to complete.

Paul Cuffe remained in Sierra Leone for three additional months. He concluded his survey of the region's resources and

---

[88] See various entries for July, August, and September 1811, Cuffe Journal.
[89] Quoted in Asa Briggs, *Victorian Cities,* p. 86.
[90] *Life of William Allen,* I, pp. 104–5.

completed his plans for American Negro assistance to the fledgling colony. At the same time, he acted as midwife in the establishment of The Friendly Society of Sierra Leone, a black-run cooperative trading organization sponsored by one of the colony's Methodist congregations.

Cuffe placed great faith in this new body. He fully expected The Friendly Society to evolve into the linchpin of Sierra Leone's economic development and that it would become the very nexus of all the colony's subsequent self-help projects. Anticipating the ideas of Booker T. Washington, Cuffe laid great stress on black self-reliance and economic independence. Consequently, he expected that with proper leadership and occasional help from English and American supporters, the Society over the years would become the instrument for effecting a rational development of the colony's economic resources.[91] In the meantime, however, it would be most useful in breaking the strangle hold that the twenty-odd European traders[92] held over the region's commerce.[93]

The American's English friend William Allen enthusiastically supported his plan and helped launch the Society by providing it with its initial capital, a gift of £70.[94] Allen, Thomas Clarkson and some other members of the African Institution organized a smaller group in London to handle Sierra Leone's exports and to funnel imports into Freetown at cheap prices. Lest anyone misunderstand their intentions, the English promoters' purposes were clearly spelled out in the organization's long-winded title: A Society for the Purpose of Encouraging the Black Settlers of Sierra Leone, and the Natives of Africa generally, in the Cultivation of their Soil, by the Sale of their Produce.[95]

---

[91] Fyfe, *History of Sierra Leone,* pp. 112–13.

[92] Professor Staudenraus believes that "The Society served as Cuffe's commercial depot in Africa" (*The African Colonization Movement,* p. 10). But see Fyfe, *History of Sierra Leone,* pp. 113, 141.

[93] The Western world had little interest in trade with Sierra Leone—always excepting the illicit slave trade. At this time the colony's principal legal export was timber (African oak and camwood), and the traffic amounted to less than £40,000 annually. Imports from Europe were slight and consisted of such essential household goods as tools, cloth, pots and pans. See Fyfe, *op. cit.,* pp. 125, 140–43, 152.

[94] *Life of William Allen,* I, p. 116.

[95] *Ibid.,* p. 139.

Heartened by London's response to The Friendly Society, and also by the evident faith Freetown's inhabitants entrusted in him, Cuffe now believed the trip to Sierra Leone was well worth the sacrifice of time, effort and money. He had become so mesmerized by his reception there that he assumed most civilized blacks in the area had become transformed into a legion of his devoted followers. There was no doubt left in his mind that the colony would measure up to his requirements as a site on which to launch the African awakening.

Early in 1812 Cuffe began making last minute preparations for his voyage home. Before departing, he managed to prepare and to circulate cautionary instructions to his "scattered brethren and fellow countrymen at Sierra Leone." Like the prophet Moses, the American was apprehensive that his people, in sight of the promised land, would revert to their heathen ways once his forceful leadership was no longer present. Fearful that Christianity had established only shallow roots in the colony, and sensing a tendency to backslide on the part of many of the inhabitants of Freetown, he urged those who wished to be saved to follow Christian teachings and to worship God in the true spirit. The faithful, he assured them, shall "find a living hope which will be as an anchor to the soul and a support under afflictions. In this hope may Ethiopia stretch out her hand unto God. Come, my African brethren and fellow countrymen, let us walk together in the light of the Lord."[96]

His final message came in the form of a short epistle. Entitled simply "Advice," it exhorted his audience to follow three basic rules of conduct:

1. Be sober and steadfast at all times, "doing justly, loving mercy, and walking humbly."
2. Teach the young, "so that they may be redeemed from the corruptions of the world . . . not swearing, following bad company and drinking of spiritous liquors."
3. Discharge obligations faithfully, be industrious, and prepare

[96] "Address To My Scattered brethren and fellow countrymen at Sierra Leone," printed in Paul Cuffe, *A Brief Account of the Colony of Sierra Leone in Africa,* pp. 8–9.

the mind "for the reception of the good seed, which is promised to all that will seek after it."

There could be no deviation from this code, he cautioned, because
"I want that we should be faithful in all things, that so we may
become a people, giving satisfaction to those who have borne the
heat and burden of the day, in liberating us from a state of
slavery."[97]

Then, taking on a cargo of African products, consisting chiefly
of exotic woods, Cuffe sailed for the United States on February 11,
1812. He dropped anchor at his Westport dock on April 19, 1812.
A few days after Cuffe's homecoming, a United States revenue
cutter seized the brig *Traveller*.[98] Its owner was charged with
having violated existing trade laws by bringing a British cargo to
the United States. America was on the verge of going to war with
England and importation of goods from Britain or her possessions
now was prohibited. The Westport sea captain, having inadver-
tently violated the law, hastily journeyed to Washington in order to
plead his case.

Again forearmed with letters of recommendation from powerful
community leaders, the persistent missionary arrived in the national capital on the afternoon of May 1. A raw and half-finished
city whose founders had laid out grandiose plans for its future
growth and development, Washington in the spring of 1812 presented a squalid vista. Streets that were broad boulevards on an
architect's map were nothing more than dusty paths that turned
into swampy quagmires after a rainstorm. Ambassadors, Con-
gressmen and Supreme Court justices all lived in clapboard board-
ing houses separated from each other by vast expanses of nothing-
ness. The Capitol was little more than an uncompleted shell, and
the White House was cold, drafty and difficult to live in.

Still, this small, cramped, frustrated, cantankerous, war-rumor-

97 "Advice," printed in Cuffe, *A Brief Account of the Colony of Sierra
Leone,* p. 9.
98 No official records of the seizure of *Traveller* by United States officials
appear to have survived. A thorough search among the records of the United
States Treasury Department for 1812 in the National Archives failed to turn
up any information. The archival holdings of the United States District
Courts in Boston, Massachusetts, and Providence, Rhode Island, proved
equally barren.

filled community greeted the black newcomer with a certain be-
mused and interested awe. Here was a man just returned from
Africa, that land of mystery, savagery and tragedy. Everyone was
curious to learn what "the celebrated Captain Cuffe"—as the
newspapers liked to refer to him—had discovered in the Dark
Continent. The interest in him was so great that Cuffe, with characteristic modesty, noted, "In traveling through the country I perceived that the people seemed to have great knowledge of me."[99]

Thanks to his friends' influence, Cuffe was granted an audience
with the nation's highest authorities. Secretary of the Treasury
Albert Gallatin, a longtime opponent of slavery,[100] greeted the
sea captain with a warmth and friendliness that he reserved for a
special few. President James Madison received Cuffe in the White
House and interviewed him in an atmosphere of extreme cordial-
ity. Thus, this black man from Westport, Massachusetts, became
the first Negro known to have been both entertained as a guest by
the President of the United States and received in his official
residence.

In later years Cuffe's experience with President Madison took
on the aura of folklore. Abolitionists seized upon the meeting as
proof of the black man's intellectual equality with the white man.
And Quaker enthusiasts printed with pride grossly inaccurate
accounts—replete with imagined quotations from their conversations—of the encounter. During the height of the furor over the
Dred Scott decision, *The Friend's Intelligencer* noted, for example,
that

> Capt. Cuffe was a Quaker, and used their plain language, and on
> being introduced to President Madison, he said: "James, I have
> been put to much trouble, and have been abused," and then pre-
> ceeded to tell the President his story . . . and added, "I have
> come here for thy protection. . . ." President Madison, after
> hearing Captain Cuffe's case, promptly ordered the Collector . . .
> to clear Capt. Cuffe . . . and although the Collector believed
> black men had no rights that white men were bound to respect,
> yet he was bound in this instance to respect the right of Capt.
> Cuffe.

[99] Cuffe Journal entry, May 1, 1812.
[100] Henry Adams, *The Life of Albert Gallatin,* pp. 86, 109–10.

Thus, President Madison regarded Captain Cuffe as a citizen of
the United States, and considered that he had rights which the
President of the United States . . . was bound to protect and
respect.[101]

But in reality, their interviews with Cuffe *did* affect both Gallatin and Madison greatly. It was obvious to them from his
manner and bearing, and from the many impressive testimonials to
his character that he brought along with him to Washington, that
this unusual man had no foreknowledge his actions violated national policy. Convinced of his innocence, and extremely concerned
with his predicament, they agreed to order his property restored to
him.[102] Cuffe, with his characteristic grace and humility, later con-
veyed his appreciation for their help in a moving letter to Madison.[103]

In the course of Gallatin's and Madison's interviews with Cuffe,
he was questioned closely concerning his recent African experiences. Secretary Gallatin, in particular, was eager to learn all he
could about Africa and the possibilities it offered as a future site
for mass relocation of American Negroes. Madison, ever on the
lookout for a solution to the race problem in the United States,
evaluated Cuffe's plans carefully, but rejected them reluctantly,
because "many objections had occurred to him against it." Still,
Cuffe's vision impressed the President so greatly that two years
later in 1814 he referred to it in a conversation concerning African
colonization.[104] Clearly, as a direct result of his excursion to

[101] "Paul Cuffe and President Madison," *Friend's Intelligencer*, XIV
(Sept. 12, 1857), p. 412.

[102] Cuffe Journal entry, May 4, 1812; Ms. copy, "Public Proclamation,"
signed by Albert Gallatin, Washington, D.C., May 5, 1812, Cuffe Letter-
book, Cuffe papers.

[103] Cuffe to Madison, Westport, June 20, 1812, Ms. copy, Cuffe papers.
I conducted an exhaustive search of the basic collection of Madison's papers
in the Library of Congress, but I could locate no Madison-Cuffe correspondence.

[104] Anon., *A Narrative of the Early Life, Travels, and Gospel Labors
of Jesse Kersey, late of Chester County, Pennsylvania*, p. 74. Madison,
according to Jesse Kersey, could find no resolution to the problem. He
believed that "difficulties would be present in every plan that could be taken
up. He said the only probable method that he could see, to remedy the evil,
would be for the different states of the Union to be willing to receive them;
and thus they would be spread among the industrious and practical farmers,
and their habits, education and condition would be improved."

Sierra Leone, Paul Cuffe came to be regarded by the government as America's African authority.

It was Cuffe's intention to visit Sierra Leone once each year. He planned to bring with him skilled immigrants and needed goods and supplies, and he expected to export African products to cover his expenses. Although he had purchased a house in Freetown in 1811, he did not propose to settle permanently in Africa, because, as he subsequently explained to an English philanthropist, "my wife is not willing to go."[105] However, Cuffe did not return immediately to Sierra Leone. The United States went to war with England in June, 1812, and Americans were forbidden to traffic with the enemy.

Despite the wartime ban on intercourse with the foe, Cuffe was eager to resume his missionary work in Africa. As a Quaker pacifist, Cuffe reasoned that his activities could not be considered actions that would assist or give comfort to the English war effort. He was merely fulfilling God's assignment. Such a task obviously transcended national boundaries or such human frailties as the need for destroying enemy lives and property; and, Cuffe wrote to William Allen, "Notwithstanding the declaration of war between these two countries, I hope that that chain of brotherly union in the true church is not shortened. I can truly say that I feel all near and dear unto me that belongs unto this church of peace and harmony."[106] The British Empire was not the enemy of this black American.

Sierra Leone continued to haunt Cuffe's thoughts throughout 1812 and 1813. He visited Baltimore, Philadelphia and New York, speaking to groups of free Negroes on the "favorable" possibilities of the colony. He also urged Negroes to form organizations in these cities to "communicate with each other . . . and to correspond with the African Institution and with the Friendly Society at Sierra Leone."[107] To disseminate news of his dis-

---

[105] Cuffe to William Allen, Westport, June 12, 1812, Cuffe papers.

[106] Ms. copy, Cuffe to William Allen, n.d. [Westport? July, 1812?]

[107] Ms. copy, Cuffe to William Allen, Westport, June 12, 1812, Cuffe papers.

coveries as widely as possible, he published a pamphlet on present conditions in the colony, "hoping the information may prove serviceable and interesting to some of my friends in the United States."[108]

There was little more he could do for the present. Several of his recent business ventures were unprofitable, and these losses caused him some concern. *Traveller's* 1811–12 voyage to Africa was "not a profitable one as to property." Cuffe's ship *Alpha* "sunk me on my half $3,500 [on its] last voyage." Another Cuffe vessel had sailed around Cape Horn on a whaling voyage, but had not returned. It was expected to reach port shortly, but "I do not see any chance for her to escape the British cruiser and I have no insurance on her."[109] Consequently, he was required to spend much time on his personal business affairs in order to preserve his solvency.

As July blended into August the sea captain again became active in the coastal trade. Several of his vessels were sent also to the Caribbean. He devoted some of his attention to improving food production on the Cuffe farm. Then, there was the new Westport Meeting House project, to which he gave considerable time and cash. And finally, he assumed responsibility for providing formal education for four African apprentices whom he had brought to America on the return voyage from Freetown.[110]

By the summer of 1813 the African missionary arranged his business interests in satisfactory order; now he prepared to renew his efforts to secure permission to return to Sierra Leone with volunteer immigrants. The war between the United States and Great Britain still dragged on. Cuffe recognized, therefore, that both governments would have to be persuaded to relax their ban on trading with enemy nationals before he could put his plans into operation. Therefore, he decided that a two-pronged offensive would have to be mounted: one in Washington, the other in London. Recalling that in 1811 William Allen and the African Institution successfully persuaded British authorities to waive re-

---

[108] Cuffe, *A Brief Account of the Colony of Sierra Leone*, p. 1.

[109] Ms. copy, Cuffe to William Allen, n.d. [Westport?, July, 1812?]

[110] Cuffe to William Thompson and Brothers, Westport, July 15, 1812, Cuffe papers.

strictions on his trading in the colony, Cuffe appointed Allen his London emissary to seek similar concessions once more.[111] Cuffe cheerfully accepted responsibility for conducting the American campaign.

On January 7, 1814, the President of the United States and both houses of Congress received copies of a "singular and rather interesting memorial" from Paul Cuffe requesting authorization to resume his civilizing mission to Sierra Leone. His petition aroused such interest that *The National Intelligencer* in response to requests of its subscribers published the complete text.[112] Hezekiah Niles also found the lengthy document sufficiently newsworthy to print it in its entirety in his widely circulated and influential *Weekly Register*.[113]

The carefully phrased memorial emphasized at the outset that its author's motives were "dictated by that philanthropy which is the offspring of Christian benevolence"[114] in offering a plan for civilizing Africans "within their native climate." The petition traced Cuffe's early interest in seeking to convince Africans that the practice of "selling their fellow creatures into a state of slavery for life as [being] very inconsistent" with the principles of equity and justice. It went on to outline his later activities in behalf of Africa, noting that he had "conceived it a duty incumbent upon him . . . to give up a portion of his time and his property" to visit Sierra Leone and to devise "such means as might be in his power to promote the improvement and civilization of Africans."

The memorialist recounted his visit to London and his meetings there with "celebrated philanthropists," who unanimously endorsed his plans for African renewal. His views had been communicated to free Negroes in Baltimore, Philadelphia, New York and Boston, and many had responded enthusiastically. In view of the widespread interest in the project, and assuming the British would cooperate, the petition solicited Congress to grant Cuffe permission to employ *Traveller* to take to Sierra Leone some free Negro immigrants. *Traveller*'s cargo would include provisions,

[111] Sherwood, "Paul Cuffe," pp. 195–97.

[112] *The National Intelligencer,* January 11, 1814.

[113] *Niles Weekly Register,* January 22, 1814, pp. 338–39.

[114] All quotations from Cuffe's petition are taken from the text as printed in *Niles Weekly Register,* January 22, 1814.

"implements of husbandry, and machinery for some mechanic arts. [The ship would] bring back such of the native productions of that country as may be wanted." Congress could be assured, of course, that "pecuniary profit does not enter into calculation in the object in contemplation . . . yet without a little aid from the trifling commerce of that country, the expense would fall too heavy on" the expedition's organizers.

Bills honoring Cuffe's request were introduced into Congress by Senator Christopher Gore and Representative Laban Wheaton, both of Massachusetts, on January 7, 1814. The Senate acted first and with surprisingly little debate voted 18–6 on January 25 to pass the bill. The legislation's fate in the House of Representatives was quite different. Here it ran into a wall of opposition.

The House Committee on Commerce and Manufactures on February 9 urged defeat for the proposal. To waive the embargo restrictions for Cuffe, the Committee noted,

> for a purpose which, how benevolently soever conceived, cannot be considered in any other light than as speculative—the efforts heretofore made and directed by the zeal and intelligence of the Sierra Leone Company having failed to accomplish the object designed by its institution.[115]

On March 18 the bill came before the House and "underwent a discussion of a very diffuse nature, and of no little length."[116] Supporters stressed Cuffe's excellent character and the benefits for the United States of "the establishment of an institution which would invite the emigration of blacks, a part of our population which we could well spare." Clearly, the bill's proponents regarded Cuffe's project as a possible opening for the elimination of Negroes from the United States. All other considerations or issues relating to the bill were secondary.

The bill's opponents were no less racist. They were as anxious to rid this country of blacks as were Cuffe's supporters. Moreover, they, too, conceded that the black missionary was noble, pure and philanthropic. However, the opposition argued that Cuffe could

---

[115] *Annals of the Congress of the United States,* 13th Congress, 1st and 2nd Sessions, pp. 569, 570, 601, 861–63, 1265.
[116] *Ibid.,* p. 1881.

take his immigrants to Africa on board a neutral vessel. Many felt it would be a gross impropriety "to permit him to carry out a cargo, which was not at all necessary to his views of propagating the gospel." Still others feared the possible consequences of relocating newly freed American slaves in British territory. But the most convincing reason offered for a Nay vote was that the enemy would never grant Cuffe a trading license unless it was considered advantageous to its interest. Therefore, they believed such legislation of necessity would aid the British. The bill was voted down, 65 to 72.[117]

The American's English ally was equally unsuccessful. William Allen did receive a friendly hearing from most of His Majesty's ministers. In fact, the Crown was willing to grant Cuffe a trading license but, with the war still in progress, it could not guarantee his ship's safety. Government officials feared that an unscrupulous and greedy naval officer just might pluck the vessel as a prize of war. Reluctantly, therefore, Allen withdrew the application for a license. He felt that the risk to Cuffe was too large.[118] Deeply disappointed but undismayed, Cuffe waited impatiently for the war's conclusion.

True to his vow, he returned to Africa once peace was declared. *Traveller* sailed for Sierra Leone on December 10, 1815, with a cargo of goods and a party of thirty-eight American Negro pioneers, some eighteen adults and twenty children. The passage over, however, was one of the worst experiences in Cuffe's many years at sea. Twenty of the fifty-six days of the voyage were filled with violent storms and squalls, with each succeeding tumultuous gale destined seemingly to be the one that would end *Traveller*'s odyssey. Everyone on board was miserable. The passengers and the crew were seasick most of the time. Many came down with various illnesses, even after "the tempestuous weather abated." Cuffe, however, was spared—he was somehow "favored with my health." All in all, it was "20 days of the most tremendous weather that I ever remember experienced of," Cuffe later reported. Still, "through mercy we were preserved." But as one who believed in

[117] *Ibid.*, pp. 1881–82; *Niles Weekly Register*, April 2, 1814, p. 78.
[118] Sherwood, "Paul Cuffe," p. 197; *Life of William Allen*, I, pp. 180–81.

signs from Divine Providence, perhaps Cuffe should have taken heed that the storms were a signal of impending disaster.[119]

Traveller arrived at Freetown on February 3, 1816, to a rather cool reception. With evident reluctance the authorities permitted the passengers to debark into this scrubby little outpost of the Empire. The prospect that Cuffe's thirty-eight émigrés were the advance contingent of a possible black exodus from the United States to Sierra Leone did not please the British officials. They had their hands full governing the present unruly population, and they did not welcome additional problems—which the Americans seemed certain to become. But ultimately they allotted the new-comers free land and agreed to their settling in the colony per-manently.

Captain Cuffe did not fare so well. Despite his most vigorous protests, he was required to pay import duties on his cargo. Since he had borne the passage expenses for thirty of the colonists, the expedition became for him a financial calamity. He lost more than four thousand dollars on the venture.[120]

This latest misfortune did not cause him to give up in despair, however. He reported in almost rapturous terms the growth of The Friendly Society in four years from a net worth of £70 to £1,200.[121] He also reaffirmed his profound conviction that once three-way commercial traffic between the United States, Africa and Europe commenced on a permanent basis, Africa's salvation would be close at hand.[122] Cuffe left Sierra Leone on April 4, 1816, intend-ing to return the following year. He sailed home a little chastened, but still firmly convinced that his great scheme eventually would succeed.

Sometime in 1816—the precise date cannot be determined—

[119] Cuffe to William Rotch, Jr., Sierra Leone, February, 1816, Cuffe papers.

[120] *Second Annual Report of the American Society for Colonizing the Free People of Colour of the United States* (Washington, D.C., 1819), p. 122.

[121] See for example, Cuffe to Samuel J. Mills, Westport, August 6, 1816, Cuffe papers.

[122] See Cuffe's lengthy letter to William Allen, Sierra Leone, April 1, 1816, Cuffe papers.

Cuffe's African rehabilitation program took on an even greater dimension, for it now became a mass emigration plan for blacks. Many forces and influences that worked on him over the years coalesced in 1816 to convince Cuffe that the only hope—nay, the only prospect for salvation—for America's Negroes was their complete removal from this country and subsequent relocation elsewhere. He did not abandon the notion of saving Africa, but now the plight of the black man in the United States assumed first place in his hierarchy of priorities. If he was not the father of black nationalism, by this decision Paul Cuffe became a leading contender for the distinction.[123]

Cuffe, despite his surface impression of simplicity, was a very complex and sensitive man. As with so many other free Negroes, from the time he became aware of race consciousness he was torn with the duality, the "two-ness," the love-hate relationship of being a black man in a white racist society. His psyche was beset with conflict between the impulse to achieve accommodation with the dominant culture and, because he could not be accepted, one of two alternatives: to rebel and tear down the oppressors' institutions or to return to Africa and live in an all-black society. His activities in 1816 and 1817, the last eighteen months of his life, disclosed that Cuffe had become a living example of one of the most important and continuous themes in American history, the struggle of black ambivalence—loyalty to either mother Africa or America.

He started out in life a convinced believer in the American Dream. As we have seen, he followed all of its principles and precepts. The sea captain had made his way from rags to riches in accordance with what had become the classic pattern. This black man lived a blameless moral life. He rose to many heights and reaped many rewards—including the friendship of James Madison, President of the United States. Yet even at the peak of his success there were constant reminders that because of his blackness Paul Cuffe was an alien in his native country.

[123] There are as many claimants to the title as there are beds in which George Washington supposedly slept. One of the latest contenders is Dr. Martin Robinson Delany (1812–1885). See Theodore Draper, "M. R. Delany: The Father of American Black Nationalism," *The New York Review of Books,* XIV (March 12, 1970), pp. 33–41.

Cuffe experienced the sting of discrimination during every phase of his career. Personal rebuffs and humiliations were a daily occurrence for a black man of even his stature. At the moment of perhaps his greatest personal triumph—the 1812 audience with Madison in the White House—the victory turned bitter-sweet when on the return trip home a boorish white man tried to humble him while both shared a coach between Washington and Baltimore. In fact, every rest stop along the way from Washington to New Bedford became a nightmare for him. Most places denied him the same accommodations given his fellow passengers, and at some stops he was refused service of any type.[124]

Two years later Congress made it quite clear to him that in rejecting his petition for a license to return to Sierra Leone the people's elected representatives longed for the day when this land finally would be rid of the despised black race. But for the war with Britain they would have gladly aided him in his "benevolent" campaign.[125]

However, Cuffe did not transform his missionary role into that of a colonizationist simply because of personal pique or in resentful response to the cruelties a segregated society imposed upon him. This was an annoying and hateful matter, but it was too petty by itself to cause him to give up on the United States. Other factors contributed to his change in direction.

The year 1816 was one of great racial tension in this country. Several purported slave plots and actual uprisings that year threw many white Southerners into near hysteria.[126] The all too recent blood bath in Santo Domingo[127] reminded them vividly of what a large-scale slave rebellion with all its attendant horrors could do. A few, so shaken by the possibility of race war, began to consider the prospect of manumission as a means for avoiding a future holocaust.

[124] See Cuffe Journal entries May 5–14, 1812.

[125] See above, p. 64.

[126] Herbert Aptheker, *Negro Slave Revolts in the United States, 1526–1860* (New York, 1939), pp. 38–39, 72.

[127] For an excellent treatment of the slave uprisings in Santo Domingo and the subsequent expulsion of the French, see C. L. R. James, *The Black Jacobins: Toussaint L'Ouverture and the San Domingo Revolution,* 2d edition, *passim.*

For Cuffe and other like-minded humanitarians, Southern neuroses offered a welcome opportunity. They were aware that many slaveholders expressed reluctance to free their bondsmen because of the ever-present racial shibboleths. But, they reasoned, offer the owners the prospect that liberated blacks would be removed from America forever, and many a Southerner would jump at the opportunity to free himself of his great burden.[128] This was a delusion. In reality, most Southerners had already come to accept slavery—that "peculiar institution"—as a permanent part of the American scene. But it was upon such quicksands of false expectations that grandiose colonization undertakings were begun.

Moreover, a handful of black emigrationists reinforced the fantasies of Cuffe and his fellow colonizers. These blacks, embittered by a forced hand-to-mouth life in the United States, were prepared to abandon their native land for an uncertain but manly existence in Africa. The wellspring of despair was so great among blacks in many Northern communities that its virus infected, at least for a moment, such a normally levelheaded person as James Forten, the important Philadelphia Negro leader.[129] When the news spread that Cuffe actually had transported colonists to Sierra Leone, several dozen prospective expatriates wrote him letters seeking information about the Dark Continent. By this time Cuffe's imagination was highly fanciful, and with little effort he convinced himself and others that these contacts were the possible vanguard for potentially tens of thousands of free Negroes desirous of returning to the motherland.[130]

Hindsight tells us that colonization was an impossible solution to racism, that it appealed only to those blacks who, abused and

[128] See, for example, Cuffe to Stephen Gould, Westport, September 20, 1816, and Cuffe to Peason Freeman, Westport, October 19, 1816, Cuffe papers.

[129] James Forten to Cuffe, Philadelphia, January 25, 1817, Cuffe papers. Most historians assumed that Forten opposed colonization from the very beginning. However, William Loren Katz and I discovered—independently of each other—Forten's temporary defection. See Katz's Preface to his edition of William Lloyd Garrison's *Thoughts on African Colonization* (New York: Arno Press, 1969).

[130] See, for example, Cuffe to Samuel R. Fisher, Westport, August 14, 1816, and Cuffe to Thomas Foy, Westport, September 7, 1816, Cuffe papers.

degraded by a hate-filled discrimination that could no longer be borne, seized upon this expedient in desperation.[131] But to those caught up in the tragedy of racism, an exodus from the United States seemed no more irrational than the madness of their daily existence in the land of the Declaration of Independence, where, supposedly, all men were created equal. Consequently, to Cuffe and his followers, a speedy departure from the United States for blacks made sense, and they attempted to develop plans for the realization of their utopian dream.

Cuffe's "realism" went so far as to provide for *two* colonies for America's displaced Negroes. A site somewhere in Africa would offer a welcome for those blacks searching for an African identity, while another center could be established along the western fringes of the Louisiana Purchase for Negroes disinterested in an African return. In this fashion a black could have freedom of choice in selecting the setting for his exile.[132]

The final impetus to Cuffe's conversion to large-scale black removal came from white colonizationists. Among the numerous reform movements that got under way after the War of 1812, African colonization was at first one of the most popular. Cuffe, of course, was the acknowledged dean of American Africanists— even if he achieved the distinction almost by default. Because of his two voyages to Sierra Leone, he was regarded universally as a fountainhead of invaluable knowledge about African geography, climate, flora and fauna, customs, opportunities for settlement, et cetera. As such, he was the logical person for colonization promoters to tap for help, and they looked to the Westporter for both inspiration and information.

Commencing in late 1816, the Reverend Samuel J. Mills and the Reverend Robert Finley, the two spark plugs of colonization, cannonaded Cuffe with letter after letter soliciting his help. They besieged him with requests for African data. Finley and Mills made it clear, also, that they would welcome his endorsement of their benevolent scheme to dump into Africa as many free Negroes

---

[131] See the discussion in Redkey, *Black Exodus,* pp. 1–23.
[132] Cuffe to Robert Finley, Westport, January 8, 1817, and Cuffe to James Brian, Westport, January 16, 1817, Cuffe papers.

as were willing to go. Better still, their most fervent wish was for
Cuffe himself to lead the wandering black Israelites to the land of
Canaan.[133]

Mills and Finley were outstanding salesmen, and their enthusiasm for colonization was infectious. Their solicitations, without
question, helped arouse Cuffe's latent feelings for black migration.
He fell in with their plans and expected to cooperate with them to
the best of his ability.

Thus, while sincere abolitionists suspiciously regarded the newly
founded American Colonization Society as nothing more than a
vehicle for protecting slavery in Southern states, Cuffe had moved
so far into the colonization orbit that in his naïveté he endorsed the
slaveholder-dominated Society. Unlike the white abolitionists, he
either failed to take note or deliberately ignored the fact that the
Colonization Society was concerned only with encouraging free
Negroes to emigrate from America, and that its members were not
interested in disturbing the status quo in the South.[134] Had Cuffe
lived, no doubt, he would have been employed by the Society as a
useful ornament.[135]

But he was never to see the African continent again. As the new
year 1817 opened, Cuffe's health began to fail. There was hope for
a time that he might recover, but by July it became obvious that he
was dying. In late August his condition became so critical that he
"took a solemn leave of his family, wife, children, grandchildren,
brothers, sisters and others. Shaking hands with all, showing
fellowship and friendship, [he] bid us farewell." Growing progres-

[133] See for example Finley to Cuffe, Washington, December 5, 1816, and
Mills to Cuffe, Washington, December 26, 1816, Cuffe papers.

[134] See Staudenraus, *African Colonization Movement,* pp. 27–31.

[135] Redkey is incorrect when he says (*Black Exodus,* p. 19) that "even
Paul Cuffe had spoken out against the new organization [the American
Colonization Society] . . . Cuffe wanted emigration for the purpose of
opening trade with Africa, enriching the settlers, and spreading civilization
and Christianity. Although these goals were also affirmed by the Society,
the difference was that Cuffe was black and his efforts could be considered
self-help. . . . Neither Cuffe nor the Colonization Society appears to have
harbored black nationalist ideas." Redkey fails to note the subtle change in
Cuffe's ideas so that by the beginning of 1817 he embraced both African
regeneration and black nationalism. See his letters to Mills, Westport, January 6, 1817, and to Finley, Westport, January 8, 1817, Cuffe papers.

sively weaker, the courageous black sea captain died during the early morning hours on September 7, 1817, "sensible to the last moments." At the age of fifty-nine he "fell asleep in Jesus and is gone home to glory, where wicked men in, nor devils, cannot afflict."[136]

Cuffe's death terminated the first phase of the black nationalist movement in the United States. It did not stir significantly again until the dark days of the post-Reconstruction era, when a combination of economic difficulties and intense racism implanted in the minds of many Negroes such a feeling of hopelessness that in their distress they embraced African reversion.[137] In the intervening half century or so no black nationalist leader of any substance emerged as Cuffe's successor. Instead, the black leadership in the free Negro communities almost to a man rejected the concept of a homeland in the Dark Continent, a black Zion in the wilderness. They and their followers preferred to make a stand in America for their freedom and dignity as human beings and as citizens of this country.

The torch of African reversionism, therefore, passed from Cuffe to the white racist colonizationists. The American Colonization Society did its utmost to realize the vision of their black compatriot, but in the end failed miserably.[138] For all the noble talk, the fanfare, the prestigious names associated with the organization, and the intense recruiting among blacks, supporters of colonization convinced only a comparative handful of Negroes to desert America for Africa. This failure illustrates clearly that for most blacks Africa might be the land that provided them with their cultural heritage, but the United States had become the site for the fulfillment of their destiny.

On September 20, 1817, *Niles Weekly Register* noted:

Died at Westport, Ms. on the 7th inst. Paul Cuffe, a very respectable and well known man of color, as a merchant, sea-captain,

[136] John Cuffe to Freelove Cuffe, Westport, September 12, 1817, Cuffe papers.
[137] Redkey, *Black Exodus, passim.*
[138] Staudenraus, *African Colonization Movement, passim.*

and philanthropist. He was a member of the Society of Friends, or Quakers, and much esteemed by all classes of people, for his morality, truth and intelligence.

No more fitting epitaph could be written for this brave and honorable man.

II

The Cuffe Journal and Letters

Although Paul Cuffe failed in his dual mission to Westernize and colonize the African continent, he did leave to posterity a priceless gift. His benefaction is the careful record he maintained of his life's work. The black Yankee had a Puritan sense of self-scrutiny and introspection that impelled him to preserve for others a record of his life, thoughts and activities. Consequently, Cuffe's papers in the New Bedford Free Public Library provide the scholar with a rare opportunity to investigate in depth an area of considerable and increasing importance that heretofore has been little known. His scrapbooks, letter-press notebooks, and account books document fully the unusual and multifold nature of his business enterprises. They record Cuffe family history; they also detail, as perhaps few other sources can do, the early struggle of American Negroes to achieve political equality in the United States.

Though the collection contains a veritable treasure trove of information for the economic and the social historian, its greatest significance lies in the account Cuffe has left us of his commitment to African advancement. This remarkable individual recorded his impressions of Sierra Leone in a journal that he maintained during 1811 and 1812 and in a series of letters that he sent to various English and American friends and supporters. Paul Cuffe was a man with a dream, but he was also a sometime realist, and his journal and letters are noteworthy for their perceptive analysis of the colony's assets, accomplishments and potential, as well as its liabilities. They give perhaps the clearest account we have of actual conditions in Sierra Leone in the early nineteenth century.

But the journal and letters contain much more. America's African expert was besieged with requests for information about the continent from American Negroes weighing the merits of returning to the homeland. Each letter was answered promptly. In the course of his response, Cuffe often would comment on the plight of American Negro slaves, the possibility of emancipation on a large scale, and various alternatives for determining the future for the mass of soon-to-be-free Negroes.

White Christian ministers exploring the practicability of large-scale Negro emigration to Africa picked Cuffe's brain for data on climate, topography, agriculture, mineral resources, trade potential, ideal sites for establishing colonies, and countless other matters. Of particular interest is Cuffe's correspondence with the Reverend Samuel J. Mills, professional fund raiser for many sectarian benevolent societies, and the advance man for the newly formed American Society for Colonizing the Free People of Color in the United States. Mills solicited Cuffe's opinion not only on African colonization but also on many facets of black-white relations in America. Cuffe's considered replies made a deep impression on Mills. No doubt, Cuffe's judgments weighed heavily as well with other promoters of the American Colonization Society.

The documents that follow are divided into two sections. The first part consists of the journal Paul Cuffe maintained during 1811 and 1812. It begins with an account of his last minute arrangements prior to departing for Sierra Leone and terminates with a notation of his return to Westport from Washington after his successful negotiations with Secretary Gallatin and President Madison.

The journal faithfully reveals Cuffe's intense religious zeal and his almost single-minded devotion to fulfilling his divine commission to bring civilization to Africa. It also confirms his basic honesty and humanity. The journal exposes all too clearly his two major weaknesses, a basic and trusting naïveté, and a life style totally lacking in a sense of humor. Furthermore, too many journal entries are limited to recording weather conditions and navigational computations, and tell us little about the captain or his cause. Such notations have been pruned judiciously so as to spare the reader unnecessary tedium.

Occasionally, laconic jottings, because of their brevity, tantalize and frustrate the reader who wants to know more about particular incidents and individuals. Unfortunately, Cuffe was not the most eloquent or verbose nineteenth century American diarist. But for the most part, the journal does offer extraordinarily detailed reports of Cuffe's daily activities during this vital two year period.

His chronicle is virtually intact. However, an occasional page has been vandalized, presumably by some very young Cuffe descendant all unaware of the importance of already-used paper he was dealing with. These excisions are noted in the text.

The second section contains a generous selection of the captain's correspondence. The letters primarily relate to Cuffe's preparations for his two voyages to Sierra Leone, his experiences there, and his thoughts in general on Negro emancipation and resettlement schemes. Since Cuffe's views on the abolition of Negro slavery and on colonization plans were developed as a result of a dialogue between him and many concerned ethical and theological humanitarians, I have included pertinent letters from his respondents.

The letters, like the journal, reaffirm Paul Cuffe's fervent commitment to improving the welfare of his fellow man. They demonstrate his sincere and abiding hatred for the institution of Negro slavery. His correspondence also acknowledges the strong sense of American nationality that had developed among many free Negroes, and, to Cuffe's acute discomfort, their forceful objection to African repatriation plans. Some of the letters in the collection document with great clarity the infinite capacity for self-deception that both white and black American philanthropists of the period possessed. These Samaritans anticipated an ecstatic Negro response to emigration schemes, but this was not the solution to the race problem that most Negroes wanted.

Other letters deal with significant aspects of the slavery question that modern scholars shy away from or discuss all too infrequently. These latter communications expose the important role that Africans played in the slave trade, both as primary suppliers of the resource and as middlemen in the exchange of their fellow Africans for Western manufactured goods.

And finally, Cuffe's letters reveal that as prospects for large-scale Negro emancipation in the United States appeared to brighten, tragically he gradually came to accept the dictum that racial assimilation was an impossibility in emerging nineteenth century democratic America.

In reading the journal and the letters it should be remembered that Paul Cuffe was barely literate. By his own account, as a youth he learned to read and write with a few weeks' diligent application to the three *R*'s. Consequently, his spelling, of necessity, was both creative and original. Punctuation did not concern him at all. He rarely employed any punctuation marks in either his journal or his correspondence. Syntactic misconstruction abounds throughout his papers. Cuffe was a master of the non sequitur, and samples of the genre are sprinkled generously over most pages of the journal and in a substantial number of the letters.

I have not tampered with Cuffe's unique style of phrasing. But for the sake of clarity, I have modernized the mariner's spelling, and I have introduced the required punctuation. These editorial intrusions have in no manner altered the content or flavor of the journal and letters. Instead, it is hoped that they will assist the reader to gain an insight into the early nineteenth century world of humanitarian idealism.

One final note of caution: In the course of his search for a better life for his fellow blacks, Cuffe met with the great people of his time, the near-great, and countless obscure Samaritans. Wherever possible, I have endeavored to identify, in the footnotes that follow, the numerous individuals whom he encountered during his travels or with whom he engaged in correspondence.

Moreover, the reader may encounter difficulties with some of the place names referred to in the text. On his trips to Africa Cuffe considered many possible sites for black relocation colonies. Some of these locations are familiar to students of African geography; others, however, are little known even to the African expert. I have managed to discover and cite in the footnotes many of the rivers, mountains and towns Cuffe mentions, but others—because of his unique phonetic spelling—remain obscure.

III

The Journal

I

PREPARATIONS

Paul Cuffe Account Book kept by himself relative to his voyage on vessel towards Sierra Leone on board the brig *Traveller* of Westport, Thomas Wainer, Master. Her crew, consisting of nine in number, all people of color, except one, [an] apprentice boy[1] to Paul Cuffe. Paul Cuffe considers himself as owner of the brig and supercargo. Mrs. Catherine Cook [and] Capt. Richardatt, a passenger from Philadelphia, [are also sailing with us] for Sierra Leone, making eleven persons in all on board,[2] namely: Paul Cuffe, Thomas Wainer, John Wainer, Michael Wainer, Jr.,[3] John

---

[1] Abraham Rodin, a Swede from Göteborg, in June 1807 apprenticed himself for six years to Paul Cuffe. Rodin's purpose was to be "learnt [*sic*] seamanship and other industry" from his Negro master. Untitled Ms. apprentice contract, May 7, 1808, Cuffe papers; see also Sheldon H. Harris, "Paul Cuffe's White Apprentice," *American Neptune*, XXIII, No. 3 (July, 1963), pp. 192–96.

[2] Cuffe here seems to be confusing crew and passengers. Actually there were eleven crew members, which would make the number of persons on board thirteen.

[3] The Wainer brothers were Cuffe's nephews, their Pequot Indian father, Michael Wainer, having married Cuffe's sister Mary in October, 1772. The Wainers were closely allied with the Cuffes, and there was a good deal of intermarriage between the two families. They also engaged in numerous joint business ventures over the years. Paul Cuffe, for example, rarely embarked on a lengthy voyage without taking several Wainers on board as officers and mates.

Marsters, Samuel Hicks, Zachariah White, Joseph Hemmenway, Charles Augustus Freeling, and Thomas Caton.[4]

We left Westport for Philadelphia 25 November 1810.[5] I [this] day [was] accompanied [to the ship] by [my] brother John Cuffe, Paul Wainer, [his] son Paul, and William Cuffe an[d] my apprentice, Abraham Rodin, who left us at 2 o'clock. All well, wind at North; pleasant weather and smooth sea.

4 December arrived at Philadelphia after a passage of 9 day[s]. Met Andrew Taylor, my freightor to Philadelphia, with barley—it was worth $1 per bushel—and called on [the] Friends in Philadelphia. They appointed a [meeting] time at [the] Arch Street Meeting House,[6] and after [a] feeling conference, they expressed satisfaction [with my plans]; and [they then] left me at liberty. Hence it [Cuffe's Sierra Leone project] fell under the head [leadership] for [of] one's former advisors, John James and Alexander Wilson.[7]

I called on them. John [James] professed that he could not see any other way better than [for me] to take a load of corn[8] that he had long held and take it to Portugal or Cadiz. I then had to tell him, the said John James, that [that] was not my business. It rather appeared to me that it was not for the profit of grain [sales] that I had undertaken this voyage. But, I had about $4000 property,[9] and would wish to proceed as far as that would carry

[4] Marsters, Hicks, White, Hemmenway, Freeling and Caton were local blacks who had sailed with Cuffe on a number of earlier ventures.

[5] The Westport captain entered calendar dates in his journal as follows: 25 day 11 mo., etc. For purposes of clarity, I shall date Cuffe journal entries in a more conventional manner—e.g., 25 November 1810.

[6] The journal frequently mentions Paul Cuffe's attendance at a "meeting," or his having gone to the "X Street Meeting House." For Cuffe, "meeting" referred to religious services, and "meeting house" was synonymous with a Quaker house of worship.

[7] John James and Alexander Wilson were Philadelphia Quaker merchants who over the years enjoyed a long and mutually profitable business relationship with Cuffe. Active in many abolitionist campaigns, and interested in African rehabilitation, James and Wilson kept in close contact with their English counterparts in the African Institution.

[8] Merchants in the nineteenth century still used "corn" as a common descriptive term for most grains. James's load of "corn" may have been wheat just as well as corn.

[9] Cuffe is referring to a cargo of general merchandise worth $4000. He ex-

me. And it appeared that if this opportunity was neglected, I might never expect to have the opportunity again.[10]

John then gave up the prospect of shipping his corn and he and I left Alexander [Wilson]. And [as we departed] he told me he believed my concern [for Africa] was real, and that he would assist me in [out]fitting for the voyage; and [he would] make no charge. I told him it felt pleasant to me, but [I would prefer] if my friends, rather than to burden them, would let me go [without their assistance].

But [James did] have prospect of gain catch his eye the next day. Falling in with a man who came from Sierra Leone in September 1810, and gave very flattering account [of conditions there], John then proposed [to me] of being paid for his subscription if the voyage would afford it. To which I was willing. On further information [coming his way], John [James] proposed to be concerned [to invest in the voyage]. I took it into consideration for some time, [but] could not make it feel pleasant to me. But on looking at it [after further consideration], I consented for him to take one half [share]. But remembering that we refused to make use of Alexander Wilson, and now to shut him [Wilson] out, I could not feel easy. I proposed to invite Alexander Wilson to take concern with us. John [James] consented to it. Alexander [Wilson] accepted afterwards.

I went to Wilmington, and [in my absence] John James changed his mind. [He] wrote to London[11] without any advice of Alexander, and objected against the coming of Alexander, which brought a great trial over me.

---

pected to sell these goods in Africa and hoped that the profits from this traffic would cover his expenses.

[10] The sea captain evidently felt that he had temporized all too long on launching his African redemption scheme. At his "advanced" age it was now or never, and Cuffe, impatient to get under way, would brook no further delays or tamely accept roadblocks set up by his friends.

[11] James evidently protested to the African Institution in London. As we have seen, the African Institution was the key organization supporting the Sierra Leone project, and Cuffe certainly dreaded the prospect of antagonizing such important sympathizers. Although John James may have given the intrepid sea captain a few anxious moments, subsequent developments suggest that "London" continued to retain complete confidence in Cuffe.

2
SIERRA LEONE: THE PROMISED LAND

The next few pages of the journal have been cut out.
Cuffe sailed from Philadelphia on 2 January 1811.
The journal entries for the first few weeks at sea con-
tain little of importance.

20 January 1811.   Wind Easterly; very rainy night with small wind. Our minds was collected together to wait on the Lord, notwithstanding we were on the great deep. . . .

31 January 1811.   High wind, SSE, and stormy. At 3 a.m. wind and sea struck us down on our beam ends. The [elements] washed John Marsters overboard, but by the help of some loose rigging he regain[ed] the ship again. . . .

11 February 1811.   Pleasant breezes; wind from SE. Three ships in sight standing on our course: the British frigate *Amherst,* a British convict ship, and a Portuguese ship, *Bonsupo,* bound to Rajerara. . . .

13 February 1811.   Gentle breezes, but fair southerly, SSE. Clear weather and pleasant smooth sea, but in the afternoon a longfooted counterswell [arose] out of NW. My time employed in pursuing Clarkson's records on abolishing slavery,[1] which [account] often battered my mind in the sin of his proceedings. And my mind oftentimes when ruminating with my friend at home [Clarkson's work], would hang very heavy over my head. But in giving my mind and dependence on the All Wise Protector, it would afford me consolation and comfort. . . .

21 February 1811.   Fresh trades [winds] and a large sea wind, ENE. The weather clear but smoky. The dust of Africa lodged on our rigging. We judged the land to be about 25 leagues off. . . .

24 February 1811.   This 24 hours begins with small wind and

[1] Thomas Clarkson, *The History of the Rise, Progress and Accomplishment of the Abolition of the African Slave Trade by the British Parliament.*

a hot sun. At 2 p.m. [the air was] almost calm. At 9 p.m. small wind from SW, and later [the wind] inclined Westerly. At 10 a.m. [25 February we] sounded and got bottom for the first ground that we got on the coast of Africa. [Bottom was] 65 fathoms. [It consisted of] some black sand intermixed with fine sand and coarse gravel. Caught one dolphin and many sucker fish. So we had an excellent fish dinner for the first time since we sailed from America. . . .

28 February 1811. At 12 meridian saw the mountains of Sierra Leone bearing SSE. [They appeared to be a] distance [of] 38 miles away. . . . [Later we could see the] dark-colored sand [of the shore].

1 March 1811. At 6 this morning weighed anchor, wind NW. [*Traveller*] stood to the southward until [we arrived at] the Cape line . . . our pilot, or [one of the] passengers mistook the Cape, although it was very plain to me which was the true Cape. At ½ after 8 o'clock we came to in Sierra Leone Road[2] where there was an English frigate—[possessor] of a letter of marque—and 2 vessels that was taken and brought in for trading in slaves, and a small schooner trading craft. [There] was 2 vessels lay[ing] on shore. Appeared to be hulks that had been condemned in slave trade. . . .

2 March 1811. At 7 this morning the Governor [of Sierra Leone] arrived from Bence Island.[3] His excellency permitted all of our cargo to being landed but the 6 bales of India goods. The Governor proposes of taking the bread and beef [I brought from America to sell], but it's not yet determined. But they like the sample well. The navy bread the Governor took, but declined taking the other [type of bread] but at the same price that he took the navy at.

3 March 1811. The Governor preferred [purchased] his beef in the choice I expected of him.

[2] Freetown, Sierra Leone. During the early years of the colony's history, Freetown was both the capital and virtually the only civilized settlement in Sierra Leone.

[3] A large, heavily forested island lying in the estuary of the Sierra Leone River, Bence Island was used by the English as a fortified outpost to protect Freetown from possible attack by sea. The island was the site of an English trading factory as early as the seventeenth century.

4 March 1811. Invitation was given me this day to dine with the Governor,[4] at whose table an extensive observation took place on the slave trade and the unsuccessfulness of the colony of Sierra Leone.

5 March 1811. This day [I had] brought [on deck the] bulk [of my cargo]. [The crew] put on board the crackerdell[5] 30 bulkheads bread. . . . [I] visited the school of 30 girl scholars,[6] which was a pleasing prospect in Sierra Leone.

6 March 1811. This day we are selling more meat, and we hired 3 Kru[7] men at $3 per month, but the capt[ain of the Kru workers] has $4 per month. The man [of] war brig arrived from the Leeward [Islands today].[8] Brought news that a number of Portuguese slave traders [were nearby] to the Leeward[s], but they could not take hold of them by law. $17 is the highest price I can get for my flour.[9]

7 March 1811. This day began with great heat, so we did not [do] much . . . but [we] discharged 10 barrels beef and 10½ barrels flour and 25 barrels bread.

---

[4] Captain Edward Henry Columbine, H.R.N., was the colony's unhappy governor from early 1809 until May 1811. Living in wretched quarters in Freetown and quarreling with some of his subordinates, Columbine longed for the day when he could leave his lucrative but strife-ridden post. Moreover, Columbine suffered a series of personal tragedies while stationed in Sierra Leone. His wife fell victim to a tropical disease, and one of his children died of the same disease a few months later. Columbine left Freetown in May 1811, intending to retire to England, but he died of dysentery en route home.

[5] *Traveller*'s skiff.

[6] There were two rival girls' schools in Freetown. Mrs. Phillis Dawes provided young belles with a broad curriculum. She taught her girls reading (3¢ per week), needlework (5¢ per week), and writing and arithmetic (an additional 10¢ per week). Mrs. Elizabeth Robinson ran a less ambitious program, her skills permitting course offerings only in reading and needlework. Cuffe probably visited Mrs. Dawes's school since it was one of the colony's showcase features.

[7] The Kru were hard-working and honest seafaring tribesmen. Their home was in an area that is now part of the Liberian coast. Scarcely able to scratch out more than a subsistence living in their own country, from time to time many Kru drifted into Freetown in search of jobs. See Michael Bainton, *West African City, A Study of Tribal Life in Freetown*, p. 5.

[8] The distance from the Leeward Islands in the British West Indies to Freetown is approximately 3,350 nautical miles.

[9] Cuffe is evidently referring to the price of flour per barrel.

8 March 1811. This day passeth with an early sea breeze. We passeth this day in landing flour and ship's cargo, and [we] bartered for 316 elephant's teeth which weighed 2,352 lbs. And [I] am to give 2 yards of cloth for [each] 1 pound of ivory. [I expect this trade] to take the entire 6 bales [of cloth][10] in proportion as it takes to pay for the ivory.

9 March 1811. Landed [a] number of articles this day, and [I] attended the Court of Admiralty at a trial of a Portuguese slave schooner. The vessel and cargo was to be condemned for the use of the captives, for [the Portuguese owners of the vessel were found guilty of] trading contrary to the [law] of nations.

10 March 1811. This morning [I] gave the brig *Pratiter* a bill for £129:19. Attended a Methodist meeting in the forenoon, and [afterwards I] dined at Widow Smalleys. . . .

11 March 1811. Landed 2 boat load shingles, and [then I] had much conversation with Henry Warren [about the future] of Sierra Leone in Africa.

12 March 1811. But little done this day, only, Thomas Wainer hired him[self] a house on shore. [He rented it] of Peter Francis[11] at £4 per month. [The house will be the site] where he proposeth of taking goods on shore [and subsequently selling the goods from his house]. The man [of] war brig sailed this day, and the American brig arrived here this day from Boston. Captain Swan, 2 months out (*Eliza*).[12] I found a plank to make the staves to the house. [The plank] measuring 25 feet, which makes 50 foot boards measured at $60 per thousand [foot boards].

13 March 1811. King Thomas[13] came on board to see me. He was an old man, grey headed. [He] appeared to be sober and

[10] The six bales of "India goods" Governor Columbine previously refused Cuffe permission to sell to Freetown residents.

[11] Peter Francis was one of the colony's more successful black emigrants. A Nova Scotian who came to Sierra Leone in 1792, Francis put his carpentry skills to good use in Freetown. He built several sturdy homes, which he rented at a handsome fee to the colony's white officials.

[12] The Boston brig *Eliza* with her skipper Captain Swan had arrived in Freetown after a two-month voyage.

[13] King Tom, as he was known in Sierra Leone, was technically the colony's landlord. A tribal chief from the Bunce River region, his real name was Pa Kokelly. In 1796 he was selected as king of the Koya Temne tribe and in this capacity he exercised a hazy sovereignty over the area known as Cape Sierra Leone.

grave. I treated him with civility and made him a present of a
bible, a history of slavery [written by] Elizabeth Webb,[14] a
Quaker, and a book of an essay on wars, together with several
others [books]. [In addition, I gave the king a] small pamphlet;
[the pamphlet was] accompanied with a letter of advice from
myself [to King Thomas] such as appeared to me to be good to
hand to the king for the use and encouragement of the nations of
Africa. He and his retinue was 13 in number. I served him with
victuals, but it appeared that there was rum wanting, but none was
given [to them]. . . .

14 March 1811. We still continue landing articles. King
George, from Bullom Shore,[15] sent his messenger on board with
[a] present of 3 chickens, and invited me over to see him. I had
concluded on going over, but on having an invitation to dine with
the Governor the other night, it is postponed until [a] second
day.

15 March 1811. This day dined with the Governor, and
landed flour, beef, etc. Rented a house at £4 per month, but was
cautioned by the Governor to be careful [whom] we paid the rent
to, as it was likely that others than the owners would call for the
rent.

16 March 1811. Continued on landing property from on
board [ship]. At 11 o'clock last evening we had an especially
hard tornado. The frigate parted her cable, and it [the tornado]
blowed down 1 or 2 houses in the town. At 6 this afternoon there
was a fire cried, and it burnt 3 houses (they being covered with
thatch grass in lieu of shingles), which appears very dangerous to
take fire as it [is] very dry in Freetown.

17 March 1811. This day being the first day of the week, we
went on shore to the church; and in the afternoon [we went] to
the new Methodist [church]; and in the [late] afternoon visited 3
families, etc.

18 March 1811. This day I went to Bullom Shore in order to

---

[14] Elizabeth Webb, *A Letter from Elizabeth Webb to Anthony William
Boehm with his Answer.*
[15] The region of low-lying shore on the north side of the Sierra Leone
River is known as Bullom Shore.

visit King George, King of Bullom,[16] who received and treated us very cordially. I was accompanied by David Edmonds,[17] John Morgan,[18] and Henry Wainer. We went in a long canoe and in my moss boat. I presented the king with a bible, a testament, a treatise of Benjamin Holme,[19] ditto of Elizabeth Webb,[20] an epistle from the Yearly Meeting, a history called a Short History of a Travel from Babel to Bethel.[21]

19 March 1811. Attended on landing [cargo] and visiting families in Sierra Leone. Found many of them without bibles; and others who had bibles [were] without the living substance of the spirit. . . . [The remainder of the entry on this page was cut from the journal.]

26 March 1811. [In] the morning [there] was some raining. I breakfasted with the Governor, Columbine, and after breakfast had conference with him on the subject of the country and [the possibility of] settling in it. [Our conversation developed] to good satisfaction.

27 March 1811. This day [we] find the island [outside Freetown harbor]; stopping our vessel [there], [we] made out over some accept[ances] for settlement with the debtors [those who purchased some of our goods].

28 March 1811. Haul[ed on board] ship 1 ton camwood of David Edmonds; and the crew employed in ship's duty, healing, hoging, and lead toping.

29 March 1811. This day received [additional quantities of] camwood, and the Kru went and cut some [of the] wood. The

[16] The Bulloms were one of the earliest and most powerful tribes known in Sierra Leone. See Peter Kup, *A History of Sierra Leone 1400–1787,* pp. 4, 6, 123, 161, 171.

[17] David Edmonds, Jr., was a second-generation Nova Scotian. An exceptionally clever carpenter, he ran a thriving shipbuilding business in Freetown.

[18] John Leedham Morgan was still another member of the colony's black middle class. A Jamaica Maroon, Morgan held a variety of minor government posts during a career that spanned more than a quarter of a century.

[19] Most probably Benjamin Holme, *An epistle to Friends and tender minded people in America* . . .

[20] Elizabeth Webb, *Letter to Anthony William Boehm.*

[21] Stephen Crisp, *A Short History of a Long Travel from Babylon, to Bethel.*

ship's people [crew] were employed in painting [the] outside of the vessel.

30 March 1811. Received 1 ton 16 [lbs.] camwood and 1 boat load fir wood; and got some water [on board ship] this day, and some [of the crew were] still employed in painting.

31 March 1811. This day attended the church, and [later on I] dined with David Edmonds. The Mandingo men[22] have the scripture at their tongue, (viz.) the Old Testament, but they deny the New Testament; they own Mohammed [as their] Prophet.

1 April 1811. Let in ballast and 1 ton of camwood of David Edmonds, Jr., and no [other] great [work was] done this day.

2 April 1811. Took in about 3 ton 16.2 [lbs.] this day. [It was] the wood of [Mrs.] Sarah Hadley, [and we purchased it] at £27.10 per ton. Slow getting debts [paid here]. I received [as a memento] James Reid's commission for Lieutenant Governor of Sierra Leone,[23] [dated] November 25, 1789, then granted by Henry Savage, Commander of the frigate *Pomona.*

3 April 1811. Thomas Wainer is much put out and is exceeding wroth [with me] for giving him what I call good advice,[24] but time will make manifest [that] God alone knows the hearts of sinful men, etc. I desire to have Him to be my preserver, etc.

4 April 1811. [We are] getting things regulated [for our departure];[25] ship [soon will be] in order for sea, etc.

5 April 1811. Things seem to regulate, but not entirely settled, but look more clear.

[22] The Mandingos were a northern tribe forcibly converted by the Emperor Askia Mohammed of Songhai to Islam in the sixteenth century. In the seventeenth and eighteenth centuries, the Mandingos, inexorably pushed from their homeland by their enemies, began to penetrate into Sierra Leone in appreciable numbers.

[23] James Reid was one of the colony's first white settlers. In 1787 he was elected governor when Governor Richard Weaver became seriously ill. In 1788 Weaver recovered, accused Reid of thievery, and resumed his post as governor. Reid stayed on in the colony and occupied other important government posts until his death in 1814.

[24] The "advice" consisted of telling Thomas Wainer to avoid serious involvement with some of the Freetown belles.

[25] Encountering difficulties with the British authorities in his attempt to sell his cargo in Sierra Leone, Cuffe planned to return to the United States. He changed his mind in late April and decided instead to try his luck with the British government in London.

6 April 1811. Got 1 boat load of wood on board, and [the crew is] getting through with our painting.

7 April 1811. This forenoon went to Baptist meeting, and in the afternoon went on board [*Traveller*]. [I was] accompanied by Thomas Wainer, John Hazwell, etc. [to the ship]—where, [once on board *Traveller*] we started a ketch off [to shore with] a petition to lay before the people for their approbation. . . . [The remainder of the entries from 8 April until 11 May have been cut from the journal.]

3
GREAT BRITAIN

Although the Sierra Leone authorities greeted Cuffe cordially, they did not welcome his efforts to introduce American goods into the colony. Furthermore, they lacked the power to grant Cuffe permission to bring his fellow countrymen to Freetown as colonists. Consequently, he was confronted with many unexpected obstacles. Cuffe finally was forced to conclude reluctantly that red tape was threatening his missionary scheme for Sierra Leone with failure.

However, Cuffe had powerful friends in London, friends who might be able to obtain for him the needed licenses, permits, et cetera. These friends could ease his way and open many official doors for him. Determined to make one final effort to effect his project, Cuffe planned to seek out his English friends to obtain their assistance. Traveller *sailed from Sierra Leone on May 11, 1811, for Great Britain, and after an uneventful voyage of 62 days docked at Liverpool on July 12, 1811.*

6 June 1811. Pleasant and fair weather. [We were graced this day] with [sight of a] rainbow at night which God placed [before us] as a token that the world should not be destroyed with a deluge or [with an] overflow of waters again. Sent up the maintop gallant yard. . . .

13 June 1811. These 24 hours begins and ends with pleasant weather, but [only with a] small wind. The gulf weed [is] plenty in the latitude from 26 to 30 degrees, and then in approaching to the northward [there is] clear sea in latitude 32°N. Plenty of sun squalls and small men of war [fish in the area]. At 12 meridian caught a tortoise. [There are] plenty of men of war [fish], sun squalls, and breakwater. . . .

30 June 1811. The fore part of these 24 hours clear with fresh wind from the east. At 3 a.m. saw a sail bearing SW 4 or 5 leagues standin[g] Westerly. At 4 a.m. saw a sail on our weather bow. At 6 a.m. [we] spoke her. [She was the] ship *Fanna,* Capt. Cates, 9 days from Liverpool. [*Fanna* was] bound to Newfoundland. Who [*Fanna*] gave us the unhappy news of an engagement having taken place between one of the United States frigates and his British Majesty's ship of war off Sandy Hook.[1]

4 July 1811. These 24 hours commences with small wind, ESE, and a swell from NNW. At 1 p.m. saw a number of sperm whales bound SW. [They] appeared to be in very good mood. . . .

11 July 1811. These 24 hours begins with thick fog, smooth sea, and a small wind. We hear noises with the horn drum and firing of the cannon. At 12 at night the wind breezed forth. At 2 a.m. made the Skerries Light[house], whose light is dark 2/3 of the time. It [the wind] bore NE, [and we] tacked ship until 3 o'clock. [We] then tacked again for the light, but the fog soon shut him in. I sounded 36 fathoms to 18 fathoms of water. [We] stood in the fog. [It was] very thick. East[ward] we made [out] land. [We] stood off [the land] 1½ hours, and then we jibed ship.[2] [We still] stood East. At 12 meridian the fog lifted, the

1 On May 11, 1811, the American frigate *President* was patrolling the waters off Sandy Hook, New Jersey. Sighting the British man-of-war *Little Belt, President* hailed her and ordered her to halt. *Little Belt* refused, and a battle between the two warships developed. *President* emerged victorious, and many Americans believed that now the United States had been avenged for her humiliation by the British navy during the 1807 *Chesapeake-Leopard* affair.

2 A helmsman frequently "jibes" a sailing ship in order to maintain a more advantageous course or to avoid hitting obstructions. In jibing, the

Skerries[3] bore SW, by compass, 4 leagues [distant]. [We] hauled in ESE giving the land a handsome berth. We fired our small arms gun for a pilot, but got none in the fog. This day [we] killed our African pig. It weighed 28 pounds. He gave us a good cook [dinner].

12 July 1811. At 1 p.m. saw a pilot boat toward the shore. Have[ing] fired her signal gun, we hauled our wind for her and she heads for us. At 2 p.m. we received a pilot who directed our course SE by E for Liverpool. At 10 p.m. [we] hove too . . . at 2 a.m. [we] passed the rocks; at 3 a.m. the Custom House boat came alongside; at 4 [a.m. we] hauled into [a Liverpool] dock. This day may be reckoned at 36 hours and called 12 July. [We] arrived safe—all well—after a passage of 62 days, this day.

Soon after we got into the dock, 2 of my men, going out of the dock gate, was met by the press gang[4] and [they were] carried to the rendezvous. The press gang then came on board my vessel and let me know that they had 2 of my men. And [they then] over-hauled [searched] the remainder of the crew, among which they found Aaron Richards, an African that I had taken [as] an apprentice in Africa to instruct in navigation. They claimed him as a British subject, and took him off [*Traveller*]. At 11 o'clock I went to the rendezvous and got the 2 men first mentioned, but they [the authorities] would not let Aaron off. [I] attended to [the] entry of the brig *Traveller;* [I] got through [with this task and

---

captain brings the bow of the vessel through the wind, shifting either from port to starboard or the reverse. I am grateful to my colleague Thomas Bader—an old sea dog—for his technical information.

[3] The Skerries are tiny islands in the Irish Sea located near the large off-shore island of Anglesey. As such, the Skerries serve as a guide to the entrance to the Bay of Liverpool and its great port.

[4] Life aboard British warships in the eighteenth and nineteenth centuries was grim. Consequently, His Majesty's Navy did not attract many volunteers, and the British, as early as the eighteenth century, began to recruit a large proportion of their common sailors via the "impressment" technique. Impressment was virtual kidnapping. Press gangs would scour the English coastal towns and sweep up anyone in their path. The victims usually would then remain in the navy until they either died or acquired a disabling injury. Now locked in mortal combat with Napoleonic France, Great Britain was not especially careful of the nationality of some of her press gang "volunteers."

then I] attended to getting Aaron [his] liberty. Used every influence as I was capable of, but all in vain. I then interceded with my
friends, but in vain.

13 July 1811. This morning the ship *Alpha* arrived, 52 days
from New Orleans, all well. My friends Richard Rathbone and
Thomas Thompson[5] was very anxious in assisting me to regain
Aaron. We got the promise from the regulating officer that Aaron
should not be sent from Liverpool. They [Rathbone and Thomp-
son] wrote immediately to London—for the liberation of Aaron—
with a petition to the Board of Admiralty.

14 July 1811. I this day put up with Thomas Thompson['s
family], and took a first day's Meeting with them. And feeling very
anxious for Aaron's liberty, I took [my] place in the stage for
London. [At] 10 in the evening we set forward for London.
Arrived in London 3 day[s later, the] morning [of 16 July at] 6
o'clock, it [the trip] making 32 hours.

The distance [between Liverpool and London] is 208 miles.
The horses were generally changed every 10 to 15 miles. My
passage [cost] was £4:17/6. These drivers and watchmen [are]
generally chang[ed] every 40 to 50 miles. It is a custom in this
country to give these people as presents (viz.) from 6 pence to a
shilling, and the servants in the public houses that tends the table 3
[pence] or there about. My expenses on the road to London was
about 23 s[hillings].

15 July 1811. This day passed with the pleasant prospect of
traveling through a well cultivated and very fertile country. How
often did I feel my mind enlivened with the peaceful desire that
this land and people ought to enjoy a universal and tranquil peace?

16 July 1811. At 6 this morning arrived in this great city of
London. I put up at an inn and took breakfast. At 10 o'clock took
a pilot [cab] for Plough Court. Whence [at Plough Court] I was
courteously received by my friend William Allen[6] who was en-

---

[5] Richard Rathbone and Thomas Thompson were Quaker Liverpool merchants active in the affairs of the African Institution.

[6] William Allen (1770–1844) was a man of science who, having developed a prosperous chemical manufacturing business, had sufficient income
and leisure time to devote to a multiplicity of philanthropic enterprises. He
was a member of the African Institution, an educational reformer, a firm

gaged about the liberation of Aaron. [I] got encouragement, [but] as nothing [concrete was] done here, I regretted [having spent] this day without going much about.

17 July 1811. This day we went to meeting, and in the afternoon Cornelius [Hanbury][7] attended me to see the great church of St. Paul and many other curiosities of London, etc.—such as London Bridge, Blackfriar's Bridge, etc.

18 July 1811. This day my friend William Allen had a note from William Wilberforce[8] desiring that I should see him at 4 o'clock. In the meantime William Allen received a letter of information that Aaron was sent for Plymouth, which made our visit to Wilberforce of the greatest importance. We accordingly waited on him, at which time the conversations soon took place of the newest events, which called for immediate proceedings. Wilberforce immediately called for pen, ink and paper, and wrote to the Board of Admiralty, and sent his man immediately to the Notary. William Allen and Paul Cuffe then went into the Parliament.

19 July 1811. This day passes with an earnest desire to hear of the liberation of Aaron, but [I] heard nothing. Cornelius [Hanbury] attended on me. [We] went into the [London] Tower and [we] had the prospect [view from the Tower] alone [to ourselves] over London. We [then] went over London Bridge to Lancaster's School[9] where was taught 1,000 scholars by one

opponent of capital punishment, and a provider of soup kitchens for the poor. Allen was Cuffe's closest English friend.

[7] Cornelius Hanbury, a member of the African Institution, was an important contributor to the Sierra Leone project.

[8] William Wilberforce (1759–1833) was the great English philanthropist, statesman and orator. He was the outstanding leader of the movement to abolish the slave trade and, later, the institution of slavery. Wilberforce was one of the founders of the Anti-Slavery Society; in addition, he championed Catholic emancipation, supported missionary societies, and promoted educational reform.

[9] Joseph Lancaster (1778–1838) based his educational system on the monitorial or pupil-teachers method of instruction. That is, the advanced student taught the less-advanced children what he had just learned from someone more advanced than himself. Pedagogical techniques were purely mechanical, the students learning by rote. But Lancaster's system, in the days before compulsory free public education, was relatively simple to operate, kept pupil costs inexpensive, and did provide some education to many children in both Great Britain and the United States who otherwise would have received none at all.

master; but about 800 was there in school [the day we visited Lancaster]. This prospect of the school was the greatest gratification that I met with.

20 July 1811. This afternoon took [the] stage for William Dillwyn,[10] at whose house I was friendly and cordially received; and [I] took great satisfaction [at my reception]. I found William and family exceeding[ly] amenable and very comfortably situated, with everything that [is] necessary to make their lives comfortable.

21 July 1811. This day [was] rainy too. [I went to] meetings about 2½ miles distance, but the carriage being covered, we went comfortably. I went and dined with George and Mary Stacey[11] who was very kind and loving. [They] appeared to live in the truth.

22 July 1811. Spent the fore part of this day in conversing with William Dillwyn on subjects of importance. After dinner William gave me 2 volumes of Clarkson's work on [the] slave trade.[12] His wife and two daughters accompanied me to town in their carriage. [The distance was] about 5 miles. At seven o'clock this evening, Thomas Clarkson arrived. No news of Aaron's release.

23 July 1811. Thomas Clarkson sets to for [attempts to arrange] Aaron's liberation. [He] makes so far as for certain persons to go with him to the Lord of [the] Admiralty, where they found the order had been some days gone [out] for Aaron's discharge. They then took immediate measures for the care of Aaron in [by] writing to their friends to assist Aaron in getting to

[10] William Dillwyn was a prominent New Jersey Quaker who relocated to England during the American Revolution. A pupil of the great Quaker abolitionist Anthony Benezet, Dillwyn in the 1780's joined a circle of London antislavery Quaker activists. Here he acted as a liaison between American and English antislavery Friends for the remainder of his life.

[11] The Staceys were leading London antislavery Quakers. George Stacey played an important role in administering the English Society of Friends, serving periodically as Clerk of the London Yearly Meeting. Mary Stacey was an equally zealous Friend and supporter of the antislavery cause.

[12] Thomas Clarkson, *The History of the Rise, Progress, and Accomplishment of the Abolition of the African Slave Trade by the British Parliament.*

Liverpool. And [they further instructed] that he should be taken care of until he should return [to *Traveller*]. You may think that was great consolation to me to think [that] if God permitted that I should have the happy opportunity of returning Aaron to his parents and fellow citizens of Sierra Leone.

24 July 1811. This day is the meeting at the Grace Street Meeting. After meeting attended to such other business as came in the way.

25 July 1811. This day [I] settled Paul Cuffe['s personal] and cargo accounts with Lubbuck to good satisfaction: (viz.) the amount current[ly due] was made out and I was charged 1 per centum commission for receiving and paying. And where the money is held subject to the drawer's order, they allow no interest. I let them know [that] I was generous in business and therefore [I] should . . . [leave] it to their goodness. They then held out the same [terms] to my friend William Allen. But when I went to settle my account and pay them in bullion, the foreman then begged me to call [back] in about 4 days. Thus, when I called, John Lubbuck was in. I put the question to him. He said that [that] was the mode in which they did business. But he observed [asked] whether I should have any more business with them. I answered: as to that, [I] was uncertain. My business was small, and as to [employ] flattery to deceive him, [that] was not my way of dealing [doing business]. He then called his foreman and [told him to] take this [my] account [and to] make it over to allow 2½ per cent [discount], if that would be satisfactory to you [me]. I tell him it would be so, and I find honesty to be the best policy.

Zachariah Macaulay[13] called at William Allen and [we] had

---

[13] Perhaps Zachary Macaulay (1768–1838) is best known today as the father of the great English historian Thomas Babington Macaulay. Zachary Macaulay had a remarkable career of his own, however, as a philanthropist, abolitionist, writer, and colonial administrator. Managing a plantation in Jamaica early in his career exposed Macaulay first hand to the evils of slavery, and he returned to England as a militant opponent of the institution. He was governor of Sierra Leone (1793–99), secretary to the Sierra Leone Company (1799–1808) and secretary to the African Institution (1807–12). A powerful propagandist for the antislavery cause, he also served as editor of the *Christian Observer* (1807–16), and turned that organ into a vigorous proponent for the abolition of the slave trade.

good conversation. He then invited me to dine with him on the morrow, which [invitation] was accepted, [I] hoping there may some good come out of it. . . .

26 July 1811. This day [I am] waiting for further advice [news]. We was contemplating on the *Traveller*'s return to Africa. They [Cuffe's friends] prepare on my return myself, but it is not yet concluded, or when concluded on [when] I shall proceed to Liverpool. [At] 4 o'clock in [the] afternoon [I] shall take [a] stage for Macaulay['s]; [he lives some] 4 or 5 miles distance in the country. Henry Hull, from America, is now in England, and expects to be in London in 3 or 4 days. . . . This day [at] 3 p.m. I had conversation with my assistors[14] concerning [my] asking for liberty for the continuation of the *Traveller* in the African traffic.

I this day went to Zachariah Macaulay's where I meet with exceeding[ly] kind treatment. Who [Macaulay] inform[ed] me that he, in company with 5 or 6 more gentlemen, had lately committed to their charge for their good management from the government about 1,000 slaves at Burish in the West Indies. The said Macaulay promised to me the continuation of his friendship.

27 July 1811. This morning [I] came to William Allen's from Macaulay's. [I was] accompanied by Macaulay, who informed me that there was a vessel to sail in [a] few days for Africa, by which conveyance I shall write to Thomas Wainer in Sierra Leone. Thomas Clarkson[15] this day sets off for home; who [Clarkson] has been a source of consolation [to me]. Thomas is a man of good deportment. My friends this day forward[ed] a petition to the Privy Council to [obtain] a license for the *Traveller* to go to Africa, commanded by Paul Cuffe or some other person. John

---

[14] Cuffe is referring possibly to a special subcommittee meeting of the African Institution.

[15] Thomas Clarkson (1760–1846) was one of the earliest English pioneers in the struggle to abolish the slave trade, devoting a good part of his adult life to the cause. An ardent advocate of African rehabilitation, he played an active role in the development of the Sierra Leone colony. Clarkson was a brilliant propagandist and his history of the struggle to abolish the slave trade (see footnote citation, p. 92), first published in 1808, over the years converted countless thousands to the cause.

Clarkson,[16] the man that carried the colonists to Africa, is a good-looking man and will work for the cause.

28 July 1811. This day I went to Grace Church Meeting, both forenoon and afternoon [services]. Then dined or ate dinner at the house of [a] Friend where I was very friendly received and used. [I was] accompanied by my attender, Cornelius [Hanbury]. There was a Friend there by the name of John Hull. These Friends desired the privilege of seeing my certificate.[17] At the perusal of the certificate, accompanied with a letter of recommendation from Benjamin Rush,[18] president of the abolition society of Phila-delphia, they acknowledged great satisfaction. John Hull, from desiring the address [of a friend] of my pocketbook [noticed the shabby condition of my pocketbook and] ordered Cornelius to get me a good pocketbook [as] a present in token of [his] love and friendship [for me]. In the evening my friend [William] Allen called his family together and we were comforted; and I believe I may say the presence of the Precious Comforter was felt to be near.

In the evening, conversation took place between William Allen and P. Cuffe [concerning] the most advantageous way of encour-agement of the improvement of the colony of Sierra Leone. I then told William that it appeared the colony people wanted [needed] help or encouragement. [I further remarked] that I had my mind still impressed [with the idea] that a channel of intercourse should be kept open between America and Sierra Leone; and that my mind was to build a house in Sierra Leone in order that if the way should open for a family to come to Sierra Leone, encouragement might be given of accommodation, and by [their] gently getting along, might the better and with more ease encourage [still other] people to go to that country. William then said if any such thing

[16] John Clarkson (1763–1828) was Thomas Clarkson's younger brother. He, too, was active in African projects, and in 1791 as a 28-year-old naval lieutenant he recruited a large contingent of black Nova Scotians to emi-grate to Sierra Leone. Like his brother, John Clarkson also maintained for many years an interest in Sierra Leone developments.

[17] Cuffe is evidently referring to his certificate of membership in the Westport Meeting of the Society of Friends.

[18] See above, p. 49.

could be got under way, encouragement would be given, and [he] made minute [note] of the proposition.

29 July 1811. This appears certain [that] my friend William Allen are making every arrangement for full information [to be sent to the authorities in Sierra Leone concerning my mission] in order that I might be at liberty to leave London [shortly].

Cornelius [Hanbury] and I dined or eat our dinner at our Friend John Sanders', and [we] was friendly and kindly used. In the afternoon [I] went to see the Friends Yearly Meeting houses. There are three in number. [They are located] in the same court-[yard] in a triangular form. They are of neat and good construction. The largest holds 1,300 [worshipers], the next 1,100, the third one 5 or 600. The latter is not made much use of. Only for the select and committee meetings. These two first [are used] at the Yearly Meeting; one is for the men, and the other for the women. But their common Meetings are held in the Meeting House that holds 1,100. The trail between these Meeting Houses are flat stones, very neat. My friend John Hull made me a present of a pocketbook.

30 July 1811. This morning Cornelius, William and Paul went to see the mint, and the works thereof were great and wonderful. [We saw] the first steam engine that put all of the first operation for the preparation for coinage in motion. [This one engine] saves the strength of 30 horses. And [we saw] the first wheel that moved the axles for the operation of the works. [The wheel] traversed at the rate of 1 mile in 2 minutes, or 30 miles in one hour, or 720 miles in 24 hours, and, of course, would perform the circumference of the globe in 30 days at that rate.

The second steam engine is 16 horses, and the third and last standing engine saves the strength of 10 horses. And all these works goes on with great ease and quietness. In fact, the works of man, although it is great, it might seem they stamp from 60 to 70 guineas in a minute, and they have 8 of these stamping machines. Thus, 500 guineas can be stamped in one hour; thus, 4,383,000 guineas can be stamped in a year, etc.

[Later this day I] view[ed part] of the [Hyde] Park: [I saw there] many kind[s] of animals, among which was the lion . . .

panther, the grey squirrel, the baboon, the monkey . . . and many other kinds too tedious to mention.

I this day took place [made reservations] in the stage Lite Port for Liverpool, at 3 guineas [for the trip].

31 July 1811.   At 4 this morning [I] arose and took morning soundings. At 5 [I] procured a hack coach to take me and [my] things to the stage office, it [the stage office] being 3 miles [away]. I was accompanied by Daniel and Cornelius Hanbury. . . . At 6 we set forward for Liverpool with 4 persons inside [the coach], of which I had an inside berth. There was 14 on the outside berth. Those riding on the outside pay half the price that those do who ride inside. We rode pleasantly on through this day, only it was very dusty. To see the well cultivated country and their well improved land, etc., [is truly refreshing]. Nothing extraordinary took place in the 24 hours.

1 August 1811.   We drove night and day, or day and night, rather. This morning [the weather is] rather cool, attended with low land fogs and cool chilly vapor risings of the low land. Breakfasted at 8 and drove until 6 [p.m.] before we dined. Through which time we drove through a town called Tedbury, whence I was credibly informed there had a woman lived, but at that time [she] was dead about 2 weeks before. She lived 4 years without eating, 3½ years without drinking, 2 years and 10 months without sleeping. This appears to be a very singular circumstance, and [it] must be the power [the work] of the Almighty Director. I arrived at Liverpool at 9 o'clock, after a passage of 39 hours. Took my package to my friend Thomas Thompson, where I was kindly received.

2 August 1811.   I arose much refreshed, and found all well on board [*Traveller*] and [that] Aaron Richards had arrived the same afternoon as I did. Saw and had much conversation with many folks, among whom was Stephen Grellet,[19] a minister from

[19] Born in Limoges, France, Stephen Grellet (1773–1855) was a French-American of noble background. His family was famous for producing some of the most exquisite porcelain manufactured in this capital of French china making. Grellet fled France during the Revolution, lived in the West Indies for a time, and then came to America in the late 1790's. He resided

America. I took breakfast, tea and supper with him at Isaac
Headwin's, in whose company and conversation [Grellet's] I was
much comforted. He was to leave Liverpool the next day for the
country. My mate and 2nd mate went to dinner with Isaac [Head-
win], and he was anxious for more to come along with them. The
crew were spoken in highest terms of for their steadiness, [their]
not given to swearing, [etc.], but I found to my sorrow that
Zachariah [White] had behaved very unbecoming in keeping unbecoming company, and drinking to excess, and [in] speaking
light of Jesus Christ [so] that he wished to have Him by the hind
legs, etc., as I was informed, etc.

3 August 1811. This morning is rainy. After breakfast [I]
went on board the *Traveller.* On my way [to the ship] I was
stopped by the [dock] gates being open. It being rainy, a shopper
[shopkeeper] asked me in out of the rain, which I accepted. I had
[a] very satisfactory stopping as [a] way [a conversation was]
opened which quickened my mind in the way which felt pleasant to
me to hold out: that honor without virtue was not true honor; and
also, from whence comes wars and fightings, etc.

I also had to hold out to William and Richard Rathbone[20] that
the flesh was imperfect, and forewarned [is to be] forearmed, and
that [the Rathbones] was not to put too great confidence in me as
I was but flesh and blood. For those young men had taken [a]
very early [and] an active part in assisting me in every way and
manner: not only making their house my home, but stepping forward to give me every aid—even petitioning the Board of Ad-

---

for several years in Long Island and then moved to Philadelphia, where he
converted to the Quaker faith. He became a minister within the Friends'
church and established an extraordinary record as an evangelist, conducting campaigns in the United States, Haiti and in Europe. Grellet was
regarded by many as one of the greatest Quaker preachers of the nineteenth
century. For Grellet's impressions of Cuffe, see pp. 51–52.

[20] William Rathbone, Jr. (1787–1868), was the eldest son of a public-
spirited Liverpool Quaker merchant. He inherited his father's philanthropic
spirit and along with his brother Richard ventured into many humanitarian
enterprises. The two brothers actively opposed the slave trade, fought for
Roman Catholic emancipation and for municipal reform. The Rathbones
were fascinated with Cuffe and became convinced that this American was
an instrument of God sent to England to lead the cause of African emancipation.

miralty for the relief of Aaron Richards. As did also my friend Thomas Thompson afford me every aid, [offering] with kind invitation to make his house my home, all which [his assistance] I felt easy to accept of. Both Thomas and his wife are very worthy, agreeable creatures.

[I] having this day seen William Bottell, the great slave dealer, as I have been told, who invited me to his lodgings. I this day wrote a letter to William Allen, and one to John Desmond, etc., and [I] took [made] a copy [of each letter].

4 August 1811. This day the weather is clear with fresh wind from NW. Attended fore and afternoon Meetings. In the former, I was favored with the Spirit of Supplication. I went home and took dinner with Thompson, and in the afternoon took tea with Joseph, at whose house I was kindly treated. Coffin, [captain] of the ship *Alpha,* and my crew was at Meeting, which was very gratifying to me.

I this day received a letter from William Allen stating that the license [for Cuffe to trade with the Sierra Leone colony] would not be obtained under 4 or 5 days. And, [he further reported] that there was some hesitation made in objection, but [Allen] rather thought it would be obtained. The *Alpha* will be dispatched [to the United States] as soon as may be [possible].

5 August 1811. This day commences in the morning rainy but clears and [becomes] pleasant. After breakfast [I] went to the vessel; all well [on board *Traveller*]. John Marsters concludes to go home. A man of color talks of going to Sierra Leone in order to help the colonists. In the afternoon another man proposes of going [to Sierra Leone] to help in any way that may be helpful: either in printing, schoolkeeping, or by other means. I think here is rather encouragement.

6 August 1811. Clear in the morning with wind NW, but in the afternoon heavy showers of rain, etc. I this day had further communication with William Thomas and a European, a printer, about going to Sierra Leone; [they] seem to be very anxious [to emigrate to the colony], and it is concluded to write to London in order to see if it may be encouraged.

7 August 1811. This day [I] took dinner with William and Richard Rathbone in company with Thomas Thompson [and]

William Roscoe,[21] a well-engaged man for the abolition of the slave trade. [Roscoe] stated at the table that to make a complete work of the slave trade that the [British] ships of war should be commissioned to take all vessels that was found in that trade belonging to whom they would. They [the British] had a good right so to do [since] they had to apprehend one man from striking another. Also, Lord John Russell[22] dined with us.

8 August 1811. This is the Meeting day. After Meeting I went home with Nicholas Waterhouse and took dinner with him. He had a very beautiful situation [home], and [he] had 13 children, with many more young people [about], in whose house I had to labor, I hope to satisfaction. I have a very bad cold, but it is getting better.

9 August 1811. I this day took dinner with William Bottell and Captain Paine, etc., formerly slave dealers. But [they] treated me politely.

10 August 1811. The *Alpha* went out of the dock at 3 p.m. I this day dined at Mary Cash's in company with Captain Barker. [He] formerly belonged at Nantucket, but [he is] now at New York, [and] sails in James Barker's ship. He sails for Savannah [Georgia] and from there to New Orleans.

11 August 1811. This day all [Cuffe's crew] attended Meeting; and after Meeting the men went home with [the] Rathbones and took dinner [with them]. . . .

14 August 1811. This day I dined with Captain Brown, Captain of His Majesty's Navy ships, who was a very civil, godly man, and his wife and family. Thoughtful people on the whole. I had a comfortable meal.

---

[21] William Roscoe (1753–1831) was a Liverpool version of the Renaissance man. Lawyer, historian, antiquarian, reformer, member of Parliament, Roscoe very early in his career embarked on an antislavery crusade. He pamphleteered against the institution and was instrumental in organizing several Liverpool antislavery societies.

[22] Young Lord John Russell (1792–1878), first Earl Russell, was at this time an undergraduate at the University of Edinburgh. He soon would launch a notable political career as one of the great Whig Parliamentary reformers of the nineteenth century. A man of breeding and superior intelligence, an aristocrat to the core, Russell's interest in meeting with Cuffe suggests something of the great stir this black man's visit to England was creating.

15 August 1811. The ship *Alpha,* Captain Coffin, is already for sea. The *Traveller* [was] hauled out on the bank to grime. John Marsters and Michael Wainer has deserted from the vessel called the *Traveller.* This day is the Meeting day, at which I attended. Doctor Cooke applied to me for a passage for 4 men to [go] to Africa.

16 August 1811. The wind blowing very fresh WNW. The *Alpha* still lays ready for sea. The *Traveller* has finished griming and is hauling for the dock again. I am now a lodger with Isaac Headwin, where I am very kindly received and friendly used. I this day took dinner with Joseph Ferress.

17 August 1811. This day the *Traveller* hauled into the docks. Doctor Cooke, [along] with Samuel Francis, came on board the *Traveller,* and [they] agreed with me for [the] 4 men's passages to Africa at 30 pound sterling per piece. And [they] bind themselves [to pay for the passage], and I to receive the passage money in Liverpool before sailing. I this day agreed to take my passage for London again.

18 August 1811. This day [I] attended both fore and afternoon meetings, and I dined with John Fields, where we had [an] agreeable dinner. And at ½ past 9 in the evening [I] set forward to London. [I was] accompanied with 3 very agreeable persons.

19 August 1811. This day [was] very pleasant on the road, [although the trip] was attended with some small showers of rain. The people [along the way] seemed much employed in getting in their harvest.

20 August 1811. At ½ past 5 arrived in London, Lombard Street [depot]. Found William Allen and [his] family all well. Cornelius and I went to John Sanders and ordered [there] 5 chests of India tea for exportation. And then [we went] to the India House and selected and ordered sundry merchandise for Liverpool [delivery]. . . .

21 August 1811. This morning is pleasant and [it is the] Grace Street Meeting day. I propose attending meeting and, after dinner, of going to Waltham Stone and to William Dillwyn's.

At 4 o'clock p.m. I departed from William Allen's after having a comfortable sitting in [the] company of a woman Friend who appeared to be a chosen vessel unto the Lord, and was [a] comfort unto us. And also [there was] a man by the name of Morris Burbeck, the Friend that Thomas Clarkson impressed me to bestow the African wood for a gain.

Cornelius Hanbury accompanied me to Waltham Stone's [house and] at William Dillwyn's, where we was cordially received. William was very unwell, and it appears that his glass is almost run [empty], and his duty faithfully discharged, whose reward will be crowned with everlasting life, world without end. Much of our time while [we] were together was taken up [with a discussion] for the good beneficial improvements of the inhabitants of Africa, for that which might attend for their good, and for the honor and glory of God.

22 August 1811. [At] ½ past 10 this morning I went to Meeting with William Dillwyn's family in their coach. Where [at the Meeting] I had a comfortable, open Meeting. After Meeting [I] went home with William Fanster to dinner. After dinner came Mary Stacey, who had good advice and delivered it in much love and tenderness. At 7 o'clock I took [the] stage for London. [I] arrived at 8 o'clock. William Allen and family was out of town. I was well provided for, nevertheless, at his house in London.

23 August 1811. I this day had a paper [a bill] of an amount of merchandise handed me for goods bought of Brown, Rogers and Brown, to [the] amount of £238:17. This day I dined in company with Captain Eben Clark, of and from New Bedford, who said he left Peter and Alexander Howard well, and [that he] hear[d] nothing [but that] my family was well. William Rotch, Jr.,[23] mentioned my name in his letter to William Allen, and mentioned nothing but [that] my family was well (William Rotch, Jr., mentioned it). His letter arrived in good time to do good, and was of consolation to me, [a man alone] in such a distant land and [only] strangers to me as [my] acquaintances.

24 August 1811. This day [I] came into London from Newington, and [I] went into the flower garden[s] where [there] was much fruit of every kind. [I] took [a] boat [ride] about Blackfriar's Bridge near the Sommerset House. This day [I] am to dine

[23] See above, pp. 24–25.

at Newert's, where we was kindly treated. His situation was very excellent—next to paradise on earth. Sent 4 letters to Liverpool.

25 August 1811. This morning [it is] very rainy. [I] came from Newington in a carriage with Joseph Bevan.[24] I went to the great Meeting where I had pretty clear openings [a good view of the proceedings] in the forenoon. [I] took dinner with William Allen's mother and [her] son Joseph, where we was very agreeably entertained. Came home to Plough Court where we had [a] good refreshing session in the evening.

26 August 1811. This morning [it is] very pleasant. Cornelius Hanbury and I went to the London and Western India Docks, which was exceeding[ly] gratifying. [We] went both to see the shipping and [the] accommodations in the docks, and also [to view] the shipping in the river that lay in tiers as we passed for 3 miles; and they continued to extend as far as I could see the river [which was] about ¼ mile wide. At 5 o'clock in the afternoon, I dined with Zachariah Macaulay, where I was very agreeably entertained. I this day received a letter from Mary Capper,[25] a public Friend which was very encouraging to the feeled [believer, because of its] cheerful review, and [I] was comforted therein.

27 August 1811. This day [I] met [with] the committee of the African Institution—who sat at 1 p.m. and expressed great satisfaction in the information [that] I gave them. And [the committee] felt also that I was endeavoring to assist them in

[24] Joseph Gurney Bevan (1753–1814) was a Quaker poet and essayist who earned his living as an accomplished chemist and druggist in Plough Court, Lombard Street, London. Bevan wrote countless tracts explaining and defending the Quaker religion. He was so successful in these efforts that many authorities consider him to be the "ablest of the Quaker apologists" of the early nineteenth century.

[25] Mary Capper was indirectly related to Joseph Gurney Bevan. Her sister married Bevan's cousin Paul Bevan, and the Bevans and the Cappers maintained a close relationship over the years. For example, after Joseph Gurney Bevan came down with a cataract in his left eye, paralysis in his left side, and in 1813 asthma and dropsy, Mary Capper would selflessly spend a good deal of her time reading to him selections from Thomas Elwood's *Journal* and Mary Waring's *Diary*. The Bevan and Capper families were devout Quakers and strong supporters of the movement to abolish the international slave trade.

maintaining the good cause with the blessing that we may reasonably hope that we may be supported with. [They also vowed] to endeavor that the subject [rehabilitation of Africa] may not fall beneath the level where we found it. I made the Duke[26] a present of an African robe, a letter box, and a dagger, to show [him] that the African was capable of mental endowments, etc.

28 August 1811. This morning [the weather] is very pleasant. This day attended the Grace Street Church Meeting. It [was] comfortable for me to sit with [a] Friend in true humiliation and supplication; and may this be the continuation of our lives through time that peace may be our lot. I have a box of books containing about 80 [in number]. These are from [the] Friend[s] and the Tract and Bible Society. I have had a place taken for me in the Manchester stage at 4 guineas [for the] 182 miles [from London to Manchester].

29 August 1811. This day [I] attended to preparing for leaving London. At 2 p.m. took [the] stage for Manchester. Rainy drive all night.

30 August 1811. This day [I rode] all day on the road. Arrived at Manchester [at] 8 o'clock. At 9 p.m. reached David Dockray's, where I found Sarah Benson[27] and her daughter Margaret.

31 August 1811. David Dockray and Paul Cuffe spent this day in seeing the [famous Manchester cotton] factories. They have got them to perfection. They light the darkest room with gas [which is] extracted from sea coal. This light far exceeds the candlelight; it is more like day light. The air issues out of a small tube. And by the blaze of a candle being put to it, it blazes and burns until the gas is stopped. This is done by turning the stop that reaches through the pipe. One woman spins 150 threads at a time.

---

[26] The Duke of Gloucester.

[27] Sarah Benson was most probably related to the Benson family who toward the end of the eighteenth century had formed with James Cropper the famous Liverpool mercantile firm of Cropper, Benson & Company. The Bensons and the Croppers became enormously wealthy from the business and, as good Quaker philanthropists, devoted a substantial portion of their fortune to the betterment of mankind. Both families were in the forefront of the struggle to abolish West Indian slavery.

This afternoon Robert Benson[28] came [to visit with me]. John Thorpe dined with us this day.

1 September 1811. This day attended Meeting, both fore and afternoon. Took dinner at Isaac Crendon's, and then went and took tea with Thomas Hale. David Bancroft, a goodly young man, took tea [with us], and waited on us home, and kindly invited me to see him.

2 September 1811. Arose this morning at ½ past 4, got breakfast, and at 6 o'clock took [the] stage for Liverpool. [I] arrived there at 10 a.m., it being 36 miles from Manchester. Found the people all well, as well on board the vessel as in the city. [I] found that William Rathbone had ordered the china. I this day wrote a letter to William Allen and state the necessity of establishing commerce in Africa and on building a vessel in Africa. And [I inquired of him] if there could be any owner [prospective purchaser for the vessel] found in London.

3 September 1811. This day passed without much being done. I went to Hannah Rathbone['s] and stopped [there] all night.

4 September 1811. This morning being a pleasant morning Hannah Rathbone's family and myself went to William Roscoe's, which was about 2 miles further [out of town]. He being a very warm friend for the abolishing of the slave trade, many subjects took place [were discussed] between us. He stated the necessity and propriety of condemning all nations that might be found in that trade. I likewise was favored to state to him the necessity there was of keeping open a communication between America, Africa and England, in order to assist Africa in its civilization; and that the two powers [America and England] to countenance it [trade with Africa], even if they were at variance [at war with each other], and to consider it [African trade] as a neutral path. And I could not see wherein the French government may not rejoin the neutral path. After leaving William Rathbone, we drove to the pottery [factory], where we saw the operation of the whole pottery work for their ware.

5 September 1811. This morning Thomas Thompson [and I]

---

[28] Robert Benson, too, was most probably related to the Benson family of Liverpool (see previous footnote).

took breakfast with William Faner, a respectful Friend, and then [we] attended our weekday Meeting. [I] signed bonds at the Customs House, and took on board [*Traveller*] 15 hogshead sugar.

6 September 1811. Very fine weather this day. [I] re-entered [the city] and landed to Coke 2 barrels flour. I this morning took breakfast with George Bings, and after breakfast [I] went to the blind school. And it was wonderful to see the operation of all kinds of work they [the blind] would go through—of spinning, weaving, matting, carpeting of many colors. And they [the blind students] being a great inspiration, both [in] practicing and learning each other.

7 September 1811. This day [I] made a collection in filing the memorandums.

8 September 1811. Attended both fore and afternoon Meeting. The Meetings [were] pretty much silent [services], but well covered with humbling truth.

9 September 1811. This day [I] made some more collections [of bills], and took on board the *Traveller* 9 crates of ware, and had many visitors: Doctor Briggs and [his] wife, Thomas Thompson's aunt, and a young woman. [I] took breakfast with William Spriggs and dinner with Thomas Thompson.

10 September 1811. This day [I] got several engagements through, and made several more small engagements. Dined this day with the widow [Smalley].

11 September 1811. This day spent in procuring sundries for the *Traveller*.

12 September 1811. Attended our morning Meeting, and [I was occupied] afterwards in ship's duty.

13 September 1811. This day spent in business on getting articles for the *Traveller*'s use: buying shoes, potatoes, and dry goods, etc.

14 September 1811. These 24 hours [witnessed] very pleasant weather. [I was engaged in] preparing [my] goods for entry at the Customs House, etc. [I] made but few entries this day on account [of] the Manchester goods not coming [as soon as I had anticipated].

15 September 1811. [Today there is] fine, clear weather,

wind SE. Attended the fore and afternoon meeting. Dined with Christopher Thompson, and I took tea with James Cropper.[29] Little [of importance] in the conversation[s]. Returned and stayed all night with Thomas Thompson, where I have made my home. His wife was put to bed yesterday with a fine boy.

16 September 1811. The goods from Manchester being not here in the evening, [it] prevented us from clearing [port] today. But [the crew] are in readiness [for a departure] tomorrow, with my articles [goods to be sold in Sierra Leone] in readiness [as well]. Dined today with Thomas Cropper.[30]

17 September 1811. Wind SE, weather very fine. Took breakfast with my passengers, and also with William Rathbone, [who] was accompanied with a Friend [from] London, where the African Convention took place. [The African Convention discussed] which was the most expedient method of civilization of Africa. [The convention concluded that] navigation and cultivation took plan[ning], and the expense of keeping a communication whereby Africa might be advantaged [was considerable].

18 September 1811. This day [I] got the 6 chests [of Manchester] merchandise delivered up. Took them on board [*Traveller*] and we hauled down to the dock gate in order to go [to sea]. And the passengers are not ready for us to clear out; and so we are detained. The African boy[31] is put on board for Africa on condition that he is to be found his provisions by them who put him on board.

[29] James Cropper (1773–1840) was a Liverpool merchant philanthropist (see footnote p. 104). A Quaker, Cropper devoted much of his free time to supporting causes the Friends endorsed. He wrote pamphlets and stumped the nation in an all-out effort to end discrimination against Roman Catholics, to bring political freedom to Ireland, to abolish the slave trade and West Indian slavery, and to establish educational facilities for the poor. Erected in his house after his death, Cropper's epitaph aptly sums up this good man's life: "In this house lived James Cropper, one, and he not the least, of that small but noble band of Christian men who, after years of labour and through much opposition, accomplished the abolition of West Indian slavery; and thus having lived the life of the righteous, he died in the full assurance of faith on the 26th of Feby. 1840."

[30] Thomas Cropper was James Cropper's brother. Although not as successful in the business world as brother James, Thomas Cropper was equally involved in Quaker-oriented reformist causes.

[31] See 19 September 1811 entry.

19 September 1811. This day cleared from the Customs House, and received our papers from the American Consul. [We] hauled out of the dock for [the] sea. We anchored at George's Dock, with the passengers on board, and [there was a] soft wind, SE, pleasant. At 12 we went out of the Dock and anchored off George's Dock. All well. Names of our passengers are George Warren, John Healey, Thomas Hirst and Jonathan Rainer.[32] The African boy [is] Bango Burso, for he came from the coast of Burso.

20 September 1811. At 10 weighed anchor; at 11 all [passengers and crew] were on board. Wind SE, [there was a] small breeze. [I] stood facing the river with William Spriggs and Rathbone's clerk [who was] on board, besides a number more of Dore and Thomas Thompson's acquaintances. And a great many attended our departure. William Rathbone, with Thomas Thompson, attended to the shore. At 12 our water boat that attended us left us. At 2 William Spriggs[33] left us. [He] ordered us to steer NW by N, finally ESE. All hands complied in clearing ships.

[32] The Reverend George Warren and his associates Healey, Hirst and Rainer were missionaries and schoolteachers sent to Sierra Leone by English Methodists with a dual purpose: to proselytize the natives and at the same time to provide them with a degree of literacy.
[33] William Spriggs was a Liverpool harbor pilot.

4
RETURN TO SIERRA LEONE

The passage from Great Britain to Sierra Leone was difficult. The first forty days of the voyage were very rough for the ship and her passengers. Rain fell almost continually; gales crashed through Traveller *practically every day. Scarcely a ship was sighted during this period. The passengers were desperately seasick most of the time. By the end of October, however,* Traveller *escaped the last of the gales and neared the African coast. Aside from the foul weather, the trip was uneventful. Cuffe's log entries*

deal   almost   exclusively   with   the   weather   and
Traveller's *position at sea.*

22 September 1811.   At 6 a.m. a squall from NNW entangled
sails; 2 reefed the topsail; some entangled yards down; spoke [to]
the ship *Salem,* of Holyhead, who wanted to report us at Liverpool.
Think rainy weather [has] left all of our company of vessels
behind out of sight. . . .

4 October 1811.   These 24 hours commences with moderate
gales, but the weather took [to] lowering. At 12 meridian there
was a schooner on our lee beam, distance 3 leagues. We were
apprehensive that she was an enemy vessel, for she gained on us
apace. At 3 p.m. she was nearly in our wake, one league off. But
then came a very thick heavy squall which lasted until in[to] the
night. We carried some extra sail, and we never saw any more of
the schooner. . . .

9 October 1811.   These 24 hours begins with strong gales. The
middle part [of the day the winds were] moderate. [The] latter
part [of the day] strong gales. At 8 a.m. [we] took in a hogshead
which [was] ironbound [and] very barnacled. Appeared to have
been very long time in the water. . . .

16 October 1811.   Clear and pleasant wind NW by a heavy
jumbled sea from the West. At 12 p.m. wind SSW and inclining
southerly with an enveloping gale. [It has been this type of wind
pattern] which has been the general [cause] of the trial of our
patience. Since leaving Liverpool our passengers hath pretty well
buried their appetites. . . .

31 October 1811.   These 24 hours commences with clear
weather and a pleasant breeze. At 10 a.m. Charles Dumor threw
the harpoon into a large black porpoise. It measure 10 feet in
length, judge it to weigh 6 or 700 pounds. [At] ½ past 10 John
Wainer threw the harpoon into another [porpoise; this one was]
of [a] smaller kind. We saved both of these fish in [by] throwing
the garbage into the sea. Many sharks appeared, and seemed to be
very fierce and ravenous. We hung a piece of porpoise over our
stern. When a shark attempted to take it away, I shot the shark
dead. After a small fling, it sunk immediately out of sight. . . .

2 November 1811. These 24 hours commences with African weather; calm and hot. From 6 a.m. to the end [of the day] we had [saw] many land riff-raff [sharks]. At 8 p.m. I was called forward by Joseph Hemmenway, [he] saying the officers and men was in a riot. And when I came forward John Wainer and Zachariah White was close clinched. Zachariah had his shirt off. I then interfered, and they separated. And since [then] Zachariah has promised to do as well as he knows [to behave himself]. . . .

8 November 1811. Today small wind, smooth sea, and hot, close air. At 6 p.m. [we] sounded. No bottom at 125 fathoms. At 4 a.m. [we] had a heavy tornado from [the East]. It last from 4 to 6 [a.m.].

This day, in taking up the passengers stores, we found in one hamper 2 bottles [that were] empty. [The bottles had been emptied] by their corks being drawn, or put in, and the porter [port] took out. Also, 8 [bottles of port] were missing. I searched the peoples' chests, but found no porter. In searching the hold where the port came from, 7 empty porter bottles were brought up, and the remainder of several more was discovered in the hold. It seems to me there had been great thirst while in the hold. . . .

12 November 1811. From 12 meridian this day, [*Traveller* sailing] in 14 fathoms water, we steered ESE. [At] ¾ after 4 p.m. saw land ahead, or rather on our starboard bow. . . . We were in 10 fathoms water. At 6 p.m. I had [the] ship stood S by E. We had from 10 to 7 fathoms water. At 9 p.m. we anchored in 10 fathoms water. [We were] very good laying at anchor, [since] the tide sat strong. Southward, it appears to be high water [at] 9 o'clock.

We got underway at 6 a.m. Wind North. Cape Sierra Leone bore E by N 2 leagues distant. At 7 the wind small, and come off [the] shore. And tide [was] of ebb, causing us to anchor.

At 1 p.m. got underway [again]. Small wind NW, and tide in our favor. We made good way [a]head. At 3 p.m. we came up with the Cape Sierra Leone; at the same time Sierra Leone's Freetown appeared [in view]. We saw several fishing boats, but none spoke us.

This day I count to contain 36 hours. It is calm and warm. Sierra Leone looks natural. Off Cocly Bay the Kruman Conce came on board—who informed us that Thomas Wainer was well. At 4 p.m. we anchored. Was boarded by Captain Brown of the brig *Protector*. David Edmonds,[1] with members of others, came on board. Thomas Wainer boarded us as well.

At 6 p.m. I, with 4 passengers, went on shore. We first went to the Governor, who appeared to use us very friendly. Thence went to [my] friend Nicholas'. Was met [there] by John Gordon. Thence to Ebenezer Smith, who received us very friendly and showed every mark of friendship. Thence to John Brown; thence to Warrick Francis; thence to Thomas Wainer.

The missionaries took their quarters to friend Nicholas' for the night. I went to David Edmonds, and then returned and stayed with Thomas Wainer.

13 November 1811. This day went to the Customs House where I see the Governor's note for [a] report to be made to the Governor of the contents of the cargo [that *Traveller* brought to Sierra Leone]. Although I had waited on the Governor the evening before, and was directed [by the Governor] to report to Charles Hopkins, [who] took up all this day in [getting around to] coming to entry [Cuffe's permit to land his cargo]. However, [I] have obtained a permit for landing the cargo. I have an officer [of Customs] put on board my vessel to see the cargo landed, it being the first vessel that ever had been so waited upon in this port, etc.

14 November 1811. This day landed 2 firkins[2] butter, 1 hamper cheese, and 2 hampers of shoes. The Governor is to have 1 firkin butter, and Esq. Smith is to have some butter [and] hams, and we are to begin landing [the remainder of the cargo] in the morning. The missionaries hired Peter Francis'[3] house £5 per month; the house are very much out of repair, etc.

15 November 1811. In the morning, it being rainy, we did not [do] much in the fore part of the day. In the afternoon landed three boat load[s of] passengers, baggage, and 10 chests beef, 2 crates tins, 1 box hats, 5 chests tea, and the box of [hard] tack, and 1 trade chest, [and] 1 keg of tallow for the Governor.

---

[1] See footnote 17, p. 85.

[2] A firkin was a small wooden vessel for butter that usually measured one fourth of a barrel.

[3] See footnote 11, p. 83.

16 November 1811.   Landed 2 casks liquor, 1 box hats, 1 cask hardware, 1 box ditto, 2 casks spruce, 3 bales of India and one of Manchester goods, and 1 load for the Board of Missions [consisting of] good 258 iron pots. (Dick Prince and Zachariah [White] and Aaron [Richards] with the Kru man was at the landing of these pots. They say they fell 2 pots short.) [We also landed] 6 baking pans, 3 crates earthern ware, 1 trunk goods, 1 box candles, 1 barrel mustard, and 1 box umbrellas . . . 1 parcel of paper, [a] parcel [of] seeds, thread, and black pepper; and [we] also put [on shore] 2 boxes we brought from Liverpool for Bokongo, and no more.

17 November 1811.   Was on shore all the good day, and went to Meeting at the Methodists and visited 2 families in the afternoon, (viz.) Thomas Richardson and Warrick Francis.

18 November 1811.   This day commences with fine, warm, or rather hot, weather. Sold 40 bushels of salt to Frederick Simpson. Landed 385 iron pots [and] 80 bushels of salt. [The salt] was put on board the schooner *Advent*. [We also] landed 18 narrow and 2 broad axes, and 1 bunch of small weights. I sold very smartly [rapidly] of the tin and hardware, so that there was constant employ [for the crew], etc. George Warren invited me to attend the Meeting.[4]

19 November 1811.   This day continued our course landing and selling [the cargo].

20 November 1811.   This day proceeded as usual; selling to those [who] would buy and [could] pay [for the goods].

21 November 1811.   These 24 hours commences as usual. Attended to business until 2 p.m. Then attended with the Mission Negroes and took dinner with Thomas Richards, at whose school much was conversed on [the] civilization of Africa. The Britoners[5] told [the group] what the Britoners would do if they were there [lived there permanently]. I advised them to set the pattern themselves; but they seem to think their [home] missions would not heave them out into [the] darkness [of Africa for very long].

22 November 1811.   This day landed 3 hogshead tobacco, 2

---

[4] Cuffe is referring to Methodist services conducted by the newly arrived missionary Rev. George Warren.

[5] The white leaders of the mission.

barrels pork, and 1 crate of wares #5. This day arrived the frigate *Marlin* from London, 44 guns. I was informed by Thomas [Wainer] that the competition today for [the purchase of our] supplies was made up [of] unusual[ly large groups], for what cause he could not say.

23 November 1811. This day continued landing as usual. Sold to Smith[6] 2 hogsheads tobacco. He had them weighed at the scale and [then] rolled them in[to] his cellar. Charlotte Simpson[7] had [bought] one. She opened hers and came and told me she liked the tobacco well. Some hours after, she came back and told me that Smith had found his tobacco not good, and [that he] told her hers was bad [as well]. I went to see Smith, but I could not speak with him until next day. I told him I would take the tobacco back. He told me it was in the cellar, and it may lay [there] for [a] few days. I told him he might give the tobacco up. He then seemed to incline to see if we had any better, or if any more arrived so as to be better or cheaper. And this appears to me to have been too much the mode of his way of dealing.

24 November 1811. This day the weather very pleasant. Went to the Baptist Meeting in the morning, and in the afternoon to the great Methodist Meeting, where I had [a] good service, in which service the lukewarm was cautioned, and [the] unconvinced closely reprimanded. And in the evening [I] had good open time in the family of David Edmonds.

25 November 1811. This day finished landing our salt. Landed this day for David Edmonds, Jr., 2 tons of salt. [We also] took to the [Edmonds'] store 14 bushels [of salt]. Landed several bales of East India goods: (viz.) 3 small bales unheaded, 2 more

---

[6] Alexander Smith came to the colony from England as storekeeper for the Sierra Leone Company in the days when the Company ruled Sierra Leone. He remained in Freetown after the Company's demise, engaging in the import-export trade. Smith was not the most scrupulous of businessmen and his transactions with Cuffe soon gave the black sea captain uneasy moments.

[7] Mrs. Charlotte Simpson was perhaps the colony's leading black female entrepreneur. Many women engaged in commercial activities during Sierra Leone's first years, but as time passed most of the colony's business activities passed under male control. Mrs. Simpson continued to thrive, however, and she maintained an extensive commercial network in the colony's back country as late as 1818.

hogshead of tobacco. Alexander Smith concludes to take one of the hogsheads of tobacco, but complains of its being poor [quality].

I this day dined with David Edmonds, and Henry Warren dined there also. A close examination took place concerning the division in the [religious] Society [or societies, in Sierra Leone], but Henry seemed fully inclined to vindicate his cause to be right, which is generally the case if we be in the wrong.

26 November 1811. We put 10 tons [and] 600 pounds camwood, and 13 barrels palm oil on board the cargo ship for London.

27 November 1811. This day put several tons camwood on board the ship for London. And our vessel's crew with the Kru men put it all on board, for which we had [received] one dollar per ton.

28 November 1811. This day had the bill of lading finished and signed, and the ship was clear of us for the sea. The inhabitants came very thick [in large numbers] and [were] quick to receive [the] books [we brought from England], which were handled very freely and received freely. And they were closely advised to make good use of the books, etc.

29 November 1811. [We turned our attention to] landing iron, tobacco, and delivering out goods to those who wish to buy. The people seem to be in pretty high spirits [anxious] to buy in a small way.

30 November 1811. This day finished landing the tobacco, and [we] delivered to Captain Boers Bones[8] 334 fine bread[s] at 9d per pound, 152 coarse bread[s] at 7d per pound, which was well received, and we was kindly had.

1 December 1811. This day being first day [of the week], I attended Meetings, [both] forenoon at the Intruding, [and] in the afternoon at the Baptist, at which places a copy of a letter from the Oneida [New York] Indians was read to good satisfaction.

---

[8] Cuffe is referring to Lieutenant Robert Bones, of the Royal Navy. Bones was much in the confidence of the colony's governor. In fact, Bones administered Sierra Leone for a brief period in 1811 during Governor Columbine's absence. His administrative and naval duties apparently did not require all his energies, and it is evident from Cuffe's log entry that Bones engaged in commercial activities as a sideline.

And some close exercising [thought provoking] hints was put forth [in the letter], both for the improving the mind of the people and [for] setting forth the power of God.

2 December 1811. This day [I] delivered the Indian letter[9] into the hands of the Methodists to copy, which copy I wish to be kept for the improvement of the people.

3 December 1811. I went on board the *Traveller* this morning. They [the crew] seemed to be all in a humor for having their discharge. Prince Edwards demanded his discharge. Accordingly, Prince is discharged. I am in hopes the rest are more reconciled. All of this ariseth from liquor, so pernicious is that spirit.

4 December 1811. I have fully and regular discharged Prince, and am in hopes the rest [of the crew] will be more reconciled. Therefore, he is not entitled to any more wages from and after [the] 3rd of this instant. We have this day finished landing iron bars and most of the pots.

5 December 1811. This day I waited on the Governor, who informed me the *Thais* would sail on seventh day [of December]. Therefore, I am to get ready to write and forward the bills on to London by the ship *Thais.*

6 December 1811. This day we are preparing letters for the ship *Thais,* Captain Sobel, for England.

7 December 1811. This day sailed the frigate for Cape Coast,[10] and a slave brig arrived, prize to the *Thais.* [It took the slave brig] 3 months [to sail] from Cape Coast to this place. Charles Dumor is quite feeble with the fever. I have paid Aaron [Richards] for weighing [merchandise] for me for 2 days.

8 December 1811. This day went to the Methodist Meeting where I saw 2 of the native captives come in. They seemed to have some of the movements of truth, [and it is hoped, therefore, that we will be able] to teach their minds. They betook themselves to

[9] The Oneida Indians' letter is not in the Cuffe papers.

[10] The Cape Colony was located at the Southern tip of Africa. Originally settled by Dutchmen and French Huguenots in the 1600's, it was seized by Great Britain in 1795. It was restored to Holland in 1802, and the British seized it again in 1806. Great Britain's title to the colony was confirmed as part of the post-Napoleonic settlement, and the Cape Colony became the nucleus for later British expansion into the territory that was destined to become the Union of South Africa.

the English mode of clothing. After Meeting, I, with 3 of the Mission, went and saw Moses Wilkinson,[11] the lame and blind man who hath been a long standing preacher, at his house. I had [there] a good open service. [Later, I] carried Charles Dumor out to rest.

9 December 1811. This day attended in making up a package of letters for England by the *Thais,*[12] ship of war, (viz.) 15 in number. Sold 3 hogsheads of tobacco at 18d per pound, to be paid one half in camwood[13] and the other half in Captain Rockel[14] wood at £25 per ton, and Sherbro wood[15] at £20 per ton.

A late colony act [has been published] stating that all the inhabitants [of the Sierra Leone colony] must be [registered with the colonial government]. Those who refused to be enrolled should not have the protection of the colony law. [Other provisions of the act state:] and no cattle to be in the streets with[out] keepers, no dogs to be with[out] a master near, or with him.

10 December 1811. This day being very busy day, and very warm day, so that it seems to take some hold of the upper part of my head. I this day delivered 3 hogsheads tobacco at $18 per hogshead. Half [the price is to be paid me] in money, the other in wood Rockel at £25 per ton and Sherbro [wood] at £20 per ton. The *Bora* this day is made up at 5 p.m. for England. I have distributed many kinds of seed and silk worm eggs [to the colonists], but I found very few [of the colonists] that knew what

11 Moses Wilkinson was one of the colony's "grand old men." Born a slave in Nansemond, Virginia, Wilkinson managed to escape and make his way to Nova Scotia during the American Revolution. In Nova Scotia he headed a Methodist congregation in Birch Town, the black ghetto of Shelburne, and later led his flock to Sierra Leone during the black Nova Scotian exodus of 1792. Though blind and lame, Wilkinson became one of the colony's leading preachers, and he was noted for his fervent and emotional style in delivering sermons.

12 The *Thais'* departure was evidently delayed for a few days.

13 Camwood is a hard timber that is used to make red dye. The camwood forests of Sierra Leone were easily accessible, and it was anticipated that a thriving camwood industry would soon develop there.

14 Rokel wood was a type of hard wood found deep in the interior of Sierra Leone along the Rokel River. Rokel timber was used principally for shipbuilding.

15 Sherbro wood is a hard wood that was used for commercial lumber purposes. Sierra Leone developers expected that English shipbuilders would make increasing use of this wood.

to do with them. The Governor told me they [the colonists] had better learn to raise cotton before they undertook silk [cultivation]. And the vaccination matters [drugs that Cuffe brought to Sierra Leone] was handed into the dispensary house, [and then] to the colony house.

11 December 1811. This day passed as usual. In the evening, I was called upon to meet with the Social Society of Sierra Leone,[16] at the house of John Reed. [We assembled] in order to consider the mode that was best for a constitution to be framed for the Society [about] to be established. In it [the constitution] was there and then talked over and [the meeting] adjourned to an evening next ensuing, and due notice to be given, and for the form [of the constitution] to be made out and laid before the Society for their consideration. . . .

12 December 1811. Charles Dumor is getting somewhat better. Yesterday, in the afternoon, Thomas Wainer was taken quite ill with the fever, and this day is getting better. But [he] is tired with the ague, etc. The *Thais,* ship of war, had 2 men run from her, but has obtained them by giving reward to the crewmen. They searched our vessel for their men, but found them not there, but found them in the bush.

13 December 1811. This day passeth much as usual, nothing remarkable. Thomas Wainer is still attended with the fever.

14 December 1811. This day [my] employment much as usual. I went to an an-due [auction] of a household lot. It sold for £370. It was a convenient lot adjoining the water, nicely [located], but rather shallow and enclosed.

Thomas continues to be closely tried with the fever. Charles [Dumor] is getting upon his legs. I attended with the Methodists at Meeting this day. David Edmonds, a respected person of color in Sierra Leone, is taken off his legs with the rheumatic complaint. Samuel Hicks is quite complaining [with the fever]. Our family seems to be getting in a weakly way. I myself feel the symptoms,

---

[16] The Social Society ultimately became the Friendly Society of Sierra Leone. This was the trading cooperative that Cuffe and members of the London African Institution hoped would become the instrument for bringing economic prosperity to the colony. See Cuffe diary entry 18 December 1811.

but am favored to keep about, for which blessing I desire ever to be therefore thankful to the All Wise Blessing.

16 December 1811. This day passed much as usual. Thomas Wainer still seems to be very closely tried with the fever. Charles is on the mending, and Samuel Hicks is still complaining, but keeps about. Sold and landed 20 bushels corn at 3/6d per bushel.

17 December 1811. These 24 hours commences as usual. Thomas and the others remain still ill. Thomas is taking bark [as medicine], but has had no doctor. The bell rung fire at 8 this morning. It burnt down 1 kitchen, but did no great damage otherwise.

18 December 1811. This day commences as heretofore. Thomas' fever seems little to break. He doth not consent to have the doctor. I sent for Samuel [Hicks] to come on shore, but he doth not consent to it. Charles [Dumor] came home last second day, and seems to be on the mending hand.

I met with the inhabitants of the colony at James Reed's, at which meeting it was agreed unto that there should be a monthly meeting held by this Society, which Society should be called the Friendly Society of Sierra Leone—whose duty it should be to take every matter unto their care that appeared to be for the beneficial good of the universe and to the glory of God, always desiring to begin and end with God. And [it was further agreed] that a record might be made of these things in order that the conduct of their meetings stand fair to the representation of the world for generations to come.

19 December 1811. This day begins much as usual. Thomas seems somewhat relieved of the fever, but is weak, and complains [of] dizziness in the head (as though there was a roaring and rushing noise in his head). He still declines of having the doctor, but is cupped by an old woman, which [the cupping treatment] I am much in unity with.

At midnight Thomas awoke me and said that he did not feel so well. I got up and sat with him. He appeared to me to be [rational] or [to] talk with good sense. He said that he had been trying to gain [behave] the right way, but it appeared to him the more he tried, the farther off he was. I pointed out to Thomas as well as I was capable [of] pointing, Christ [is] to be the way of everlasting life, and [that he should] not let the enemy discourage him from seeking unto Christ. For He will be sought unto by all who would be saved, for He is worthy.

Warrick Francis kindly offered his house for me or Thomas to be at in sickness, which is a favor I hope he will be rewarded for with the blessings of heaven, amen.

20 December 1811. This day [passed] as heretofore stipulated. Thomas Wainer's fever, I think, is turned, but leaves him very weak and pensive. Anna Edmonds came this afternoon and directed a plaster of flies nut[s—a widely used poultice for fevers] to the back part of his shoulders, and it was done, which I think to be [of] great service [to Thomas]. I got another woman to attend [to Thomas] this night through. The plaster made him very restless, but afterward it gave him ease. Charles Dumor is getting something poorer. Samuel Hicks rather recruits [recovers].

21 December 1811. These 24 hours begins as pleasant as can be with the Harmattan Winds[17] off the land, which generally is late [in the day] winds. And in the middle of the day [the wind blew] NNE to calm, which makes the air very close and hot. At 12 o'clock this day there was a sale of a house and lot of land nigh the East Bay. Set up at public auction, I bid it off at £60. At 3 p.m. they made out a bill on me for the Sheriff['s] sale. I paid them the cash and took the Sheriff's deeded receipt for the payment, [along] with his [the sheriff's] promise for the security on Sunday.

Thomas Wainer is low and weak, but is on the mend. He at sometimes sweats terribly, and anon [then] is chilly. I bid on 5⅙ acres of land on King Tom's point as high as £4 [per acre], and it was bid off at 4 guineas per acre. I this day sent 8 books to James Reid's [house] on the abolishing of the slave trade. At ½ past 6 this evening an American brig arrived: 58 days from Boston.

22 December 1811. At 4 this morning, or at least a few minutes after I awoke or Thomas called me, the clock struck 4; Thomas told me he thought that I should not stay long[er in Sierra

---

[17] The Harmattan Wind is dry, parching, charged with dust—a land wind that is indigenous to the west coast of Africa.

Leone]. And requested me to [return to the United States shortly
in order for him to be able once more to] see his family, (viz.) his
wife and children. I gave Thomas assurance of my assistance, if
God permitted. I then endeavored to point out to him the great
necessity there was of our being prepared and given up to the [ser-
vice of] the true and living God, looking unto Christ for our
redemption always, and at all times being given up to His Holy
Will; often retiring in our closets to pray unto the Lord our God
whose mercies endureth forever; and He will abundantly pardon
all those that put their trust in the Lord Jesus Christ, etc. In the
morning Thomas arose, was shaved, shirted, and walked out as far
or to Warrick Francis', and was quite recruited, but in the afternoon was not quite so well.

23 December 1811. This day, or last night and today, the
schooner *Adventurer,* of this port and from Sherbro [Island],
arrived with 28 tons wood in-shipped [imported] by John Kizzell;[18] and [also arriving today] was the brig *Manerua* from
London, and the sloop, or ship, of war from London. No [impor-
tant] news [was reported by the ships]. We lost Captain Benson;
[he was] very sick at Gonce. I took 1 puncheon[19] of palm oil,
about 90 gallons, on board the brig *Traveller,* and landed some of
Kizzell's wood on the keel, and some [in trade] for nails, at his
landing.

There was a meeting of the inhabitants [of Freetown] called
together today to take the oath of allegiance to [the] Crown. [The
oath] obligated [the oath takers] to obey the King's decrees in all
cases, but the inhabitants refused signing. It was then told to them
that they forfeited their houses and lots of land, but all this
[threats] did not prevail on the men.

---

18 A native of Sherbro Island, John Kizzell as a young man had been
carried to South Carolina and into slavery. He managed to escape during
the American Revolution and after the war followed the Tories into exile
in Nova Scotia. Then he came full circle and joined the Nova Scotians who
made the trek to Sierra Leone in 1792. Kizzell proceeded to build an extensive business network in Freetown and on Sherbro Island where he lived
for a number of years. Kizzell was a devout Baptist, took an active part in
the colony's political life, and became the Friendly Society's first president.

19 A puncheon was a large cask of varying capacity, but the usual standard
was 111.6 gallons.

Charles Freebury was taken [ill] last night. Hither I sent the doctor to him at 3 o'clock. M. Zachariah is sick. I took him on shore. Luckily, they are both under doctor's host [care]. I went to meeting with Hannah Z.

24 December 1811. This morning the sick much as usual. The doctor attends them all. He prescribes a poultice for Thomas' knee, but it has not [had] much effect yet.

This day finished landing John Kizzell's wood, but could not get hands [helpers] enough to get it off the keel. The government men find fault that the wood is not off. Allen [Alexander] Macaulay[20] is to have 3 tons; he has promised this 2 days [ago] to take it [away], but does not perform [as he promised]. I was obliged to land some [wood] at Nichol's[21] landing, and was obliged to leave it in [the] water for 2 days for want of help.

I this day paid a short visit to the new missionaries, who seemed to be well pleased with the place. They told me that the [Mission] Society had 100 children under their tuition at Rio Pongas.[22] I then endeavored to hold out [to them] the necessity that good may be done [here], even in good morals and industry, etc., etc.

25 December 1811. This day being Christmas morning, the night [before] the inhabitants spent in a very noisy way in firing of guns, singing and the like. The sick much as before mentioned. Thomas has a bad swelled knee; otherwise, to [all] appearances, [he] would be quite smart.

---

[20] Alexander Macaulay was Zachary Macaulay's brother. He had been interested in Sierra Leone from the time of the first colonization attempt and later on served the Sierra Leone Company as a ship's captain. Some time later, Macaulay settled down in Freetown and engaged in the mercantile business. He went "native" and maintained a Nova Scotian mistress, much to the distress of his brother Zachary.

[21] George Nichol was a European carpenter who came to the colony in the employ of the Sierra Leone Company. He married a mulatto heiress and parlayed her inheritance into a considerable fortune. Nichol owned a sizable quantity of real estate in Freetown, built two houses in the capital on speculation, and lived in a stone and brick house that fronted on the harbor and cost more than £3,500 to build.

[22] The Rio Pongas is located in Guinea some distance north of Conakry, the capital. In the early nineteenth century the area was inhabited by the Susu tribe. English missionaries expended considerable energy in an effort to convert the Susu to Christianity, but for the most part their efforts ended in failure.

At 6 this morning James Carr[23] and myself went to J. Carr's place, about 1½ miles on a point up the river from Sierra Leone [Freetown], to view a quantity of dry hides he had there—cattle, deer, sheep and goats. I proposed to barter with him for them, (viz.) sugar for skins. I delivered him a sample of the sugar for his consideration.

At 12 o'clock I went to see my 2 sick men, (viz.) Zachariah and Charles. Hannah told me they were gone in[to] the backyard. She went after them, and I after her. They were not to be found. But there was a rum drinking, noisy house stood to the east and west-northward [to Hannah's house]. It appeared they were there. I told Hannah it was not worth my while to hire a nurse, doctor, etc., for men that was well enough to stand houses of mirth.

26 December 1811. The day after Christmas the people kept up a noisy stress with their drums, dance, and clapping their hands. Thomas Wainer continued much as usual. His knee badly swelled. Sent a boat towards Bullom Shore to get some leeches or other blood suckers [for Thomas Wainer]. [The expedition] got back at 10 or 11 o'clock at night. Brought 11 of the animals. The smoky Harmattans still continue. Still employed in getting Kizzell's wood up; [I have] 6 men employed [on this one task].

27 December 1811. This day business much as usual. The sick getting better. Thomas this day has the leeches or blood suckers applied to his swelled knee. They were put to [the knee] by the help of a glass beaker. If they seemed to be loath to take hold [of the infected area], wet the skin with [a] little milk. When they have filled themselves, they will let go. Then have a plate [ready] with [a] little fine salt [on the plate]; put them [the leeches] in the plate and touch them to the salt; they will immediately throw out the blood and become limp. Then put them in clean fresh water, and they will be fit for use again.

After they [the leeches] came off, wet cloths took out of warm

---

[23] James Carr was an Englishman who came to the colony as an accountant for the Sierra Leone Company. Carr stayed on in Sierra Leone after the company's collapse and engaged in the sale of produce. He turned to the slave trade for a few years, then came back to Freetown, where he settled in with his Nova Scotian mistress and managed a plantation a few miles outside the city.

water was applied [to Thomas' knee], which keep the blood running for 6 hours, etc.

28 December 1811. This morning [the infection on] Thomas' knee broke; it run very much. John Macaulay[24] came in the evening and opened it [a] little [more] with his lancet. It vented pretty freely, but I think he did not open it enough.

There was a poultice [for the infection] ordered of oat meal and corn fodder and beef relics. But in the morning the head doctor came [and] ordered the same taken off [Thomas Wainer's infected knee], and [he ordered an] oat meal poultice applied, which kept the matter pretty freely running. [We] dressed it [the infection once] in 2 or 3 or 4 hours, which afforded free discharge, which relieved the patient.

Zachariah and Charles this evening went on board [*Traveller*] after staying on shore 5 days. Charles Dumor kept to the nurse 1 week, etc.

There has been 2 or 3 musters [calls] in Sierra Leone to enroll the inhabitants, and for them to take the oath of allegiance [to the Crown], but they seem to have pretty general objection [to the entire affair].

29 December 1811. This morning smoky Harmattan weather as usual. The comet[25] seems to descend about the middle of the 12th month in lat[itude] 8½ N. The comet bore nearly west [of] his regular course, and travel seems to be into the SW, varying from $1.^d 15^m$ to $2^d.5^m$, but his most general route seemed to be about $1^d.30^m$ in 24 hours. But his course was regular [a]round with the stars this day.

In the morning went to Methodist Meeting. At 2 p.m. saw [to

[24] John Macaulay was a recaptive recently brought to Sierra Leone. He was of the Hausa tribe and had been reared as a Muslim. However, he practiced Christianity when relocated in Freetown. Macaulay was very strong physically and earned the nickname Atapa, which was Yoruba for "kicker."

[25] Cuffe evidently is referring to the Vintage Comet. This spectacular comet, first observed by the great English astronomer Sir William Herschell, lingered in northern skies for 510 days, from March 26, 1811, until August 17, 1812. In October, 1811, the Vintage Comet's tail spread over approximately one hundred million miles of space; it was perhaps fifteen million miles in breadth.

having] Thomas' knee dressed [properly]. It discharged very freely. Put on new poultices, which gave him much relief. And I am in hopes that Thomas will be soon about, and [that he] will remember to thank and praise God for his deliverance, from time to time.

James Smith applied for some turpentine spirits for a bleeding at the stomach. I sent him some spirits of turpentine, and ordered [him] to take 5 drops night and morning. We called our little family together this evening, [the healthy] with the sick, and had very agreeable time. [there were] 2 or 3 Kru men with [us] who seemed to behave exceedingly well, indeed. They, I hope with the blessing of God, will experience His Divine Goodness to [be] engrafted in their hearts.

30 December 1811.   This day we send out bills to people for payment, but [only a] small collection made. Thomas Wainer is still confined to his bed by the badness of his knee. The doctor ordered warm poultices to be made and applied, and they caused a very free discharge [of the infected matter]. But Thomas concerted [claimed that] it rotted his flesh, and would not have them put on any more. But [then Thomas Wainer himself] applied green earth [to the infection]. But I believe it would be much better if [the infected area] was more opened so as to let the [infected] matter out; but he chooseth not to be cut up, so he must have his own way. He will be best satisfied.

The government decrees seem to interrupt the minds of the inhabitants much. That is to say, [the government decree requiring] that of enrolling themselves so as to be subject to the commanding officer['s] directions to be in readiness to march on any expedition whatever. Some has signed, and some has not.

31 December 1811.   Thomas Wainer remains much in the state as before mentioned. The fever seems to have left him, but the knee remains quite unwell. The doctor allows him to eat, and ordered a berth to be made out of chamomile[26] flowers and bark. For 10 or 15 minutes at a time, Thomas' wound seems to discharge pretty freely and is not painful but some. And that is not so

---

[26] Chamomile is an herb with strongly scented foliage and flowers which is used medicinally.

much to be wondered at as the defect is large and sometimes collecting.

I measured an African canoe: 40 ft. 9″ long, 2 ft. 9″ deep, 5 ft. 3″ broad, and [it] measured 6 tons 14/95 of a ton. I have bartered my sugar with G. Nichol's for wood: sugar at 6d [per pound] and wood at £25 Rockel and Sherbro at £20 per ton delivered.

1 January 1812. Thomas Wainer much as before mentioned; [he is] confined with his knee. The doctor has not prescribed any new medicine, but continues the bath and the applications of the pepper leaves as proposed by him and his nurse. We are in hopes Thomas will be about soon, but I think it may not be so soon as we wish.

Zachariah is very earnest to marry, and wants to hire my house. But I tell him if he could be steady and keep with the brig, he would never do better. But if he must marry, and nothing would do but marrying, he must desert [ship], for I could not discharge him. But I did not think I should hurt him with the crewmen [permit Zachariah to cause dissension among the crew], etc.

I carried a pair of steps to my house this day, and one board measure 8 ft., to mend the steps to go in and out of the house. Alexander Smith came this afternoon and notified me, he said, that he was sorry to say that he should be obliged to put [give] wood to me for payment, notwithstanding I had positively agreed with him for the payment of 2 hogsheads of tobacco at 18 s[hillings] per pound for cash or bills on England. And as he did not agree with me for barter, I considered it all cash, and made discount of 5 per cent on the pairs of satin stripes [that I had sold him] on that account. But it showeth that he means to take advantage [of me].

2 January 1812. This day begins with fine weather. As usual, wind in from seaward. Thomas got up today and went [about] with crutches. But his knee is much out of repair. The doctor attends on him yet, but does not [do] much [for Thomas] to real advantage.

I landed 9 hogsheads sugar for George Nichol. In weighing [the sugar] it all fell short from 28 to 46 pounds in a hogshead. Sold it at 6d per pound; took wood in pay at £25 per ton.

At 12 o'clock at night we were alarmed with information that

the natives was coming to invade the town, that they had got as far
as Carol Bay. The Governor this day went to Bence's Island,[27]
and [so too did] the Chief Judge. Therefore, the care [defense of
Freetown] fell on the Major. They set patrols out, and the officer
of the man [of] war that was on shore sent off for them [the man
of war] to be in readiness to attack them [the natives]. However,
this all passed by to appearance without any real foundation.
Nothing remarkable took place at [during] this alarm.

3 January 1812. Thomas Wainer seems to be better, but he
still is under the doctor's hands. I am trading safely [cautiously];
[therefore], no great doings. Landed 3 hogsheads sugar for
George Nichol this day. I have borrowed a horse to go in[to] the
mountains tomorrow, if God permits.

I went to [James] Carr's place, about 1½ miles [out of town].
I went [out] in a boat with Carr, but walked in [back to town] by
land. It is a very pleasant walk. Carr informed me that a leopard
had taken 2 of his sheep of late. Pineapples grow exceeding[ly]
well [here], although the country is rather barren. The soil is
reddish, but rocky nigh to the top of the ground.

I saw some of the guinea grass. Carr told me that the cattle eat
the grass well. I reached to the top of some of it with my umbrella;
it [the grass] appeared to be 9 or 10 feet high. Notwithstanding
the soil is poor, they can and do raise 2 good crops of Indian corn
and buckwheat [each year].

4 January 1812. This 24 hours pleasant weather. In the
morning it was calm; at 12 o'clock wind NWE; small breeze.
Thomas Wainer last night became a good deal fuddled-headed. But
today his knee has run a good deal, he [is] better, and his knee
stronger.

At 7 this morning I set forth for the mountains on horse back,
attended by Lazarus Jones, George Warren and Jonathan Rainer.
Went about 3 miles to Governor Little's plantation. It is inhabited
now by the Governor's native captives. [There are] about 12 or
15 huts [about the place]. Plenty of coffee bushes standing, but
they are overrun with forest. They have corn fed plenty of fowl.

We returned by way [of] Warrick Francis' and Lazarus Jones'

27 See footnote 3, p. 81.

plantations. Lazarus showed us a plantation where he lived a few years ago, but it has got so that it looks as though it had never been cleared. He paid £1 per acre for that land. Their [Sierra Leone] plantations abound with corn fed [fowl]; they prefer them to [wild] game on account of [the ease of] feeding [their] stock, etc. When they plant those roots [used for feed, all] they [do is] break a piece off the stalk and put it in the ground, etc.

5 January 1812. This day Thomas Wainer is much better. The wound on his knee is attended with [a] warm bath and an African pepper leaf keep on it as a plaster. The corrupted matter has to appearances pretty much discharged itself, and he begins to walk about without crutches, etc.

6 January 1812. Thomas Wainer and his knee is much on the mend. So I am in hopes he will be about [completely recovered] in a few days. John Kizzell has arrived this day at 10 o'clock, The [Friendly] Society met with John in the evening. William Allen's letter[28] was read [to the meeting] and approved of with a degree of love and unity.

The missionary[ies] from the Rio Pongo has made a visit to me this evening. They say they have 100 children under their care, but the natives was much disturbed that they were cut off from their former privileges, and no means [had been] procured for them to clothe themselves and, etc.

7 January 1812. Thomas Wainer seems to be getting better, and is getting his account in [order]. The inhabitants is very anxious I should take their boys [as] apprentices. But I advised them to keep them at home and learn their industry themselves, unless they could get government protection for them. Otherwise, I should be in danger of losing them [to impressment raiders].

8 January 1812. Thomas is about house without crutches. The doctor still visits him. I have this day taken 3 tons of rice of Thomas [Kizzell] at $40 per ton. Here was arrived 1 prize Portuguese 3 mast[ed] slave schooner. Was captured off the Cape de Verde[29] with about 50 slaves on board. I hope this may be warning to them [the Portuguese] to flee from the evil to come.

---

[28] A thorough search of the Cuffe papers failed to reveal this letter.

[29] Cape Vert (or Verde) is located off the hump of Africa near the site of present-day Dakar.

9 January 1812. Landed 1 cask sugar for James Carr and took on board [*Traveller*] 1 large iron compass. Thomas Wainer has been as far as the Black house, etc. [I] had [received] 1 old cart from Nichol, etc. Also landed 9 bushels coal for the blacksmith, with promises of pay for them on the Governor's promise to pay his bill.

10 January 1812. This day in the fore part of the day Thomas was very smart [felt well], but in the afternoon [he came a] good deal down with the fever. His nurse fondles good deal over him. I have had [some] talk of taking another of the colonists to learn him the useful art of navigation so as [for the navigation student eventually] to become useful to the colony, etc.

11 January 1812. This day Thomas is pretty smart, but in the afternoon [he] is tried with the return of ague and sickness to the stomach. Nothing very remarkable [happened here today]. The Methodist mission was prosecuted by the Judge Thorpe,[30] for holding meetings[31] whilst the [Anglican] church was assembled, but they [the Governor?] suppressed it by writing to the Judge to drop it.

12 January 1812. Thomas seems to remain sick to the stomach. [He is racked] with loud gaggings and heavings.

I went to the Methodist Meeting this afternoon at 2 o'clock, where I had a good service, where the truth was lively reigned. And many were closely warned not to satisfy themselves of feeding on empty husks of vanity; but to return home to the Father's house, where there is bread enough and to spare. [The Methodists warned] also against [their parishioners] becoming their own executioners in drinking in the baneful poison, and for their lascitudes of gain, of holding it to their neighbors' mouths that they became drunk, and feeding our children with it, and taking the last draught themselves so that they may be called self-murderers [that are] never to be forgiven.

13 January 1812. This day I commenced taking in [on board *Traveller*] camwood. I have taken in this day 11 tons, 200, 2 quarters, and 14 lbs. Thomas Wainer seems to mend slowly. The

30 Dr. Robert Thorpe, Chief Justice of Sierra Leone.
31 Sierra Leone regulations evidently prohibited non-Anglican gatherings during Sunday services of the established Anglican church.

Harmattan continues without [bringing] rain or any great wind. The sea breeze blows in but very faint, and some days not at all, and then not until very late.

The Methodist missionaries are fined[32] from Judge [Thorpe] for keeping meetings in church hours, which has been prohibited by himself since [his] coming here. The fine was £20, which they [the Methodists] said they paid. I fear this will have a tendency to stagnate the civilization of Africa [rather] than to promote the good cause. God only knows what is for the best good. May God be pleased to be our preserver and our own guide, etc.

14 January 1812. Thomas Wainer went up to Pompey Young's[33] this morning, but in the afternoon he had quite a return of the fever. But got better in the evening. At 12 o'clock [I] opened the vender; sold for cash at sight of the bills. Sold about 190 pounds sterling worth. Our servant Kruman Jack was suspected to be guilty of knavery. We lost 6 knives and forks, setting ones, and 4 handkerchiefs, etc. In the evening we heard the iron move. We found Jack near the place [where we discovered part of the loot hidden] on Surron's Harbor. [He] ran away swiftly.

15 January 1812. Thomas Wainer [is] more comfortable [today]. At 4 this morning [we] hove in very heavy sea on the shore, and [we] continued the day through so that we injured our boat on shore in taking the wood off, etc. The vender continued the day through or until 2 o'clock. Sold to the amount of £157:15s.

16 January 1812. Thomas went on board [ship] this morning, and spent the day [there]. He seems to be better. [I] spent the day chiefly in adjusting accounts. In the evening attended with 2 other friends to wait on Anthony Davis and his wife to talk with them about their son going with me. He [the son] was not in. [He] was out somewhere. They seemed very earnest for him to learn [an] industry, and [they believed] that he could not learn here. I told them [that it] was in the parents [to teach their son a

---

[32] Cuffe on January 11 apparently underestimated Judge Thorpe's determination to promote Anglicanism within the colony.

[33] Pompey Young was a Nova Scotian baker. Although he had a number of rivals, Young at this time was considered by many to be Freetown's "premier" baker.

trade]; that they did not put industry in practice; if they would,
here [Sierra Leone] was as good a chance as in the known world,
for they could raise 2 crops a year [here] and the weather called
for but few clothing; that there was a chance for their advancement
[here].

17 January 1812. This day continues as usual. Thomas mends
slowly. [I am] getting some things forward. A ship arrived here
today from Cape DeVerde laden with salt (11 days passage) for
George Nichol.

18 January 1812. Thomas Wainer much as usual. Continued
[my] business today. There has been a heavy swell on the shore
for several days. It is agreed [that I am] to give an answer to the
African Institution for the letter[34] [they] sent to John Kizzell. In
this [letter] I have to reprimand very closely on ourselves the
necessity for encouraging industry, and defending the case of
ardent settlement.

19 January 1812. This morning small wind, but [the sky is]
hazy; [the wind blows] NE and WNW. Eat breakfast and dinner
with D. Edmonds, and then took morning Meeting with Warrick
Francis, at which place [the morning Meeting] there appeared to
be what they called a convert. I fell to, and did encourage her that
as she was set free, [therefore,] to go and sin no more. In the
afternoon I had good open service in which they [the worshipers]
was closely warned to flee from sinning against light and reason,
and to avoid that monster of spiritous liquors, and that of idleness.
[They were further cautioned] that the great work of the reformation [of the individual] depended on their faithfulness. [The
remainder of this entry has been cut from the journal.]

20 January 1812. This day commenceth with close, sultry air,
small of[f]shore wind. But in the afternoon [the wind blew from]
WSW, and in the evening, NW. I went to the West Bay in the
morning to take a survey of the water streams [in the area]. And
it appears that there is a stream that will do for a undershot wheel.
And another stream that has a fall power of over 20 feet perpendicular. And I believe by carrying the stream in [a] trough 30 or
40 rods there may be a wheel of 30 feet erected which may go [be

[34] This is evidently the William Allen letter that was read to the meeting
of the Friendly Society on January 6, 1812.

operated] for the year round. Logs may be brought to the mill. Likewise, it is very good [site] for a gristmill. . . . [The remainder of this entry has been cut from the journal.]

21 January 1812. In the morning the wind easterly; in the afternoon [the wind blew] in from sea, from WSW. This day arrived the noontine Captain Wood in the American brig *Manchester,* of Boston. Now, from the services at forenoon, [I] rung the bell for vendue. [Many] things sold of[f] tolerable well. [I] got on considerable, but did not get through [selling everything I desired to sell today]. But think I may get through in 4 days more. Have got pretty well through with the pots and iron bars, etc.

Samuel Hicks seems to be getting uneasy, and seems to [be preparing] to leave the vessel. I tells him that if he goeth, he must run from the vessel. If he doth, I do not think that I shall kill myself in running after him, the sad tick. It is a pity that men as they grow old[er] should grow in sin; but the lives of one are not apt to stand still, they are apt to go back or forward. If they take the straight forward road they become good citizens; but if the reverse, they become more the children of the Evil One [rather] than the Heavenly Father.

22 January 1812. This day commences with the wind in from the seaboard at WSW. At 9 o'clock this morning arrived [in port] a fine pilot [*sic,* meaning *pirate*] boat [which appeared] like a built schooner. [The pirate boat] was taken by His Majesty's ship, and sent to this port with [its] slaves [still] in [the boat]. She was taken in Gambia.[35] I do long to see the slave trade discouraged, and wish that men [the slave traders] could feel their causes to be put in the slaves' stead. I believe they would [then] feel themselves condemned by their own consciences.

I this day called on Alexander Smith and let him know that I was arranging my business as fast as possible [in order to be able] to leave the colony [shortly], and wished the favor of him to settle his bill [with me]. He told me that he could not pay cash, nor bills, and that he made it his pointed rule not to make any further engagements than he was able to perform. Therefore, [Alexander Smith] would give me no encouragement of any payment but [in]

---

[35] Gambia is located to the north of Sierra Leone. Several hundred miles up the coast, it is situated on the hump of West Africa.

wood. Although he had rarely enjoyed cash or bills, he further said
[that he] had a £20 bill I could have.

23 January 1812. The wind fresh [from the] West, which
makes [for] a heavy sea on the shore. Thomas Wainer is getting
about quite smart. He is endeavoring to settle his business affairs
so as to be [able to sail] off with us. I am having vendues [public
auctions] in order to get through with my business [quickly] so as
to be off soon.

The Friendly Society met this evening, but there appears to be
more debating than business done. It appeared that the many of
them are willing to lade[n] other men's shoulders with burdens,
and they themselves to be excused [from making any contribu-
tion]. But if we in Sierra Leone would [only] rouse ourselves to
more industry and sobriety we would get forward the better, and
make the better progress. They seem to be much agitated because
the Governor will not permit foreigners to land tobacco and rum.
And I rather conceive this prohibition to be a maxim to make us
look about ourselves and endeavor to help ourselves. And as we
are made to seek, so may we find.

24 January 1812. This morning the wind light off [the] land
wind, but in the afternoon [there are] freshets [of a] sea breeze.
Thomas Wainer seems to have a slight return of the fever; [in
addition, he is troubled] with the symptoms of the ague.

The brig *Manchester,* Captain Wood, from Boston, got underway to go out [to sea]. After he had departed about 2 miles, they
from the fort gave him a shot, which brought him to. He left his
Customs House dues unpaid, but he came back and paid his shot
and Customs dues. He is bound to the Leeward [Islands]; [he
sails first] to Cape Minso Radow, [and then] to the Leewards.

I this day paid a visit to the Governor. And had communication
[with him] on the matter of improvement among the inhabitants
of Sierra Leone, and on the propriety of [my obtaining] grants of
land, and [of my] building a saw mill, and on his opinion on what
encouragement would be given to those who would afford [offer]
their aid and assistance to Sierra Leone. The Governor proposes to
me on supplying him with lumber from America.

25 January 1812. Thomas is [a] little worser and complainy
towards evening. [My] business going on in a slow way. Disposed

of all the scrap [items] for ivory, [selling] at a low price for the scrap and [buying at] a high price for the ivory. We propose of sailing next week for America. We are getting through with [our] business pretty well. I understand Samuel Hicks talks of coming back [to the ship] again, but he had made no application to me. [The remainder of this entry has been cut from the journal].

26 January 1812. Calm, or rather offshore, air [today]. At 12 the sea breeze set in from the West. At 8 I went on board the brig and took dinner. And then came on shore and spent the afternoon from reading and visited [my] friend Edmonds. And [then I] sat [a] spell with John Gordon's family.

27 January 1812. I this day in the morning, the weather being good, hired 4 Kru men and 2 riggers, the riggers at 3 s[hillings] per day, and the Kru men at 9 p[ence] per day. So the *Traveller* bent her 2 new topsails, rove the rigging, filled [her] water [casks], etc. In the evening the [Friendly] Society met and agreed unanimously that the copy of the letter[36] laid before them should be sent to answer the one received from them in England. David Edmonds, Jr., and J. Gordon resigned their membership [in the Friendly Society]. I left some small accounts with several persons on credit [in order] to prove their faith [honesty]. [The remainder of this entry has been cut from the journal].

28 January 1812. Weather much as usual. In the morning small air off shore; in the afternoon small breeze came in. The vessel's crew employed as usual mending sails, etc.

Samuel Hicks agrees to go in the brig *Traveller* to America. And agrees to submit to my consideration what I may allow him for such services as he has forfeited—according to the law of the United States—and also for such services as he may do [for me] here after.

Alexander Smith refuses to pay me according [to the manner] we agreed for what he owes me. I refuseth to take my pay in any other way than that which he and I agreed. [The remainder of this entry has been cut from the journal.]

29 January 1812. The air dry [today], and clear as to clouds, but hazy. Thomas Wainer continues on the mending. Charles

---

[36] This letter is not in the Cuffe papers.

Dumor is gone on board [*Traveller*] but [he is still feeling] rather poorly. Zachariah is [still] somewhat sickly, [and he is recuperating] on shore.

Daniel Jones offers his services of working his passage to America, but is refused on account of [our crew list] being full. I have offered him the [passenger] berth, but since [I made my offer] I have got 2 [new] crewmen and 1 or 2 others.

George Warren came to me this day to get my affidavit that he did not preach, pray, or read in the Meeting on the 5th of January. As it appeared from his own mouth [that] he did [do] so, and as I did not go to [a] Meeting for such critics [of the Sierra Leone administration], I feel cautious of having anything to do with it. And [I prefer] to leave each one to work his [problems out in his own] way, for I consider the loss of a little money[37] to be but a small thing to the loss of true peace and happiness.

30 January 1812. Wind in the morning light; [the] air [came in from] off shore. In the after part of the day wind in from seaboard. Weather fair and serene; air close and musty, or sultry. Thomas Wainer seems to continue better.

I this day called on Alexander Smith for payment that was due me from him, but could not get it. For he refused unless I would take camwood [in payment], which was not part of our agreement, for as I particular agreed with him for cash or good bills of exchange. Therefore, I feel to leave the debt with him, unless he will pay according to agreement, and [I shall] petition for further address [*sic,* meaning *redress*] from some other quarter.

Captain Biggsby has lately had his vessel condemned for slaving. He some 5 years ago carried 2 boys off that belonged to Sierra Leone, all which he gave bonds for their return. And as he has not returned them, he is this day cast into prison in Sierra Leone.

I this morning took breakfast with G. Warren, and advised him to let me entirely off as an evident [witness] to his cause, as I did not like to have anything to do with it.

31 January 1812. Getting forward [in preparations for departure] slowly. And [there is] softly weather, soft and pretty fine. The doctor sent in his bill [today]: £12 for Thomas Wainer; £6 for Charles Dumor; £4 for Zachariah; and £2:10 for Charles

---

[37] Warren's fine before Judge Thorpe.

Freebury. The doctor attended those about a week [in] all, without [except for] Captain Wainer. He [Wainer] was attended [by the doctor] considerably longer. After showing Captain Wainer his bill, he refused paying without a particular [itemized] bill. Thomas Wainer seems to have deep disputes with his servants in paying them off. But I have heard no dispute between him and Betsy Mary Jones.[38] [They] have very close shots; I thought I should not like to have shots hove so nigh my head.[39]

1 February 1812. All is well. [I] entered on board [*Traveller*] this day at [the] Bay, and based [the brig there], where we was kindly received by John Wainer. I this day went to Cocoa Bay in order to survey [ascertain] if there was suitable places for making salt [there], but found no place without [except] they were artificial made. The land itself appeared to be right leachy or sandy land. I was attended with John Kizzell, William Munro,[40] George Warren, Jonathan Rainer.

I called on my friend G. Warren to pay for 6 slates and 1 Hamilton mop [that I had sold him], but he utterly refused to pay me. I then offered to leave it to his partner Jonathan Rainer, but he denied that. But said that he had given [me] a coat, and [that] ought to be offset. I told him what I gave [him in the past, but] I never called for pay. However, I gave the debt up to him, and the said Warren accepted it. William Munro has a very pretty place, indeed.

2 February 1812. The weather in the morning much as usual: moderate, and seems close heat. One Lawrence, a man belonging to Bagru River,[41] sent his plant gardener on board [*Traveller*] with a plant that worms will not eat; and some bark to make

[38] Betsy Mary Jones was apparently Thomas Wainer's housekeeper.

[39] Cuffe is suggesting that an illicit relationship may have existed between Miss Jones and Wainer. Cuffe further implies that it is unwise to mix business with pleasure in one's own home. In any event, Cuffe was far too strait-laced a man to ever have entered into any such relationship.

[40] William Munro was an English Methodist missionary who came to Freetown at the beginning of the nineteenth century. Unlike many of his fellow missionaries, Munro did not regard his assignment in Sierra Leone as being simply a tour of duty. He expected to remain there for the rest of his life employed in the service of God. Munro died of yellow fever during a severe outbreak of the disease in the colony in 1829.

[41] The Bagru River is located on Sherbro, that most important trading and timber island south of Freetown.

bitters of; and some root that was good to cover the bite of a snake, and also to prevent the snake from biting you; also a quarter of mutton for our dinner.

I shored, and went to church. It was hot [in the church]. Nyländer,[42] in his exhortation, appeared to be sanctified, but the ceremonies [within the] institution appeared to be formal, or in the letter of forms.

I dined this day with David Edmonds, and I [then] went on board [*Traveller*]. Then Thomas Wainer and John Wainer went on shore.

3 February 1812. Came on shore at 9 o'clock this morning, and went into settling [accounts] with the people. Made pretty good [head]way, but got not through [all the accounts]. Met with the Society this evening, to pretty good satisfaction.

Samuel Hicks presented [to me] a power of attorney from Warrick Francis dissolving all other authorities, and making himself [Hicks] the sole executor to his [Francis'] last will and testament. I then being present [familiar] with both parties, [I] was asked my advice. I then advised, as Samuel Hicks was [a] foreigner and stranger, to be cautious how he put trust in foreigners, but [instead to] try to look nearer home among his neighbors. It appeared that Francis had a daughter in America, and [he] would wish to get her [back] to Africa. Whether Samuel proposed marriage or not, I cannot tell, but I conclude there was policy in it [in other words, his decision would be based on self-interest].

4 February 1812. Business commences this day as usual. In the morning proceeded to business as usual. Zachariah White came to me this morning [and requested permission] to come to America with me, he being sick [of Sierra Leone]. I told him if he would consent to obligate himself to be under my direction until we got to America, and would consent to put himself under guardianship of John and Paul Cuffe, and would sign a bond to consent to abide [by their] advice, even if it was to go 'round

[42] The Reverend Gustavus Rheinhold Nyländer was one of three German missionaries sent to the colony in 1806 by the Claphamite Church Missionary Society.

Cape Horn or to the Indies, accordingly [I would then take him along with me]. He agreed, and signed a[n] agreement.

I also gave a note [bill] to Alexander Smith for payment, but it was noncomplied with though I would take wood [accept wood in lieu of cash]. But I let him know by a letter that I should be put to the disagreeable necessity of going without settlement with him. He then said I should be settled with before I went, but [he] wished to know in what way I wished to be settled with. But that part he and I have already talked over, (viz.) cash or bills.

I also went to the Governor with Anthony and George Davis, and had George Davis bound to me to serve 3 years. He accordingly was bound to me.

5 February 1812. The business of the morning, as soon as I came on shore, was to visit the water of the western bay where there is a fall of running water that falls 25 feet perpendicular. And at the distance [of] 44 or 50 rods it run into a basin. This basin is connected with the sea where logs, etc., can be conveniently brought to the mill. I am confident that there can be a wheel erected [there] for receiving the water over it 30 feet or more if occasion required it. It was our judgment that 50 feet of water would pass [over the wheel] in a minute during the driest part of the season, and in the rains [there] would be no lack of water for a mill of any description.

Notwithstanding the Governor bound George Davis yesterday [to me], he sent and took his name from the paper today. [The Governor accounted for his action by] saying it was because he [Davis] had not taken the oath of allegiance.

6 February 1812. All seems to be in motion [for our return trip home, but] my motion is but very slow. A[lexander] Smith this day preferred accommodation [with me negotiating] through Thomas Wainer, which was agreed unto. He then agreed to give [me] 2 tons wood and £72:12 in bills, all which I agreed unto, although I really wished [that when I was ready] to leave Africa [I would be able] to have my pay in cash or bills. But when men are like lions, we must be careful how we get our hands in their mouths. And if we should by chance to [have put our hands in a lion's mouth], we must endeavor to get [them] out [in] the best way of prudence. I hope this may be a lesson of instruction to me, and not be unuseful to others.

7 February 1812. Many are called [to God], but few are chosen. The choice lies with us either to choose [God] or to refuse [Him]. Alexander Smith has insisted on a new stipulation, and for peace sake I have complied with it, but [I am] far from agreement [with the new settlement]. I thought [it] better to compromise than to let the business run to a resentment too far.[43]

8 February 1812. This day employed in adjusting accounts and stating and regulating [my account] books. All [the crew is] employed. I this day took and gave a lease on my house and lot of land to William Henry Savage[44] at 5s[hillings] per week, and he paying all public taxes assessing thereon whilst [the house is in his] possession. All this was agreed unto, but not in an actual [signed] lease, etc. At 10 o'clock in the evening, I packed up and moved on board the *Traveller*.

9 February 1812. I spent all this day on board [ship] writing, etc. In the afternoon the Captain and [the] Lieutenant [of His Majesty's Navy] came on board and inquired how I should make my course [from Sierra Leone to America]. [They wished to know] whether I should stand to the northward, or stand in the open [sea]. I cannot feel much liking to their conversation. What their meaning may be [the purpose for their inquiry], I cannot say. They likewise informed me that there was 2 French privateers on the course, and that there was one [French privateer] off the Grand Canaries [Islands] having Spanish soldiers on board, and [that this particular privateer] had robbed several vessels. I do not much like such compliments.

10 February 1812. We [are] being nearly ready for sailing. Was on shore [today,] left 2 sets of bills with William C. Maxwell, Governor of Sierra Leone. [Governor Maxwell is] to for-

---

43 Obviously, Cuffe was forced to accept wood instead of cash as payment of Alexander Smith's debt. See entry of 6 February 1812.

44 William Henry Savage was destined to become one of Freetown's most successful businessmen. An Englishman by birth, of mixed parentage (his father was a black man and his mother was white), Savage came to Africa in 1808 as a schoolteacher. For a time he dabbled in the slave trade, then went into the import-export business. He was admitted to the bar in Sierra Leone, and in 1821 he became the colony's first black notary public.

ward [the bills] by Captain [William] Rotch [, Jr.], [who is to sail] for Liverpool, to William Rathbone. He [the Governor] then handed me his letters for his sister [who was residing] at New York. I made David Edmonds my attorney, and left notes and bills with him to amount of 333 s[hillings]. And the Governor assured me every encouragement will be given to those who may remove thither [from America] and become citizens thither.

11 February 1812. At 8 a.m. [we] unmoored [*Traveller*]; at 9 weighed [anchor] and sailed [from Freetown]; at 10 the boat came on back from setting the people on shore; at 12 meridian passed the Carpenter of the Cape with [a] small wind, NNW; all well. . . .

5
HOMEWARD BOUND

For unknown reasons the authorities began to suspect Cuffe's motives as he prepared to leave for the United States. Toward the end of his stay they seemingly shadowed his every move in Freetown, and when Traveller *put out to sea, they followed for some time. The British gave Cuffe some anxious moments, stopping and searching his vessel and ultimately deciding to tow* Traveller *back to Freetown for further investigation. But whatever misunderstanding or misgiving may have developed among the authorities was resolved by the intercession of Governor Maxwell, and Cuffe was permitted to resume his voyage home. The remainder of the sixty-three day trip was uneventful, and* Traveller *and crew arrived safely in Westport on April 19, 1812.*

15 February 1812. At 6 a.m. [we saw a] sail ahead, standing stern on, bearing WSW. Breeze being small, and the tide setting NE, I anchored, which made the speed [of the two vessels] the quicker toward each other.

At 8 [a.m.] the sloop of war, the *Abrina,* Captain James Tildwell, sent his barge and lieutenant on board [*Traveller*]. We hove up our anchor and got underway. The wind breezed, and after overhauling our papers and people, the lieutenant went on board the ship of war.

But [the lieutenant] soon returned. And now called for the papers for [the] 2 Africans that I had on board, (viz.) a crewman and George Davis. The lieutenant then told me if I had shown him these papers before, he should not had need to come on board again.

But the lieutenant soon returned again. [This time he came] with a command for me [to surrender] the crewman, George Davis, and Aaron Richards. They [*Abrina's* commander] called for the logbook, all account books, my 2 chests and 2 trunks, and [they] put the end of the hawser on board and took the brig [*Traveller*] in tow, and stood for Sierra Leone.

I endeavored to give the Captain all the satisfaction as I could, but in vain. We continued our course for Sierra Leone. He [the Captain] said these [people] should not have been taken away without the Governor's approbation, all which I allowed. And [I] told the Captain the reasons I could or did not have the Governor's permission in them all, etc.

16 February 1812.   There is a gentle breeze from SW [today]. We are still standing for Sierra Leone.

At 3 o'clock the Captain ordered the ship to be wore, and [that it should] stand to the westward. And then [the Captain] took me in the cabin and told me [that] from reading my logbook and other documents [he concluded] that it was so good evidence to him that my motives to be good, and that I had not taken this pains for [personal gain or] interest, but [instead that I was motivated solely] from principles. Therefore, he should discharge me and let me go. I thanked the Captain, and assured him that he had the [proper] feeling [as to the] motives of my mind.

We was all sent on board [*Traveller*]; the hawser [was] looped; and [we were] left once more to steer our course, and he his. We both stood to the westward on a [brisk] wind; the ship [*Abrina*] outwinded us and outwent us, she being at or near sunset [some] 3 or 4 miles to the windward.

[Then,] she bore down on us again; we [however, were still] continuing [on] our course. [The sloop] was soon alongside [*Traveller*], when I was again boarded by the lieutenant, who told me that he had come for me again. And that I must pack up all my things as before, and go on board the ship [*Abrina*]. And [I was instructed to] carry these others with me as I had carried [them] before. When I came on board the Captain told me he had over-hauled [reviewed] his instructions, and [that] he had no right to let me go. But [instead, he believed that he] should [be required in order to fulfill his duties] to carry me [back] to Sierra Leone.

I told him I was sorry for that; but [my arguments were] all to no purpose. We again stood for Sierra Leone. The lieutenant visited the *Traveller* again and brought the 10-year-old boy on board [*Abrina*]. The Captain then seemed to be more strongly confirmed that I was [engaged] in a clandestine trade. I opened the whole of the subject to the Captain, but all in vain. To Sierra Leone I must go, and to Sierra Leone he carried me. Feeling friends may give a place in their minds to the exercise [disturbed state of feeling] this put me in, although the Captain used me kindly. . . .

18 February 1812. At 5 p.m. [we] passed from 6, 7, 8, and to 9 fathoms water, at which time we made the Cape.[1] . . . At 10 a.m., [we] anchored off the town. The Captain went on shore and returned in about 1 hour. [He] called me in[to] the cabin, and then and there told me that he had been to the Governor, and had found all to be right and correct. Therefore, I was set at liberty to go, and [the Captain] told me that he would send his boat to take his men [from *Traveller*], and [that he would] carry me and mine on board [*Traveller*]. I thanked him, and told him I chose to go on shore, I and my men. He told me, very well, his boat should wait on me which she did.

I paid a visit to the Governor and was friendly received [by him]. The Governor then gave me his permission to take George Davis and Moses Jenkins, 1 [a] boy of about 10 years, and the other boy, about 17 years of age, and Aaron Richards. [The] order for his [Aaron Richards'] discharge from the Admiralty,

[1] Cape Sierra Leone.

and his real discharge from the commander, will satisfy all inquiring people that all is right and [is being] honorably conducted, and will suffer us to pass unmolested. Amen!

19 February 1812. At 4 p.m. the brig [*Traveller*] anchored in the harbor. Then, having my [Customs] discharge, [I] borrowed George Nichol's boat and [I] went on board the *Traveller*. And [I] gave orders for all of our empty water vessels to be sent on shore. And [they were] to be filled with water and got on board [by] that evening. [The water bottles had to be on board *Traveller* that evening] in order [for the brig] to leave the port at 3 o'clock in the morning, as the tide served at that time. And [I] ordered the boat to be on shore for me at 10 o'clock, which was attended unto.

I gave orders for all [hands] to be on board [*Traveller*] at 10, or 12 at the furtherest. But after getting the water on board, Samuel Hicks leaves the vessel without ever returning again. Although we waited until 3 in the morning with a watch on deck, we did not hear him hail [us], nor see anything of the said Samuel. We accordingly got underway, and [we were] happy that we got underway as we did, for had we not got underway at that time, the wind come on shore so [that] we should have been obliged to have lain [becalmed], I know not how long.

I looked out of the Cape in the morn until 7 or 8 o'clock in the morrow before I bore away, [I] not knowing but [that] he might get in with the fishermen. But alas, no Samuel. Yet, I wish him well, and hope he may amend his habits to refrain from such of his ways as are not beneficial for him to retain. . . .

> The man of sin,
> Who wicked hath been,
> Hath run his race,
> But got no grace.

Captain James Tildwell came to me in the evening [before we sailed] and made a handsome apology, offering his assistance very kindly. . . .

23 February 1812. Pleasant weather [today], and gentle breezes. At 2 p.m. the chase vessel came up to [us], lowered her boat, and sent [an investigator] on board. After examining our ship and crew, we was discharged to pass on [our way]. She [the chase vessel] stood to the E[ast] for Island de Louis. She was the man of war schooner late from England and [from] Sierra Leone. [We] sounded 18 fathoms of water. [We sighted] plenty of fish, but caught none. . . .

25 February 1812. These 24 hours commences with moderate gales and clear weather. At 3 a.m. a squall from the North [struck *Traveller*]. Took in the steering sails and reef [sails]. It [the squall] lasted 1 hour:

> If the wind comes before the rain,
> Clear the topsails and hoist them again,
> If the rain comes before the wind,
> Lower the topsails, and take them in. . . .

28 February 1812. Wind [is] cool but pleasant, and [there is a] smooth sea. [There are] plenty of the stinging men of war [fish]. We saw a school of black porpoises, but caught none. The stricker white mare's tails clouds began to appear and the thick smoke [appeared] to be somewhat clear[ed]. At 10 a.m. stood our anchors, thinking we may not need them until we arrive the other side of the Atlantic Ocean. . . .

4 March 1812. These 24 hours commences with swift breezes and clouds. At 6 p.m. it began to rain, and continued to rain until 4 a.m. [It was a] moderate rain, the first we have experienced for some months. Opened our hold and got up wood, water, and pork. [There are] plenty of flying fish [in the area]. Some fly on board [where] they meet with kind reception. . . .

4 April 1812. The 24 hours begins with a fine leading breeze. We improve it to the best advantage with all sail set, etc. At 8 p.m. took in [the] steering sails and [we] run under easy sail. And [we] kept good look out for [the] Bermudas. After 12 p.m. [we] sounded every hour by carrying the lead forward and heaving the lead without heaving the vessel to. Although [the] Bermudas bore N76°E, distance [of] 300 miles, I conceive there [would be no] harm in keeping good lookout [for them]. I stood the deck [watch] this night myself.

5 April 1812. These 24 hours commences with clear weather and pleasant gales or small winds from North. At 2 p.m. spoke the ship that [we] saw in the morning. It was the *Caledonia,* Capt. Roberts, of Philadelphia, from China. He gave us his longitude: 70°-45″W for the last 24 hours. At 6 a.m. spoke a schooner from Baltimore, in longitude 71°-30″, who informed us that the Importation Act was off, and that there was 2 French frigates and 1 brig on the coast. At 9 a.m. spoke a Sierra Leone [-bound vessel] further away; got no information from him. [At] 11 a.m. saw a topsail schooner standing southerly. . . .

16 April 1812. Small wind and smooth sea. Steered N by E easterly. At 7 a.m. spoke a Cape Harbor pilot boat. Sent a letter unto John James, and [then I] shaped our course for Block Island [off Rhode Island]. Very smooth sea and many sails in sight. It appears that the embargo is in force and at the same time the unimportation is on.[2] . . .

19 April 1812. (60 days at sea.) These 24 hours commences with pleasant weather. At 2 p.m. spoke a pilot boat belonging to Hamesset Hale, by name of Daggett, who agreed to take me to New Bedford and out again for $25. I gave the captain [the pilot] particular directions to keep off about South from Seaconnet Point, and [that he should] not get to within 4 leagues of the land.

We caught 2 fine cod off Block Island. This day's account contains by this account 36 hours.

At 1 p.m. the pilot and myself (viz.) set sail in for New Bedford. [We were] steering NE and NE by N. At half past 6 o'clock saw land. [We then] cast [the anchor] overboard. We jibbed as soon as possible, and [we found that] it was Westport shore. It being night [we had been uncertain of our location]. Wind was blowing fresh, and [there was] thick fog [everywhere]. We went into Westport. Found my family well. In 30 minutes after we got in the harbor we had a very hard thunder squall. I felt thankful that I had so nicely escaped [the squall's effects].

[2] On March 2, 1811, the United States Congress adopted a bill reinstituting nonintercourse with Great Britain.

6
TRIBULATION AND TRIUMPH

Cuffe encountered difficulties with the American authorities the moment he landed in the United States. He had innocently violated the recently enacted Non-Intercourse Act with Great Britain and, consequently, Customs agents impounded Traveller *and its cargo. The sea captain journeyed to Washington, explained to the satisfaction of President James Madison and Secretary of the Treasury Albert Gallatin the circumstances for his having brought contraband back from Africa on his return voyage, and secured the release of his cargo. Cuffe's entries for this segment of his journal are perhaps the most fascinating of the entire document, and certainly the most poignant.*

20 April 1812. At 4 this morning I prepared [to take the pilot boat] to New Bedford, where, I was informed, that I might have the brig *Traveller* entered [in Customs] with African produce from Africa. I made all possible dispatch home in order [that I might] return unto the *Traveller*. The wind [was] blowing hard to the NE. The pilot thought [it] not advisable to leave our port that night.

21 April 1812. At 4 [I] arose, got breakfast, and stood toward the sea. At 10 arrived off Seaconnet Point. Saw the *Traveller* standing off[shore] south of Brenton's Reef. We went on shore to get our dinners until she [*Traveller*] should stand abreast [of the shore] off Seaconnet Point.

But when we had gotten [completed] our dinners with Jeremiah Austin, we returned unto our [pilot] boat, and we set off [to join *Traveller*]. But to our surprise, the brig bore up for Newport [in Rhode Island]. To our [further] surprise, when we came up [to *Traveller*], she appeared to be in the possession of the cutter of the Customs, Captain John Cahoon.

I received Captain Wainer in the pilot boat, and [we] came on shore. Called on the Captain of the cutter. He directed me to the Collector [of Customs of the Port of New Bedford], where I interceded closely for the acquittance of the brig *Traveller,* but to no purpose.

22 April 1812. At 7 this morning I went to the Collector and informed him that all the vessel's papers was correct; [furthermore, that] there was a correct manifest of all the articles that was on board. He then sent the Captain [of the cutter], the officer [of the cutter], and the pilot [of the port], on board [*Traveller*], and [they] found all the things to be correct [and] as I had told him, etc. The brig arrived [in New Bedford] at 4 in the afternoon.

23 April 1812. This day, being advised to make a petition to the Secretary [of the Treasury], I engaged accordingly John Vase, Amasa Robins, etc. [to act as my attorneys]. A petition was made,[1] and letters of recommendation procured. The petition was presented to the Collector, amended and approved of, copied over, and delivered to the Collector, who approved thereof. At 6 p.m. [*Traveller*] came into the wharf.

24 April 1812. At 6 o'clock this morning, I, having gotten liberty to take my wearing apparel, etc., out [of *Traveller*], got Captain Edward Philip's [boat] alongside [my brig], and got all of our small stores on board Captain Philip's [boat]. [We] took our departure from the *Traveller,* [and we headed] for Westport.

I, feeling the need of the help of friends, applied for a letter of recommendation [and] was favored to obtain [them] from Simeon Martin, Governor Constant Taber, Judge G. C. Champlain, formerly [a] member of Congress, John Coggeshall, I. Vernon, Thomas G. Pitman, Walter Channing[2] . . . [The remainder of the entry has been cut from the journal.]

---

[1] I have been unable to locate a copy of the petition.

[2] Walter Channing (1786–1876) was a member of an illustrious New England family. (His brother William Ellery was the distinguished Unitarian clergyman.) Born in Newport, Rhode Island, Channing attended Harvard College but was denied a degree because he had participated in a student uprising in 1807. However, he received an M.D. degree from the University of Pennsylvania in 1809, and Harvard in 1812 awarded him still another M.D. Channing soon became a leading physician and in 1815 Harvard appointed him to its first chair of obstetrics and medical jurisprudence. He became Dean of the Medical School in 1819 and held the post until 1847.

25 April 1812. At 9 o'clock this morning, having obtained all the documents needed that could be obtained here [in New Bedford], went on board the packet [scheduled to sail] for Providence. Left Banniston's Wharf at 10 [a.m.]. Arrive at Providence at 2 in the afternoon.

Providence—where I called on Obediah Brown, [and] where I found letters of recommendation from William Rotch, Jr. Obediah let his father, Moses Brown,[3] know that I was at his house. He immediately came [to see me]. He, [along] with Thomas Arnold, went with me to the Judge,[4] and the Judge went to the United States Attorney General.[5] They both, from the nature of the cause, expressed their concurrence [in my activities], and they asserted [so], accordingly. My friends Moses Brown and Thomas Arnold favored me with their names to my general letter of recommendation.

26 April 1812. [I am] being now in readiness for setting off for the seat of government [Washington, D.C.]. Waiting for the stage this day, attended both fore and afternoon Meeting. Took dinner with William Almy,[6] but made my home with Obediah Brown.[7] At 3 o'clock my son Paul arrived with the papers. [The

---

[3] Merchant and philanthropist, Moses Brown (1738–1836) was the founder of the cotton-spinning industry in the United States. Enormously wealthy, this devout Quaker devoted a large portion of his estate to the advancement of American education. He was a sponsor of the Rhode Island College which later changed its name to Brown University in honor of the Brown family's benefactors. Moses Brown was instrumental in establishing a Quaker school in Rhode Island in 1780 that later became the famous Moses Brown School. He was active in promoting the establishment of libraries, peace societies, and in the furthering of abolition sentiment.

[4] Federal Judge David Leonard Barnes, judge (1801–1812) of the United States District Court, Rhode Island district. I am indebted to Mr. Neale D. Murphy, Clerk of the United States District Court, Providence, Rhode Island, for this information.

[5] David Howell, United States District Attorney for the District of Rhode Island (1802–1812). I am indebted to Miss Bess Glenn, Archivist in Charge, Justice and Executive Branch, National Archives and Records Service, Washington, D.C., for this information.

[6] William Almy was Moses Brown's son-in-law. He, too, played a leading role in the various family enterprises and philanthropies.

[7] Obediah Brown (1771–1822) followed in his famous father's footsteps. A shrewd merchant and businessman, he occupied much of his time in philanthropic enterprises. Obediah patronized all of Moses Brown's charities, and like his father, he was a vigorous opponent of Negro slavery.

remainder of this entry has been cut from the journal.]

27 April 1812. Set off from Providence 10 o'clock in the morning in the mail [stage]. [By] 1 o'clock arrived at Fisher's, 15 miles from Providence, where we dined; [also] at which place I saw my worthy friend Bowling Green, [the] doctor. At 7 [p.m.] we arrived at Norwich [Connecticut], where I took supper, and [we then] set off on our journey [once more].

28 April 1812. 3 o'clock this morning [we] came over [the] Seabrook ferry. Took breakfast at 5 o'clock. Arrived at New Haven at 11 o'clock, where I took a sleep until 1 [p.m.]. And then dined, and once [again I prepared] to set forth at 2 o'clock. Here I parted with William Coit of New York. [He had been] very agreeable company. Took supper 10 miles to the south of Norwalk.

29 April 1812. Arrived at [the] New York stage office [at] 4 o'clock this morning. Paid my passage to Philadelphia ($8), [and we] set off at 5 o'clock.

Arrived at John James' in Philadelphia at 8 in the evening. Found the family in [good] health. I opened my business with John. He seemed to be much discouraged, but upon true reflection [he seemed] to be encouraged, which was some compliment to me.

When and where we dined [during my journey to Philadelphia], the servant came and told me my dinner was ready in the other room. I told him as I rode with the company, I could eat with them. So, we all sat down and ate at one table. This is the only objection that I meet with. There appeared to be a Southward man there, not of the best character, who seemed to be good deal tried [that I sat at the same table with him], but we got through [the meal] well.

30 April 1812. I got up at 4 o'clock this morning. Went to the stage office. The pilot had gone. [He had] set off at 3, and [so I] returned to J. James' to wait until 7 o'clock for the mail [stage].

It is 120 miles to Baltimore [from Philadelphia]. I paid the fare to Baltimore, 8 dollars. Left Philadelphia at 7, arrived at Wilmington at 12. Found James Brian and family well. Left Wilmington, arrived at Havre de Gras [Maryland] at 7 o'clock, where we had to pass over a water [obstacle for] 1¼ miles.

1 May 1812.   Arrived at Baltimore at 5 this morning. At 6 left Baltimore for Washington. Paid $4 for a passage [of] 42 miles, and paid half dollar for 1 hour['s] lodging. Arrived at Washington at 2 o'clock, enquired for Samuel Hutchinson, where I was kindly received. Made my business known [to him]. [His] advice was taken and seeked for.

In traveling through the country I perceived that the people seemed to have great knowledge of me, etc. I left Providence at 10 [o'clock] Sunday morning, arrived at Washington 6 days following, the time being 100 hours. It makes me 85 hours on my passage, or 3 days and 13 hours, and stopped 15 hours by the way.

2 May 1812.   Made the inquiries which appeared [to me] to be most advisable, and at 11 o'clock [I] waited on the President [James Madison]. [On my visit to the President I was] accompanied with my friend Samuel Hutchinson. From the President, [I] waited on the Secretary [of the Treasury, Albert Gallatin[8]], and then on those that I had letters [of recommendation] unto: [from] all which I obtained favorable countenance and [an] assurance of an answer on second day [within two days at] 12 o'clock. I likewise went to Congress' Representative House. The construction was magnificent.

This day was a very rainy day, but I got very well [a]long with [my] business. The Secretary observed to me that French brandy could not be imported from a British port, but [he] observed [wondered] whether it would be inconvenient to me to have it [the brandy] entered [in Customs] for [re-]exportation. I then told him my funds was small, and [that] it [a deal of this nature] would lock up [all] my funds. All [the] people [I visited] appeared very friendly, indeed.

3 May 1812.   Attended Meeting at Washington, intending in the afternoon to go to Alexandria [for the] afternoon Meeting.

---

[8] Coming from an old European aristocratic family, Albert Gallatin (1761–1849) served the young United States republic brilliantly as a financier, politician, diplomat and statesman. He was Secretary of the Treasury in the Jefferson and Madison administrations, holding the office from 1801 until 1814.

But rain prevented our calling on George Drinker. [Therefore, I] spent the afternoon and evening in the family of Samuel Hutchinson to good satisfaction.

4 May 1812. This morning very rainy. Little after 12 [noon] I waited on the Secretary. The President had sent for him. We waited in Samuel Brooks' office until 1 o'clock, then were sent for into the Secretary's office.

The Secretary very openly and freely invited us to sit down. He then told me that all of my property was remitted, or [was about] to be restored to me without reserve. I thanked him for his services.

He then observed to me [that] anything the Government could do to promote the good cause that I was pursuing, consistently with the Constitution, they would certainly be always ready to render me their help. Or, any information that I could give, or point out ways that [the slave] traffic might be discouraged, they were ever ready to receive such information.

I then thanked him for his firmness, and told him [that] as I was traveling in a path of peacefulness, I at present had no such information to communicate. I further observed to the Secretary that if I should continue my aid towards Africa, and [if] I saw it from the advice of friends necessary to apply to [the] Government [for assistance], whether it would be recommendable. He freely told me that by all means [help would be forthcoming], and any assistance that they could render me, agreeable to the Constitution, they should render me every aid to forward my views.

I took [a] place in the Baltimore hack stage. [The ticket] cost 3½ dollars. My much esteemed friend Samuel Hutchinson very kindly attended with me to all the [Governmental] Departments, and was eye and ear witness to what is afore written.

5 May 1812. Embarked this morning at 5 o'clock. Started from Davis' at 6 o'clock, arrived at Baltimore at 3 in the afternoon.

When I took my seat [in the stage], being the first in, I took the after-seat. When the passengers came, in came a bustling powder-headed man with stern countenance. "Come away from that seat," [he demanded]. I was no[t] startled, but sat still. He then bustled along and said, "I want to put my umbrella in the box." I arose. He put his umbrella in [the box]. He then saith, "you must go out of this [seat], for there is a lady coming in."

I entered into no discourse with him, but took my seat [again]. He took his beside me, but showed [me] much evil contempt.

At length the woman and [a] girl made their appearance. I then arose and invited the women in the after-seat, saying, "we always gave away to accommodate the women." We [then] set forward on our journey.

On our way, at the tavern [stop], I was overtaken by William Hunter,[9] member of Congress. He was very free and conversant with me, which this man, mentioned above, observed. Before we got to Baltimore, he became loving and openly accosted me. "Captain, take the after-seat," [he said to me]. But, from the common custom, I thanked him, and wished him to keep his seat. I believe if I am favored to keep my place, [then] my enemies will become friendly [to me]. I note this for [my] encouragement, and of [my] memory.

When I arrived in Baltimore they utterly refused to take me in the tavern, or to get me a dinner, unless I would go back among the servants. This I refused [to do]. Not as I thought myself better than the servants, but [I refused to accede] from the nature of the case. Thought it not advisable.

I found my way to a tavern where I got my dinner. Friend Bernard Gilbert went with me, and was friendly. Jesse Talbot, a very worthy, approving Friend, [also] had paid every attention to me. By this time I seemly had friend[s] on every side. I stayed at the house of Elisha Tyson,[10] who appeared to be [a] real friend to people of color.

6 May 1812. I was prevailed upon to spend a day in Balti-

[9] Lawyer, orator, and champion of religious freedom, William Hunter (1774–1849) was United States Senator from Rhode Island from 1812 to 1814. He later served as United States Minister to Brazil from 1834 to 1845.

[10] Elisha Tyson (1749–1824) was a fourth-generation Quaker who, along with other members of his family, owned a very successful chemical manufacturing business in Baltimore. The Tyson family were the first in the United States to manufacture bichromate of potash; they also had important investments in Maryland copper mines.

more. I [, therefore,] this day attended the Preparative Meeting.
After Meeting, took dinner with Evan Thomas[11] and his son
Philip. And afterwards, called on Daniel Coker and George Col-
lins, teachers of the African school.[12] They teach 107 children.
This is a good prospect.

I, with my friends Elisha Tyson and Evan Thomas, took tea
with these people of color, and had much agreeable conversation
on the mode of aid to Africa. I think some good may be done by
this communication. A correspondence [between Coker and Col-
lins and Sierra Leone] is agreed to.

I this evening saw Susannah Horn and her companion. I stayed
with Jesse Talbot [until I was] to be called on by the stage, but
[I] was much disappointed in being left behind. I am still with
Jesse [while I am] waiting for conveyance.

7 May 1812.   Arose at 2 o'clock [this morning]. At ½ past 3
went to the stage office, but the stage went at 2. Great disappointment, indeed. I attended [unexpectedly, therefore,] the Eastern
Meeting this day. Susannah Horn was there. Took dinner with
Hugh Judge. Visited John Oberstatts' [home], where was a number of Friends, among whom was the first Friend that took care of
me, and he was exceeding kind [to me].

8 May 1812.   At 2 this morning took stage for Wilmington.
Arrived to James Brian's [at] 1 o'clock [this afternoon], where I
was kindly received. Visited [here] but few families. Stopped all
night with James Brian. My friend had taken great pains about me,
[e.g.] in writing to my assistance, [etc.] and was about to come in
person to [my] assistance to Washington, which shows [his] great
humanity.

9 May 1812.   At 8 this morning took stage for Philadelphia;
[the fare was] $1½. Arrived at ½ past 12, was kindly received by
my friend John James, at whose house I made my home. The
family was kind [to me] in every respect, etc. John, with me,
visited several families, which was comfortable. Took tea at

11 Evan Thomas, a member of the Society of Friends and a strong supporter of Negro legal rights in Maryland, was Elisha Tyson's cousin.
12 Negro children attended segregated schools in almost all American
communities. To Cuffe, the "African" school referred to the school for
American Negro children in a particular community.

Joseph Clarke's house, who is a warm Friend in the cause of truth.

10 May 1812. Attended Meeting in the fore noon at Avery Street Meeting, and in the afternoon at 4 o'clock at the North [Street] Meeting. In the evening visited Ann Mifflin;[13] it was [a] comfortable [visit].

11 May 1812. This day attended with John James in adjusting our accounts at the accounting house and at the Customs House. At 6 o'clock in the afternoon [I] attended to [a] meet[ing] with the African Association in order to give them [my] account of Africa. I was attended by my friends John James, Joseph Clarke and Alexander Wilson, where [at the Association meeting] we had agreeable conversation. At which conference, I believe there was something operating that [some] good will come out of [it] toward [aiding] Africa. It was proposed that there should be a Society gathered for the purpose of aiding, assisting, and communicating with the Sierra Leone Friendly Society, as well as with the African Institution in London, for Africa's good, etc.

12 May 1812. Called on Alexander Wilson for advice [concerning my] accounts. Came to no settlement with John James, but left my accounts with him. The ship's account he is to have made out, and [he will] send it on to me.

In the evening called on Doctor [Benjamin] Rush and Sarah Jean. Attended [upon them] with the company of Absalom Jones[14] and James Forten.[15] They expressed great satisfaction in

[13] Ann Mifflin was a member of a socially prominent Quaker family. Wealthy Mifflins dotted the New Jersey-Pennsylvania-Delaware shore area. The family had long been active in the cause of Negro emancipation, and at the time of the American Revolution most members of the family liberated their slaves. Ann Mifflin carried on in the family tradition and supported many antislavery projects.

[14] Absalom Jones was one of Philadelphia's outstanding black leaders. Born into slavery in Delaware, he eventually managed to purchase his freedom from his master. A thoughtful introspective man, Jones had a tremendous love for learning and a compelling desire to assist his fellow blacks in improving their status in American life. Suffering discrimination in the white man's church, in 1792 Jones and some supporters founded the first Negro church in America, the First African Church of St. Thomas. The building for the church was erected and dedicated in Philadelphia in 1794.

[15] James Forten (1766–1842) was Philadelphia's leading Negro and a close friend of Paul Cuffe. Orphaned at an early age, Forten came to the

my communication with them. I likewise called to see Thomas Worcester. He seemed to be willing to settle everything right.

13 May 1812. At ½ past 4 this morning I set out for New York in [an] accommodation stage. There being no fore notice given, [the stage ride] made [for] dull [company] in getting [a]long. I arrived in New York at ½ past 8 o'clock in the evening.

I, being a stranger [in New York], could get no entertainment at the stage tavern; but a kind man took me to Jacob Barker's [house]. Jacob friendly received me, and kindly entertained me, and told me there was a plate and a place for me [to stay]. However, I thought [that it would be] hard to throw myself on his hands, [and so I] took my chance among [my many New York] friends. But mostly lodged with Richard Dean, who used me very cordially.

14 May 1812. I this morning saw in company [met] with Abraham Barker, John Murray, Jr.,[16] and Robert Bounds, etc.— whose advice [to me] was [that I should send out an announcement] to call the Africans together at 4 o'clock in the afternoon at the African school house, where there is 100 children taught. [Cuffe's friends argued that the Negroes should meet] to consider which might be the best way to afford Africa some assistance.

At which meeting [which took place at 4 o'clock] we was favored to make many observations for future information. It rested thus, that there should be a [New York] society embodied, uniting with that of Philadelphia, Baltimore, etc., for the further promotion of Africa, of which Sierra Leone at present seems to be the principal established colony. About 20 people of color met, as

---

attention of the great Quaker abolitionist Anthony Benezet, who provided him with an education. Starting out as a humble errand boy, Forten eventually became a successful sailmaker and earned a fortune that has been estimated at nearly $100,000. Forten was a Quaker, a pacifist, a supporter of temperance and women's rights causes, and a zealous opponent of slavery.

[16] John Murray, Jr., was the son of one of early nineteenth century New York's greatest philanthropists. His father, a successful import-export merchant and a major shipowner, was active in myriad humanitarian causes which included providing educational facilities for poor children, assisting New York's large Indian population, and relieving the distress of prisoners in debtors prison. John Murray, Jr., followed his father's example and played a prominent role in New York philanthropy for many years.

above mentioned, and nearly as many friends [white supporters of the Sierra Leone project]. [The meeting] ended to good satisfaction.

p.s. As I was traveling in the street with my guide he kindly introduced me to 2 Methodist preachers—who accosted me thus: "Do you understand English?" I answered them there was a part [of the language that] I did not understand, (viz.) that of one brother professor [of Christianity] making merchandise of and holding in bondage their brother professor [of Christianity]. This part I should be glad they would clear up [for] me. We bid each other farewell, with[out engaging in] any further conversation.

15 May 1812. I employed my time this day in journeying [to] see [a] friend. And took breakfast with [my] sister Freelove [Cuffe], and [I also spent the day in] seeking out my friend George Trumbull, but could not get to see him. The next day I wrote and sent him a letter informing him that I had brought letters for him from his wife's brother, the Governor of Sierra Leone.

16 May 1812. The wind continuing Easterly, which is very contrary for my homeward journey. I this day improved my time in simply stating the question before mentioned,[17] [this time] to the United Society [which was] assembled for the Methodist Society in New York. [I wanted] to clear [up] this stumbling block, of a brother selling and instancing [the sale of] a brother. This statement I laid before such of the members as was in the way, as the Conference did not sit in the forenoon. They seemingly treated [my question] with rather a coolness.

At 6 o'clock in the evening, I called on the Bishop [Francis] Asbury,[18] and laid the subject before him with some earnestness

---

[17] See "p.s." entry, 14 May 1812.

[18] Francis Asbury (1745–1816), English by birth, and a disciple of Charles Wesley, came to the American colonies in 1771 to preach the Wesleyan gospel. In 1772, Wesley appointed him general assistant or superintendent, and Asbury proceeded to organize the Methodist Church in America. This dynamic "master of religious strategy" became the self-proclaimed bishop of the American Methodist Church in 1784. He was an indefatigable promoter of the new faith, and he maintained a tight rein over the Methodist organization until his death.

[so] that it might be read for their further consideration. Thomas Eddy[19] also accompanied me [to Asbury's], [and Eddy] lively stated to the Bishop the evil of the use of spiritous liquors, and that of festivals.

17 May 1812. Wind still easterly. I this day attended [the] Pearl Street Meeting. It was both [an] open Meeting in the forenoon, but in the afternoon [a] silent Meeting. I took dinner with my sister Freelove, and tea with John Murray, Jr. And stayed the night with Thomas Eddy, and took breakfast [with him] the next morning. The night past was very rainy. Caleb Coggeshall invited me to come to his house.

18 May 1812. The wind still easterly; dull weather. I this day called the second time on John Howland for John Wainer's wages, but he was not in.

At 4 o'clock went to George Trumbull's. [I was] accompanied with William Trumbull and Richard Dean. They lived in Greenwich [Village], about 2 miles from the southern part of the city. They was pleasantly situated and treated me with a great deal of hospitality.

On my return, called to see Doctor Ross, a man that resided 7 years in Jamaica. In which time he saw [the] most terrible abominations inflicted on the slaves, [they] being gibbeted, bound on a plank, [thrown] down a steep place, whipped, hanged, burned and racked. Lord have mercy, have mercy, I pray Thee.

19 May 1812. This morning wind [is still] easterly. Employed in writing letters and copying minutes on the oppression [suppression] of slavery. [The minutes] which I delivered into the hands of Doctor Ross of New York, [were] for [him] to make such a use of as the Society of Friends thought well of.

At 12 o'clock Captain Curry called for me. I took dinner, and

---

19 Thomas Eddy (1758–1827) was a Philadelphia Quaker who ultimately settled in New York City. He became one of New York's principal insurance brokers and made a fortune in underwriting. Eddy was a humanitarian who participated in all the leading philanthropic causes of the time. He was active in Negro emancipation and improvement societies, supported free education for the poor, and worked to establish an asylum for the insane. His greatest concern, however, was for prison reform and he spent more than twenty-five years crusading for the revision of New York's medieval penal code.

[then] set forth. [I was] attended with the company of Richard Dean and Philea Green's husband to the vessel.

At 3 o'clock got underway; at 5 vessel passed Hellsgate; at 7 o'clock passed Frog's Point [Throgs Neck], in sight of the light on Sander's Point, where we had to keep for the island [in order] to clear the stepping stones. And when near the island, [we were required to] haul more for the light[house] to clear the Executioners [rocks] which lieth nearly 3 miles from the light of Sander's Point. Wind light, but fair. All well on board, etc. So ends these 24 hours with thanks to God, amen.

p.s. Here [there] is a man that has taken great pains to find me. His name is Captain Barber who [at one time] was taken care of by a man of my name and color. And out of respect and gratitude to recompense him, he took all this pains. I note this in my minutes in order that the people of color may see and consider what consolation we may see and feel for well doing. But when we commit evil, there is grief, and confusion attend us instead of comfort.

20 May 1812. These 24 hours commences with easterly wind, and cold, raw wind. At 9 a.m. strong breeze off Crannery Neck, about 4 leagues to the East off Lord's Neck, or Huntington. We continue to bear to the windward. Several sail in sight. Some standing before the wind, and some downwind. We continued our course to the eastward, tack and tack, until 7 o'clock, and then bore up for Sachorn's Head. Dark came on so fast [that we] was obliged to come up for New Haven, where we arrived at 9 o'clock. Anchored, wind E by S, blowing fresh, and clouds looking heavy.

21 May 1812 (New Haven). These 24 hours begins with light winds. At 9 a.m. thunder and showers of rain. At 11 a.m. moderate weather broadens, and wind hauls southerly. Reefed sails and got underway. Wind SE. At 6 p.m. the fog set in thick. [There also was] lightning, thunder, heavy clouds with small gusts of fresh winds. This 24 hours ends with the little above remarks.

22 May 1812. At ½ past 1 in the morning the full light bore east, 3 leagues distant. Wind W by S, good wind, 3 sail in sight, [all 3] standing before the wind. ½ past 8 arrived into Newport. When landed, found [my] well engaged friend in good health. I called on the Collector [of Customs]. He told me that he had orders to return [my] vessel and cargo without taxing [me the] costs. But on my departure I had to give Embargo bond, and I had to pay wharfage [fees]. And [I] should know no other cost. I called on those that signed my letters of recommendation which was [so] serviceable to me [during my visit to Washington].

23 May 1812.   Left Newport last evening. Arrived at home at 8 o'clock. Found all well, for which I desire ever to be thankful, world without end, amen. [The remainder of the entry has been cut from the journal, and the Paul Cuffe diary thus ends abruptly.]

IV

The Letters

----⋅⋅⊱∞⊰⋅⋅----

To the Honorable Council and House of Representatives, in General Court assembled, for the State of the Massachusetts Bay, in New England:

The petition of several poor Negroes and mulattoes who are inhabitants of the town of Dartmouth humbly showeth, that we being chiefly of the African extraction, and by reason of long bondage and hard slavery, we have been deprived of enjoying the profits of our labor or the advantage of inheriting estates from our parents as our neighbors the white people, and having some of us not long enjoyed our own freedom, yet of late, contrary to the invariable custom and practices of the country, we have been, and now are, taxed both in our polls and that small pittance of estate which through much hard labor and industry we have got together to sustain ourselves and withall. We apprehend it therefore to be hard usage and will doubtless, if continued, reduce us to a state of beggary whereby we shall become burdensome to others, if not timely prevented by the interposition of your justice and power.

Your petitioners further showeth that we apprehend ourselves to be aggrieved in that while we are not allowed the privilege of freemen of the state, having no vote or influence in the election with those that tax us, yet many of our color, as is well known, have cheerfully entered the field of battle in the defence of the common cause, and that (as we conceive) against a similar exertion of power in regard to taxation too well known to need a recital in this place. That these, the most honorable Court, we humbly beseech thee to take this into consideration and set us aside from paying tax or tax fees. Or cause us to be cleared, for we ever have been a people that was free from all these things ever since the days of our forefathers.

And therefore we take it as a hardship that we should be so felt by none in these difficult times, for there is not to exceed more than five or six that hath a care for us in this town. And therefore in our distress we send unto thee, the most honorable Court, for relief under the peaceableness of the people and mercy of God that we may be relieved, for we are not allowed in voting in the town meetings in, nor to choose an officer. Neither there was not one of us ever heard in the active Court of the General Assembly in, nor, we poor despised miserable black people have not an equal chance with white people—neither by sea nor by land.

Therefore we take it as a hardship that poor old Negroes should be rated which have been in bondage some thirty, some forty, and some fifty years and now just got their liberty—some by going into the service, and some by going to sea, and others by good fortune. And also poor distressed mongrels which have no learning and no land and also no stock, neither where to put their head. But some of them shelter themselves into an old rotten hut which thy dogs would not lay in.

Therefore we pray that these may give no offence at all by no means, but that the most honorable Court will take it into consideration as if it were their own case. For we think it as to be a hardship that we should be assessed and not be allowed (as we may say) to eat bread. Therefore we humbly beseech, beg, and pray thee to plead our case for us with thy people and God, that those who have the rule in their hands may be merciful unto the poor and needy. Give unto those who ask of thee and he that would borrow of thee, turn thou not away empty. And God be merciful unto the poor and give unto those who giveth ought unto the poor, therefore.

We return unto thee again, most honorable Court, that thou wouldst consider us in these difficult times, for we send in, nor come unto thee, not with false words, neither with lying lips. Therefore we think that we may be clear from being called Tories, though some few of our color hath rebelled and done wickedly.[1] However, we think that there is more of our color gone into the wars according to the number of them in the representative towns than any other nation here.

Therefore, we most humbly request therefore that you would take our unhappy case into your serious consideration, and in wisdom and power grant us relief from taxation while under our present depressed circumstances. And your poor petitioners as in duty bound shall here pray, etc.

Dated at Dartmouth   John Cuffe
February the 10th 1780   Adventure Child
             Paul Cuffe
             Samuel Gray
             Pero Howland
             Pero Russell
             Pero Coggeshall

This is the copy[2] of the petitions which we did deliver unto the honorable Council and House for relief from taxation in the days of our distress. But we received none.

Given under my hand, etc.   Jno Cuffe
Dartmouth June the 26th day of 1782

A REQUEST

To the Selectmen of the town of Dartmouth, Greetings:

We the subscribers, your humble petitioners, desireth that you would in your capacity put a stroke in your next warrant for calling a town meeting so that it may legally be laid before the

[1] Benjamin Quarles, in *The Negro in the American Revolution,* estimates that at least five thousand black men served in the patriot armies. However, an even larger number of Negroes rallied to the British side. See pp. ix, 134–57.

[2] The original document is in the Massachusetts State Archives, *Massachusetts,* Volume 186, pp. 134–36. I am grateful to Mr. Lee Flaherty of the Office of the Secretary of the Commonwealth of Massachusetts for furnishing me with a Xerox copy of the petition.

town by way of vote to know the mind of the town whether all free Negroes and Mulattoes shall have the same privileges in this said town of Dartmouth as the white people have respecting places of profit, choosing of officers and the like, together with all other privileges in all cases that shall or may happen or be brought in this said town of Dartmouth, or that we have relief granted us jointly from taxation whilst under our present depressed circumstances and your poor petitioners as in duty bound shall humbly pray, etc.

Dated at Dartmouth April 24, 1781   JNO CUFFE
                                             PAUL CUFFE

A true copy of the request which Jno Cuffe and Paul Cuffe delivered unto the Selectmen of the town of Dartmouth for to have all free Negroes and Mulattoes to be counted equally with the white people or to have relief granted us jointly from taxation, etc.

Given under my hand and seal,

Dartmouth June 5, 1781   JOHN CUFFE

Philadelphia 8 June 1808

ESTEEMED FRIEND:

Since thy last being in this city the remembrance of thee has so frequently occupied my mind as to excite an inclination to write to thee, and particularly respecting thy sympathy expressed with the poor afflicted inhabitants of Africa, to which I am further induced by having lately received information from a respectable friend of mine in London, that divers persons of eminent stations and characters in that city are so affected with a desire that the prohibition of the slave trade may be improved for their benefit by promoting the civilization of the people of that country have with this laudable view formed an Association and raised a considerable sum of money to engage persons of sobriety and other necessary qualifications to go over to Africa to instruct them in the art of agriculture and other proper employments which they think from the nature of the climate and the soil of the land may be readily affected to great advantage if the natives can be gradually brought to a right disposition to change their former course of living as has been already in some degree promoted with a favorable prospect of further success among the Indian natives of this country. I also received a pamphlet written on this interesting subject by a Committee of this society[3] which explains their views and the practicability of carrying them into execution.

And by a late letter from the same friend he further informs me as contained in the following extract from it—viz.:

> I have had a conversation with Zachariah Macauley (the late Governor of Sierra Leone) in which he said that, if Capt. Cuffe should incline to make a voyage to Sierra Leone, although no longer under the Company's government, he will take care that he shall there receive every encouragement which its governor can afford." It seems that, notwithstanding the Company has surrendered the Government to the Crown, the original objects in forming the colony are likely to be strictly attended to: Macauley is Secretary to the more recently established "African Institution," and fully sensible that its important views would be much advanced if any free black people from your continent of good conduct and religious principle could be induced to offer their personal assistance.

Thus far I have thought it advisable to communicate the intelligence to thee without further comment on the subject, except adding that I find the names of Thos. Clarkson, Wm. Wilberforce and Granville Sharp are among those well disposed persons for advancing the benefits intended by the new society called the "African Institution" and am

Thy real friend
JAMES PEMBERTON[4]

[3] Pemberton is referring to the London-based African Institution.

[4] James Pemberton was a wealthy Philadelphia Quaker long active in Negro amelioration causes. A friend of Anthony Benezet, Pemberton was a member of the Philadelphia Society for the Relief of Free Negroes Unlawfully Held in Bondage, and in 1787 became vice president of the successor organization, the Pennsylvania Society for Promoting the Abolition of Slavery, the Relief of Free Negroes Unlawfully Held in Bondage, and for Improving the Condition of the African Race.

[P.S.] To Paul Cuffe
I desire thee to mention my love to my friend Wm. Rotch and wife, also his son William and his [wife].

Westport
14 September 1808

WORTHY FRIEND JAMES PEMBERTON

In reply to thine of 8 June I desire ever to humble myself before my Maker who hath, I trust, favored me to the notice of my friends. And I desire that God will bless all our friends who hath been made willing to rise to our assistance without whose providential hand we must ever been miserable.

As to poor me, I feel very feeble and almost worn out in hard service—and unable of doing much for my brethren the African race. But blessed be God, I am what I am, and all that I can conceive that God please to lay upon me to make an instrument of me for that service I desire ever to be submissive that His will may be done, etc. I shall not lose sight of the above but endeavor to write thou again on the subject. If thee will write me any further information [that] be given, it would be kindly extended by one who wishes well to all menkind, etc.

PAUL CUFFE

Philadelphia 27 October 1808

ESTEEMED FRIEND:

I received a few days past thy acceptable letter of 14th inst. which I am desirous early to acknowledge, and to inform thee that not long since I had some further intelligence on the subject contained in my last, from which and a printed copy of a second report made by a Committee of the African Institution in London to a general meeting of that Society, I perceive they are earnestly attentive to pursue the laudable object of promoting the civilization of the blacks in their own country with a view to draw them off from the wild habits of life to which they have been accustomed, by instructing them in the arts of agriculture, mechanic labour, and domestic industry, by which means they hope to be instrumental in preparing the minds of those uninstructed people gradually to become qualified to receive religious information.

This Association is, I observe, composed principally of those distinguished characters who have long labored with unabated attention in promoting the abolition of the iniquitous slave trade of which number are some who stand in conspicuous stations, among whom is the Duke of Gloucester now nominated President of the Institution; he is a nephew to the King of England and in his Parliamentary capacity has manifested a laudable firmness to the abolition in opposition to his royal relations who injudiciously took part and favored the other side.

The long subsisting enormous evil being removed through the favor of Divine Providence on the endeavors of the friends of humanity, they now apprehend a further service is required to improve on this blessing for the benefit of those poor inhabitants of Africa and for that purpose have adopted a plan as nearly similar to that which Friends are engaged in for civilization of the Indians on the borders of these American states as different circumstances admit; and the soil and climate of Africa being more favorable for agricultural purposes, the projectors indulge themselves with hopes of success in their plan not only for the benefit of the native inhabitants, but in a more extensive way.

Thou will be sensible that the undertaking is very important and those concerned to promote it are anxious to receive all the assistance and encouragement they can from the friends of humanity at home and in America; now if thy concern for the good of the poor untutored people continues and finds thy mind impressed with a sense that any portion of the work is allotted for thee to perform, I hope and trust thou will give it thy most serious consideration, and should it ripen to such a degree as to bring thee under an apprehension of religious duty to perform it in such way as that wisdom which is superior to human may point out, a consultation with thy friends on the occasion may be seasonably

useful, tending to thy strength and encouragement; so referring to
the Allwise Councillor for direction herein

> I remain
> Thy loving friend
> JAMES PEMBERTON

Paul Cuffe
Westport

Westport 10 June 1809

ESTEEMED FRIENDS JOHN JAMES AND ALEXANDER WILSON[5]

I have for some years had it impressed on my mind to make a
voyage to Sierra Leone in order to inspect the situation of the
country, and feeling a real desire that the inhabitants of Africa
might become an enlightened people and be so favored as to give
general satisfaction to all those who are endeavoring to establish
them in the true light of Christianity. And as I am of the African
race I feel myself interested for them, and if I am favored with a
talent I think I am willing that they should be benefitted thereby.

I have had an opportunity [to correspond] with our esteemed
friend James Pemberton on the subject (who is since deceased),
and I received a letter from him which informed me that he had
given information of my concern to the Sierra Leone Company.
They wrote to him that if Paul Cuffe should make a voyage there
that he should have every privilege that its government could afford.

When this comes to your consideration, if you think it expedient
to write to England to inform them that I have some concern in
navigation, which if I concluded to settle there I would wish to take
with me so that the inhabitants might be benefitted both with
agriculture and commerce; and that in case I engage in the whale
fishery whether I could have encouragement such as bounty, or to
carry the productions of the country duty free to England.

If times should be so settled between this and next fall so as to
be advisable to undertake such a voyage, it looks pretty clear to be

[5] See footnote 7, p. 78.

put in execution in case there should be encouragement. I think there are several families of good credit that may like to go.

I am your assured friend
[Signed]   PAUL CUFFE

Philadelphia 21 June 1809

DEAR FRIEND WILLIAM DILLWYN[6]

The foregoing is a copy of a letter we received from our friend Paul Cuffe by which thou wilt perceive that now on the opening of the intercourse, the concern formerly felt by him on account of his brethren in Africa has again revived, and we feel rather pleased that it has fallen to our lot to address thee on the present occasion, as we are united with the concern; and believing that having its origin on a good ground, it will, if rightly pursued, ultimately tend under the Divine Blessing to the benefit of many, especially our fellow men of the African race.

Paul Cuffe, in whose mind the concern has been begotten, is a man known to some of us for many years. And we believe him to be one who is measurably acquainted with the work of truth in his own mind which has manifested itself in a circumspection of life and conversation, which has recommended him to the notice and love of many, not only among Friends (with whom he is now in membership), but also to others of various descriptions both in public and private society.

We expect that our friend James Pemberton in his correspondence with thee has possessed thee of Paul's views. But lest this should not have been the case, we may briefly remark that if he meet with proper encouragement from the African Institution to whom through thee he wishes to apply, he will make a voyage this fall to Africa that so by being on the spot he may be more in a situation to judge whether it would be prudent for him to move his family and business, and encourage some sober religious people of his own color to do the like. He is a man of some property, and in whole and in part is concerned in several vessels, some of them employed in whaling, and others in other mercantile pursuits.

[6] See footnote 10, p. 92.

Therefore, if way should open in his and their minds to move, their business will of consequence be removed with them. Therefore they wish to know whether in this case they could have secured to them all the rights and privileges that British subjects enjoy in their trade and business. This precaution we fully approve of, and could not encourage them in the undertaking without their having a reasonable prospect before them of making a comfortable support for themselves and families and something more. Yet it is our belief that Paul's concern reaches beyond this, and that he has more at heart the improvement of the natives in civilization so as gradually to open and prepare their minds for the introduction of the principle of Truth and that they may in time be made partakers of the many gracious privileges and benefits that a subjection to its holy influence bestows, and that freedom which it alone gives. Nevertheless, in this first voyage it will be necessary, if the African Institution approve of and encourage the undertaking, to afford him some pecuniary assistance, either by engaging to defray the expenses that may be incurred or give him a freight from this country or some other way whereby he may be remunerated.

Our friend John James has patronized him here for a number of years past, and assisted him in most of his commercial concerns and holds part of the ship *Alpha* with him which ship is now on an European voyage. John is still disposed to continue his friendly care and assistance to Paul in the transaction of his business, but in the commencement of the present undertaking, it will be really necessary that succor should be afforded from some fresh source. Some time back J. James had received from J. Pemberton an order to supply some good Cotton seed for the use of the African Institution, but the intercourse being stopped by the laying of the embargo, prevented his accomplishing it, and the old chain of communication being broken by the removal of our esteemed friend J.P., it will be necessary if the company desire it to give fresh instructions to have the seed procured, and in this case if Paul's way is opened to prosecute the voyage he could take it with him.

Paul has recently paid us an agreeable visit. In the course of his business, and previous to his going away, J. James and some others who had gone with our friend Benjamin White to Wilmington to see him embark on his religious visit to your nation had a seasonable and solid opportunity with Paul in which their minds felt united with him, and freedom to encourage him in the prosecution of his weighty concern. We expect that in the course of Benjamin's visit thou wilt have an opportunity of seeing and conversing with him. And from him thou wilt receive further information on the subject.

If the African Institution had any desire to see and converse with Paul, or think it would be any advantage to the good cause they are so honorably engaged in, we have little doubt that he would be willing to call at a port in England either on his outward or return passage, as they might direct. And if he could not be loaded here on account of the Institution direct to Africa, perhaps a freight could be procured to England and from thence they might give him a freight to Africa. We suggest this for their consideration, and if they are disposed to encourage it we would wish to hear from thee as soon as convenient. With tender love to thee, thy wife and children We remain

Thy affectionate friends,

[Signed] { JOHN JAMES
{ ALEXANDER WILSON

Philadelphia 24 June 1809

PAUL CUFFE
ESTEEMED FRIEND

I hope this will find thee arrived safe with thy family. Above is copy of thy letter to us and our letter to W. D. of London to be communicated to the African Society there, which thou wilt show to our friends William Rotch, Senior and Junior, for their judgement on the business. If there should be anything that you should have to remark we wish it may be communicated. With love to thee and family and also to them. I remain with affectionate regard

Thy friend
JOHN JAMES

NOTE

I find by the records of the Westport monthly meeting of Friends that Paul Cuffe requested and became a member of that meeting in the year 1808.

In the year 1810, he laid before said meeting a prospect of making a voyage to Africa and after appointing a large committee to advise with him on the subject he was left at liberty to pursue his prospect and furnished with what they termed a letter of recommendation.

In the year 1815 he informed his friends that he had a prospect of making another voyage to Africa, which met with similar encouragement.

Westport 1 mo 6th 1851   JOHN MACOMBER

[Westport], June 1810

ESTEEMED FRIENDS[7]

Taking into consideration my former prospects of a voyage to Sierra Leone, if God permits, and my friends see with me, it looks as though such a voyage, or visit may be undertaken this coming fall. It would feel very pleasant to me if some solid Friends could feel truth to open the way to accompany me, as I may have need of advice; yet I trust the good and all wise Adviser never fails those who are truly dependent on Him, and on Him alone. Etc.

COPY OF A LEASE

DAVID EDMONDS[8]

Know all men by these presents that I, Paul Cuffe, doth covenant and agree to let and lease unto Henry W. Savage,[9] a house and lot of land that I bought at public auction of Charles Hopkins, auctioneer, or Sheriff, on account of the government in confederation.

Whereof I, Henry W. Savage, doth covenant and agree to pay unto Paul Cuffe on order the sum of five shillings per week, the

[7] Cuffe to a Friend in Philadelphia, printed in Anon. ed., *Life of William Allen with Selections From His Correspondence,* Vol. I, p. 135.

[8] See footnote 17, p. 85.

[9] See footnote 44, p. 138.

first payment to be monthly, in the same way so long as the premises are improved by the said Henry W. Savage.

Further, the said Henry W. Savage agrees not to keep [a] bad house, such as frolicking, drinking, or harboring bad company.

In witness whereof, we have hereunto set our hands this first day of the first month, one thousand eight hundred and twelve.

PAUL CUFFE [Seal]

HENRY W. SAVAGE [Seal]

The said H. W. Savage is to pay all the taxes that may be assessed on the premises whilst the said Savage is in possession.

Witnesseth   DAVID EDMONDS

Washington May 2, 1812

ESTEEMED FRIEND MOSES BROWN

I arrived in Washington on sixth day of the week, 2 o'clock in the afternoon. Was much fatigued. Rested at the house of our friend Samuel Hutchinson.

He this day went with me to have an interview with the President and the Secretary, etc. I am to have my answer Sunday 12 o'clock. I am not able to write anything particular, but may say things look favorable, and the people seem friendly indeed.

I am thy sincere friend

PAUL CUFFE[10]

To all to whom These Presents Shall Come, I, Albert Gallatin, Secretary of the Treasury of the United States, Send Greetings:
Whereas a statement of facts bearing date the 25th of April 1812 with the petition of Paul Cuffe owner of the brig *Traveller* of Westport thereto annexed touching a certain forfeiture and penalties incurred under the statute of the United States entitled an Act to Interdict the Commercial Intercourse Between the United States and Great Britain and France and Their Dependencies and For Other Purposes, has been transmitted to the Secretary of the

[10] The original is in the Rhode Island Historical Society Library.

Treasury by the Judge of the United States for the District of Rhode Island pursuant to the statute of the United States entitled an Act to Provide Mitigating or Remitting the Forfeitures, Penalties and Disabilities occurring in certain cases therein mentioned as by the said statement of facts and petition remaining in the Treasury Department of the United States may duly appear and whence I, the said Secretary of the Treasury, have naturally considered the said statement of facts and petitions, and it doth appear to my satisfaction that the voyage was not only innocent but was undertaken for most laudable and benevolent purposes, that there has not been throughout the transaction any intention of fraud or willful negligence, and that the vessel was brought into port by the revenue cutter while the owner was on shore consulting on the steps which might consistent with law be pursued with respect to said vessel and cargo. Now therefore know ye that I, the said Secretary of the Treasury, in consideration of the premise, and by virtue of the power and authority to me given by the last mentioned statute, do hearby decide to remit to the said petitioner all right claim and demand of the United States and of all others whomsoever to the forfeitures and penalties aforesaid without payment of the costs.

Given under my hand of office in the City of Washington this fifth day of May in the year of our Lord one thousand eight hundred and twelve and the thirty-sixth year of the independence of the United States.

> [Signed] ALBERT GALLATIN
> *Secretary of the Treasury*

Newport, May 22, 1812

MUCH ESTEEMED FRIEND MOSES BROWN

Arrived this morning in Newport by water from New York. And may inform thee that through thy assistance, as well as the benevolent aid of my friends in general, I found no great difficulty of having my property delivered up to me again at the seat of government—for which I feel to acknowledge thy kindness in every respect.

With sincere desire that I may not be left to violate that confidence that has been hitherto placed in me—in much love I am thy assured friend

PAUL CUFFE

P.S.
Please to remember me to the judge,[11] that I very cordially acknowledge his kindness.

P.C.[12]

New Bedford, June 6, 1812

ESTEEMED FRIENDS MOSES BROWN & THOMAS ARNOLD
Excuse me for taking the liberty of troubling you to inform me whether the clearance from the Secretary exempts me from a duty on the cargo & vessel.

As in the clearance no authority was given to the office for my entry and it rather appeared to me that all entries was void without a special order from government.

If in looking over the clearance that it is your opinion that the judge's advice is needed, I wish you to do me the favor to call on the judge for his opinion and inform me accordingly.

p.s. I have entered and unloaded my vessel and secured the duties.

I remain your assured friend

PAUL CUFFE[13]

Providence, June 10, 1812

RESPECTED FRIEND
I received thine of the 6th with [a copy of] the Secy. of the Treasury's clearance of thy vessel.

[11] Judge David Leonard Barnes. See footnote 4, p. 147.
[12] The original letter is in the Rhode Island Historical Society Library.
[13] The original letter is in the Rhode Island Historical Society Library.

In answer to thy question "Whether the clearance from the Secy. exempts from a duty on the cargo & vessel," I have not shown or conferred with the judge about the matter. I have conversed with it of the mind [in my mind] that the Secy. directly decide[d] to remit to the petitioner "all right claim & demands of the United States and of all others whomsoever, *to the forfeiture and penalties aforesaid, without payment of costs."* So thou observed he says nothing about the duties, which the act of Congress he refers to, does not authorize him to remit.

Judge Barnes had shown me the decree from under the hand of the Secy. when it first came and observed that he was very favorable in relinquishing the cost, which he said was seldom done. The seizure being relinquished has no effect on the payment of duties which are payable the same, as if no seizure had been made, and thou had been admitted to an entry in the first instance. It was not necessary for the Secy. to give any authority for thy entry [of] the vessel. His relinquishment of the seizure left the vessel in a state to enter as other vessels are, and it became the duty of the officers of the Customs to enter her & secure the duty as in the common case.

I was pleased with the answer of the question and of thy clearance, and hope it may prove a source of humble gratitude to the Father of All Our Mercies.

I conclude respectfully thy friend

[Moses Brown][14]

Paul Cuffe to James Madison—President
Westport 20 June 1812

JAMES MADISON PRESIDT.
OF THE UNITED STATES

I stopped short of my duty in not calling to acknowledge the favor that I received from the seat of government, for which I desire to be excused.

---

[14] Draft of a letter; the original is in the Rhode Island Historical Society Library.

But upon serious reflection, feeling that there is an acknowledgement due unto the rulers of the people—certainly there is greater acknowledgement due unto the Father of all our mercies.

May the blessings of heaven attend thee. May the United States be preserved from the calamities of a war—and be favored to retain her neutrality in peace and happiness.

These are the sincere desires of one who wishes well to thee, and all mankind

PAUL CUFFE

(Copy of a letter that I was impressed to send to the President after my return from Washington)

London July 1, 1812

DEAR FRIEND PAUL CUFFE

Enclosed we send for your consideration the minutes of two Committees of the African Institution, and we accompany them at the request of the members of the same with such explanations as we think will enable you to ascertain the object, which the Institution have in view, as they relate to your services.

The Resolution which the first of these Committees entered into, was, as you will observe, on the 16th of January 1812. By the word "grant," as there expressed, you are to understand that the land to be granted to you will become your own property, which you may either farm yourself, or let out to others, and which of course you may sell, alienate, or divide by will, if you fulfill the conditions annexed to the said grant. The first condition is that it is to be settled by persons by whom or by whose means it is to be put into cultivation. This condition will show you, that the Directors have in view the encouragement of industry and cultivation in these parts, as they relate to tropical produce. As to the quantity of Land to be granted to you, this is made to depend upon your own Resources and Exertions, for you would have in the first instance as much as you could people, or rather, as much of it as you could put and keep in a state of cultivation by persons either resident upon or near it. And as a further encouragement to the promotion of Industry and agriculture in these parts this grant would be enlarged to you when the first had been fully settled, but not before. The next condition relates to the sort of settlers, and on this point we shall speak when we come to the next minute. We may first observe here that you have little doubt of obtaining the above grant from the government here, if you should feel inclined to accept it on the terms offered. The Resolution which the second of the committees entered into was on the 5th of June following:

The first object contained in this Resolution relates to your own settling in Sierra Leone. How far you could make up your mind to this, is best known to yourself; but we are of the opinion that a rigid residence there is not intended, an occasional resident would be necessary, that you might project, and occasionally to see the Execution of what you so projected. This Residence you might accomplish if you thought it proper either to keep open yourself a communication between America and Sierra Leone, or to sail yourself between Sierra Leone and England, or to try to establish a whale fishery on the African Coast. In all these cases you would be both absent from, and yet often present at, the Colony. You might perhaps think it desirable to carry over and settle some of your own family there. All, we apprehend, that you would be required to do would be to reside occasionally, so as to project and execute, so that the spirit of the grant might be fulfilled. If you choose to establish all your family, and to close your days there yourself, so much the better for Sierra Leone and its neighborhood.

The second object relates to the settlers, and here the first condition is that they be willing to place themselves under the British government. You yourself having been at Sierra Leone are a judge how far you could recommend the situation. The inhabitants are free; they enjoy religious toleration. All matters are decided by a jury; and they compose the jury themselves. With respect to the other conditions, they are in the first place to be such as you are to search for [prospective settlers] in America and to carry from thence to Sierra Leone; by this it is intended that they are to be persons of color selected from that continent.

They are to be, secondly, of free condition, and good known character. This condition requires no comment.

They are to be, thirdly, persons of some property. By this it is not meant to be understood that all who might wish to embark should be of this description. But undoubtedly the more, the better; because such persons might be enabled to purchase, or to hire, land of you; and in this case, besides working themselves, they might be enabled to employ others in the cultivation of their lands. They might hire Grumettas[15] or free African natives for this purpose, or such of those as had been redeemed from slavery, out of the captured slave ships.

They are to be, fourthly, such as are acquainted with some of the useful mechanical arts, or with the cultivation of tropical produce; but more particularly with the cleaning of Rice. On this head we may observe, that there is already so many Carpenters and Handy Craftsmen among the Nova Scotians at Sierra Leone, that the Directors would in this instance rather give the preference to those who were acquainted with the cultivation of Rice, Indigo, Cotton and Tobacco. Those however who are to be selected, must have a knowledge of cleaning the Cotton and the Rice, and preserving and packing up the Tobacco. Now of this description of settlers, they who were persons of property, might, as we before said, purchase or hire farms and thus cultivate these articles; and with respect to others who had little or no property, their use would be principally to instruct others in their art. This they might do by going out to teach the native villagers, or to teach the Nova Scotian and Maroon settlers to raise the same produce, for which instruction they might be paid; or they might have the management of little farms to be paid by their employers, or they might work as laborers themselves. And here it may be proper to observe, that persons of color acquainted with masonry or putting lime and stone together in building might be great gainers by going, as government probably will erect stone buildings and as many of the settlers also will do the same, when their present houses are decayed.

With respect to the number to be searched for, and taken over, it need not be great. To carry over a Colony is not intended; nor is it necessary to carry over as many as would work the whole grant

---

[15] "Grumetta" was a slang expression used in Sierra Leone to identify free native laborers.

of land to be made to you, because not only Grumettas may be hired under the instructions of these for this purpose, but great numbers from the captured slave ships. It seems therefore only necessary that a few very choice persons possessing the requisites above mentioned, should be taken over in the first instance; for the Directors can only try an experiment at present. Perhaps a dozen persons would do in the first instance, or 18 at most, when it is considered how many laborers they would find at Sierra Leone and in the neighborhood. And it is here we apprehend that the Directors, when they affirm that every reasonable encouragement ought to be given to you, mean to lend their chief assistance. They would cheerfully contribute towards searching out for such persons of color and of bringing them together to embark; also towards the passage of the poorer, who might go out as steerage passengers; and also towards supplying them with Instruments of agriculture when they arrive there.

As to the minute relative to the whale fishery, this is a matter of future consideration; but as to the grant, Settlement and Settlers, we beg you would take these into your immediate consideration, and send us an early answer.[16]

With our best wishes we remain your friends

THOMAS CLARKSON
WILLIAM ALLEN

Westport July 15, 1812

RESPECTED FRIENDS WILLIAM THOMPSON AND BROTHERS

The enclosed is a account of sales of the goods shipped in the brig *Traveller,* Paul Cuffe, Capt.

When I arrived on the coast of America the Embargo and the Non-importation law being [in] force, I left the brig at sea and went to see what steps could be taken. Before I got on board again our revenue cutter took possession and carried the brig into Newport,

[16] This scheme was not implemented because Cuffe failed to secure Congressional permission in 1813 to take passengers to Sierra Leone. However, he patterned the plans for his epochal 1815–1816 voyage around the ideas Clarkson and Allen expressed in this most important and revealing letter.

Rhode Island. I petitioned the government and they considered the voyage to be undertaken for benevolent purpose and gave up the vessel and cargo with taxing no cost, etc. But I was oblige[d] to be at very considerable charge which I made every charge which I hope will be considered to be right.

I have advised my friends, Wm. and R. Rathbone, to pay to you the amount of the sum of £261-11-6. As I expect I have property there and know of no way of getting it here, and that at these critical times feeling the want of it, have given orders for it to be paid in Liverpool instead of paying it to Francis Thompson in New York—and I hope it may answer both of our purposes.

I hope the declaration of war between the two powers will not be able to separate us from the brotherly love of the true church, etc.

I am your ever well-wishing friend

PAUL CUFFE

As I was returning from the Congress by way of New York, Francis Thompson stated to me that if 50 per centum could be obtained on the goods [it] would be considered a fair sales, which I obtained. All however that is not right shall be righted hereafter.

Should not the Rathbones honor the bill, you need not take any law, but return the bill and I will endeavor that you shall be reimbursed. I was under the necessity of making the best turn I could to keep the vessel and cargo of goods from being condemned.

I am PAUL CUFFE
and his wife ALICE CUFFE

I have these Africans at school regular, which, if the war should continue for any length of time will be a bill of considerable expense. However, if necessity should call for it, I hope the [African] Institution will not let me be too much the sufferer by it.

NB. I have regular taken the advice of my friend. A day ago I saw William Rotch, Jr. and he united with me in opinion and thought proper that I should write to thee on the subject as before stated.

PC

PS Paul Cuffe thinks well of establishing mercantile intercourse on the coast of Africa to replace to the Africans a trade in
lawful and legal terms in lieu of the slave trade, for it seems hard
to them to be deprived of all opportunities of getting goods as
usual. As to presents to appease them that way, I cannot see much
into more than some trifling things.

PC

Further, I think much on the establishing the whale fishery in
Sierra Leone. But as my funds are at stake, and the unsettled state
of things between the two countries at present, there cannot be
much said on the subject.

COMMONWEALTH OF MASSACHUSETTS

Bristol   By this public instrument and declaration of protest, be it
known and made manifest to all whom it doth or may concern that
on this eighteenth day of July in the year of our Lord one thousand
eight hundred and twelve Before me Abner Brownell, notary
public by legal authority duly commissioned but not sworn, and
dwelling in Westport in said county of Bristol, and one of the
justices of the peace for the said county, duly commissioned and
sworn, personally appeared Paul Cuffe, Master of the brig *Traveller* and John Wainer, mate, both of said Westport who being by
me duly engaged, did depose protest and say that on the twentieth
day of September just past, they sailed in said brig from Liverpool
for Sierra Leone, and that they did not stop at Madeira, neither
touch nor anchor at any port or harbor until they arrived at said
Sierra Leone and there did they actually land the cargo of said brig
and the four passengers which they had taken on board

PAUL CUFFE   ⎫   *Master and Mate*
JOHN WAINER ⎭   *of the Brig*
                 Traveller

wherefore I the said justice from the fact above stated and the
special instance and request of the said Paul Cuffe as well in behalf

of himself as in the behalf of all and singular, the owners, underwriters and others concerned in or on the said brig and cargo and everything thereunto appertaining have certified the above as do by these present solemnly protest against all actions, damages, losses, costs and interest suffered and sustained or to be suffered and sustained, in consequence of any bonds, policies of insurances, or any other obligations whatsoever, relating to stopping at Madeira, or any other port or harbor, between Liverpool and Sierra Leone.

In testimony whereof, I have hereunto set my hand and affix my seal at said Westport, the day and year first above written.

ABNER BROWNELL, *Justice of the Peace*

[n.p., n.d., Westport? Late August 1812]

DEAR FRIEND WILLIAM ALLEN

Having obtained all the information that I can at present, I shall at this time write to thee and hope it may reach thee in safety. As here appears to be an open declaration of war of the United States of America against Great Britain, I see not how I am to get the *Traveller* to Sierra Leone in Africa, as there appears to be several families that have made up their minds to go to Sierra Leone in order to render Africa some assistance.

When I was at the seat of government they then told me that they would render me every assistance that they could consistent with the laws of the United States. I believe if there could be a license obtained from the British government, it [might also] be obtained from this government, if thee can intercede with the English government to grant a license for the brig *Traveller,* a cargo, crew and passengers, names not altogether ascertained.

If the above liberties can be granted, I shall endeavor to send the *Traveller* to Africa this fall. As here appears many minds much influenced to see Sierra Leone, I should wish for the way to be kept open.

Notwithstanding the declaration of war between these countries, I hope that that chain of brotherly union in the true church is not shortened. I can truly say that I feel all near and dear unto me that belongs unto this church of peace and harmony. Beloved friends, may we all unite in observing on earth peace and toward men good will, and glory to God on high, amen.

NB The ship *Alpha* sunk me on my half 3500 dollars last voyage, and my bark ship that has gone round Cape Horn on a whale voyage has not yet returned, but is looked for every day. But I do not see any chance for her to escape the British cruiser and I have no insurance on her; and the *Traveller*'s voyage to Africa thou art sensible was not a profitable one as to property.

And many of these people that might, and I dare say would, be serviceable if they could get to Sierra Leone, I am willing to do all that I can do. There is few that has property to assist themselves, etc. Again, can grants of lands, houses, or some small aid or privilege be granted to those who may leave their land for the promotion of Africa?

Any error or omission in my statement, please to excuse and correct. The above, I believe, is a true statement of facts. In love, I am thy well-wishing friend

PAUL CUFFE

P.S. Still think that a sawmill is much needed in Sierra Leone, and I shall endeavor to send materials for one and a man who understands of tending one. The most that stands in the way will be a millwright to erect her. I have it on my mind to send out a plow and a wagon to assist in carrying loads through the streets instead of being carried on men's heads.

PAUL CUFFE

The following singular and rather interesting memorial, which was on Friday presented to congress, is published at the request of several subscribers, who probably feel an interest in the success of Mr. Cuffe's expedition. It is impossible to say what fate awaits it.

Nat. Int.

To the president, senate, and house of representatives
of the United States of America

The memorial and petition of Paul Cuffe, of Westport, in the state of Massachusetts, respectfully sheweth, that your memorialist actuated by motives which he conceives are dictated by that philanthropy which is the offspring of Christian benevolence, is induced to ask the patronage of the government of the United States, in affording aid in execution of a plan, which he cherishes a hope may ultimately prove beneficial to his brethren of the African race within their native climate.

In order to give a complete view of the object in contemplation, it may not be considered trespassing too much on your time to premise some of the leading circumstances which have led to the present application. Your memorialist, being a descendant of Africa, and early instructed in habits of sobriety and industry has gratefully to acknowledge the many favors of a bountiful Providence, both in preserving him from many of the evils which the people of his colour too often have fallen into, and also, by blessing his industry with such a portion of the comforts of life as to enable him in some degree not only to commiserate, but to relieve, the sufferings of his fellow creatures, and having early found implanted in his heart the principles of equity and justice, he could but view the practice of his brethren of the African race in selling their fellow creatures into a state of slavery for life as very inconsistent with that Divine principle; and in his mature age, having been greatly interested in the abundant labor of many pious individuals, both in this country and in England to produce a termination of the wrongs of Africa, by prohibiting the slave trade, and also to improve the condition of the degraded inhabitants of the land of his ancestors, he conceived it a duty incumbent upon him, as a faithful steward of the mercies he had received, to give up a portion of his time and his property in visiting that country, and affording such means as might be in his power to promote the improvement and civilization of the Africans.

Under these impressions he left his family, and with a sacrifice of both time and money visited Sierra Leone, and there gained such information of the country and its inhabitants as enabled him to form an opinion of many improvements that appeared to him essential to the well being of that people. These he had an opportunity of communicating to several distinguished members of the Royal African Institution in London, and he had the satisfaction at that time to find that his recommendations were approved by the celebrated philanthropists the duke of Gloucester, William Wilberforce, Thomas Clarkson, William Allen and others, and has since learned that the Institution have so far acceded to his plans as to make some special provision to carry them into effect. One of these objects was to keep up an intercourse with the free people of color in the United States, in the expectation that some persons of reputation would feel sufficiently interested to visit Africa, and endeavor to promote habits of industry, sobriety and frugality, among the natives of that country.

These views having been communicated by your petitioner to the free people of color in Baltimore, Philadelphia, New York and Boston, they, with a zeal becoming so important a concern, have manifested a disposition to promote so laudable an undertaking, and several families whose characters promise usefulness, have come to conclusion if proper ways could be opened to go to Africa, in order to give their aid in promoting the objects already adverted to. Your petitioner, still animated with a desire of making the knowledge he has acquired, and the sacrifices he has already made, more permanently useful in promoting the civilization of Africa, solicits your aid so far as to grant permission that a vessel may be employed (if liberty can also be obtained from the British government) between this country and Sierra Leone, to transport such persons and families as may be inclined to go, as also, some articles of provision, together with implements of husbandry, and machinery for some mechanic arts and to bring back such of the native productions of that country as may be wanted.

For although pecuniary profit does not enter into calculation in the object in contemplation, nor does it afford any very promising prospects, yet without a little aid from the trifling commerce of that country, the expense would fall too heavy on your petitioner, and those of his friends who feel disposed to patronize the undertaking. Your petitioner therefore craves the attention of congress to a concern which appears to him very important to a portion of his fellow creatures who have been long excluded from the common advantages of civilized life, and prays that they will afford him and his friends such aid as they in their wisdom may think best.

With much respect, I am, your assured friend,

PAUL CUFFE

Westport, 6th month, 1813.[17]

Philadelphia; February 15, 1815

DEAR FRIEND

It has pleased the Almighty Disposer of all things, to once more bless this late distracted country with peace, which to you and all christians must be welcome news indeed. It is out of the power of man to describe the great joy that was manifested by all classes of society, in this city; indeed, the people for some time appeared to be almost frantic, for the interference of Divine Providence in staying the sword of the destroying Angel, permit me to congratulate you. . . .

I approve very highly of your proposition of building a ship for the African trade by the men of color, so as to come in common stock, and shall lay it before the Society[18] when next we meet; and write you their opinions. We have had a very severe winter. The Delaware is all frozened over and has been for some time, so that sleighs and sleds are passing and repassing constantly. Still there is great preparations making here for the first market. It is with much pleasure I can inform you that the news from Washington is that the Treaty of Peace has been unanimously ratified by the Senate. Charlotte and the family joins me in love to you and family.

I remain very affectionately yours
JAMES FORTEN[19]

---

[17] Reprinted from *The National Intelligencer* in *Niles Weekly Register,* January 22, 1814, pp. 338–39.

[18] Forten, a close Cuffe confidant and at this time a supporter of a black mission to Africa, headed the Philadelphia African Institution. The Institution was Philadelphia's leading black organization.

[19] For more information on Forten see footnote 15, pp. 153–54.

Providence, February 23, 1815

SIR, it is with much satisfaction that I congratulate you on the happy event of peace, and it gives greater pleasure that you have now an opportunity of putting your benevolent plans into execution. I feel concerned for the welfare of our brethren in Africa and all other parts of the earth wheresoever they are scattered. And although I may not live to see it, yet I believe the day is approaching when we shall not only become a nation with the other nations of the earth, but also when Ethiopia shall stretch out her hands to God and be saved. There is several of us here who are anxious to visit our brethren in Sierra Leone and settle among them, yet we are willing and wish to place ourselves in a situation to be useful to them. I do not know how many of us there are. Some of us have family.

[Unsigned letter to P. Cuffe]

COPY

Our Friend Paul Cuffe (who is a Member of our religious Society) informs this Meeting that he has a prospect of making a voyage to Africa on Business. And in a particular manner, with the laudable view of endeavoring to promote the temporal and civil improvement and comfort of the inhabitants of some parts of that Country; which having our solid deliberation, we feel desirous that he may be enabled to accomplish his object, to the peace of his own mind; and leave him at liberty to pursue his prospect, recommending him to the friendly notice and regard of those amongst whom his lot may be cast.

Signed by direction, and on behalf of our Monthly Meeting of the religious Society of Friends held in Westport, State of Massachusetts the 16th of the 11th month 1815

By EBENEZER BAKER, *Clerk*

Westport 4 December 1815

DEAR FRIEND WILLIAM ALLEN

Thine of the 6th of the 5th mo. I have received. With every reason [I] might have expected to have received further communication in a short time, but considering thy time to be occupied on subjects of greater magnitude, this might have been omitted—but from the concern I trust that I have felt, and the encouragement that has been held out. I have with advice and concurrence of friends ventured to pursue the object, and have on the 2d instance cleared from the custom house with the Brig *Traveller* a small cargo and thirty-eight passengers, (viz.) 18 as heads of families, male and female, and 20 children. All which I hope may be well received in Sierra Leone by the governor—as well as the Friendly Society as they are provided with certificates as good characters. They are not too well provided with property as would be desirable; neither are they so much acquainted with the treatment of tropical produce as would be desirable. But believing them to be serviceable to the colony, I shall sail, through God's permission, the first wind after tomorrow.

I have all the iron work for erecting a sawmill, a wagon and a plow. There hath been many serious inquiries concerning this voyage. They in Boston went so far as to ask for a statement of their expenses to Sierra Leone. I stated to them $100 per head and finding them ship stores. They viewed the . . . list in order for collection as it appeared which was as follows (viz.) 32 in number old and young. 3 out of the 32 was not charged, which left 29 passengers at $100 per head, $2900. I have not, neither have I any encouragement of receiving anything at all through that channel, but have received by a private hand through the channel of Wm. Rotch, Jr., $100. One hundred dollars will go but little way in paying their conveyance from Boston to Westport and thence to Sierra Leone. And other unavoidable expenses that I have been at for this 3 years past.

The four passengers from Philadelphia has paid their passages at the rate of $100 each. And the two from New York has paid $130 toward their passages. One of those families from Philadelphia has paid his all, the other has about $250 dollars. I mention this for thee to look with me and see how these people are to be provided for when they arrive there. Provided they obtain grants for 10 acres of land, they must have it one year under improvement before much can be expected to grow. Thy needy writer hopes thee will consider his cause and unite with him to serve as is consistence, etc.

One of the young men that I had under my care from Africa has not conducted himself altogether so well as would be desirable. He has left this quarter some time past without my consent, but I hope he has or will find his way back again to Sierra Leone. The other and the boy goeth to Sierra Leone with I hope pretty good improvement both in education and morals.

I do not expect to make much stay myself at Sierra Leone, but to return with the brig to America unless it is recommended for me to return by way of England.

I am thy affectionate friend

PAUL CUFFE

Sierra Leone 6 February 1816

ESTEEMED FRIEND WILLIAM ALLEN

I arrived at Sierra Leone on the 3rd instant after a passage of 56 days, all well. Nine families, (viz.) 18 heads of families and 20 children, was well received both by the governor and the Friendly Society, though I was not permitted to land tobacco, soap, candles, nor naval stores.

I was very sorry to find no particular instructions at Sierra Leone from the London African Institution. The few articles I am permitted to land pay such a duty that the expenses of the voyage will fall very heavy on me. But having the passengers so well received was great consolation to me. The governor saith they shall be entitled and have grants to them [of] the same quantities of lands as the former settlers had. I am in hopes of hearing from this yet before I leave this place. The Friendly Society seems to express great satisfaction in the assistance they receive from thee. I am informed 2 of them have been to London. I shall encourage them to be punctual in making their remittance. As I have been some aiding in encouraging the establishment of the Friendly Society, I feel still to advise for the continuation of the Society.

I think it best not to make to[o] great advances, and, whenever any correspondence take place, for it to be with the Society and not to an individual, unless it is an individual capacity. I hope these may meet thee and thine in health as they leave me. At this time [economic conditions] in Sierra Leone was well placed for obtaining payment, but I was sorry to say that out of £333, I may lose nearly one half of it.

I am thy assured friend

PAUL CUFFE

Sierra Leone February [*n.d., 1816*]

ESTEEMED FRIEND WILLIAM ROTCH, JUNIOR[20]

I arrived safe on the 3rd instant after a passage of 56 days. I experienced 20 days of the most tremendous weather that I ever remember experienced of. The ship and crew seemingly were in jeopardy, but through mercy we were preserved. All the ship's crew was attacked with a short fit of sickness which took place after the tempestuous weather abated. But I was favored with my health: and medicine, and close attention unto them, though, they all recovered, and now are enjoying perfect health, for which as well as all other preservations I desire ever to be truly humbled before the Father and fountain of all our mercies.

His excellency the governor received us very courteously. The passengers and their baggage were permitted to be landed. But I were rejected from landing any. If nothing favorable appears in a few days I shall leave Sierra Leone for America.

I hope these may meet thee and thine in health as these leave me at this time.

I am thy assured friend

PAUL CUFFE

[20] See pp. 24–25.

Since writing the above the governor has authorized the custom house office grant permission for part of the cargo to be landed, so I cannot positively say what my route may be.

I have had no instructions from William Allen but am in hopes it may come in a few days.

N.B. Send this letter to my wife as time do not permit at this instant a letter to her, etc.

Sierra Leone 1 April 1816

Esteemed friend William Allen

Thine of 1st of 1 mo I have received, together with the invoice of £257. This difference or balance due thee I shall endeavor to remit according to [your] directions. I received the goods the 30th, and as I was on the point of sailing and so many goods arriving, I was obliged to sell mine on eight months' credit, and even then made but small sale. I arrived at Sierra Leone the 2 mo 3 1816. By reasons of not answering thine of the 5th mo last was from thy mentioning that of the Institution meeting on the 16th, then thee intended writing more particularly. I have to acknowledge Governor Macarthy's[21] kindly [attitude] towards me. He was very kind to me and took a great interest in showing me every favor he could did. Not too much point directly against the British navigation act.

The chief judge[22] arrived in good health, and I had the pleasure of dining with the governor & judge. They expressed their desires that the way may be open for me to return to London. But as this

[21] A Frenchman by birth, and Jacobite by heritage (his great-grandfather fled to France with James II), Charles MacCarthy left republican France during the Revolution. He joined the British army and rose to the rank of Lieutenant Colonel. Appointed Lieutenant Governor of Sierra Leone in 1814, MacCarthy became Governor of the colony in 1816. Renowned for his mild rule and his fanatical loyalty to the monarchy, MacCarthy served as Governor until his death in 1824. The historian of Sierra Leone calls MacCarthy's reign the era "of happy relations between African and European . . . a golden age of the Colony." (Fyfe, *History of Sierra Leone*, p. 147.)

[22] Dr. Robert Goold Hogan was appointed Chief Justice of the colony in early 1816. He replaced the puritanical, ill-tempered, reformist Chief Justice Robert Thorpe (1808–1815), who had managed to antagonize almost every settler and royal official in Sierra Leone.

African produce was so low, and I had not obtained license, it appeared safe to return to America where a communication could be opened between London and Sierra Leone in order to advance the colony. If I could wish to be made use of to improve the morals of the inhabitants of Africa, I am sorry to say that subject when I at first entered upon appears must fail.

In keeping open a communication from America to Africa once a year, circumstances will not admit of keeping a vessel in this concern without employing some as trading stock. As the act now stands, I do not see but I must drop this prospect. However, I hope to receive further advice on the subject. I have been permitted to furnish my passengers with provisions, considerable amount toward their support for the present year. That of my not being permitted to make trade in Sierra Leone with much of my articles, all which make against the interest of voyage, all which I hope [you] will take into consideration on my behalf so far as thee approves of my proceedings.

The people I took over to Africa were all common laborers. They were no mechanics, but are inclined to cultivate the land. They are most inclined to make trial with tobacco for the present year. There are 5 of them that has about 10 acres of ground cut away now, burning the rubbish. The season is so far advanced that I think they will not be able to make any progress this season. One of them has indented, taken to work the governor's plantation. The 7th hath undertaken to farm for one of the citizens; the 8th has undertaken to farm with the Congo people, as he is one of the nation, a little out of Sierra Leone. He intends when convenient opportunity to go to Congo. The 9th and last is a native of Senegal; thinks of getting to Senegal. He inclined for traffic, although he is acquainted with mason work.

This Congoman is a man about 40 years old, has a wife but no children. He has paid his passage, so is not inclined on to receive any assistance, but is inclined to stand on his own ground. He has some property in Philadelphia; so has drawn in my favor for about $150 for supplies he's received from me. His name, Antony Survance. He was sold among the French at Santo Domingo, & at the time of their revolution he got over to America & thereby obtained his freedom. And since has acquired education so far as to write a good intelligible hand, read pretty well & very well in arithmetic. Also has made himself acquainted with the rules of navigation. However, it appear he will not make a mariner on the count of his seasickness on. Also, he had about $500 of his on [credit? debt?].

I have heard him say in his conversation whether the black man had not 2 eyes & 2 ears & white men had no more, & could he not see with his eyes, hear with his ears, etc.

Samuel Wilson is a man about 36 years of age, has a wife but no children. He was from Philadelphia & has paid his passage, but had no property left but a little household furniture; is a professor of the Methodist. He is an industrious man & proposes to be acquainted with raising tobacco of which he thinks of making a trial this year.

William Guin, the man that works the governor's farm, is about 60 years of age, has a wife & one daughter about 17 years of age from Boston. Paid nothing; he is a member of the Methodist.

Perry Lockes, 30 years old, has a wife & 4 children, 2 boys & 2 girls. The eldest boy 11 years old, the youngest girl 5 years old. He is one of the 5 that has cut the 10 acres of ground. Also he is the member of the Methodist society & is licensed to preach. I believe him to be an honest character, but has rather a hard voice for a preacher, etc.

Samuel Hughes, one of the 5 that farms in Co., from Boston, has a wife & 4 children, the eldest 14 years old, the youngest 18 months. He is about 50 years old. He is a hard working man, a farmer.

Thomas Jarvis, about . . . 50 years old, has a wife & 5 children, eldest 11 years, the youngest 18 months.

Peter Wilcox, about 40 years old, has a wife & 5 children, eldest 11 years, the youngest 8 months. He is 1 of the 5 that farms together. He professeth to be a tanner.

Robert Rigsbary, about 36, has a wife with one child about 12 years old. He is from Boston, is one of the 5 that farms together. He is a member of the Methodist order.

The year's ration for 7 families amount to £411:14:5. I have taken receipts for all that I have advanced, so if it is allowed unto or for them, I should wish to be remembered for my advances, etc.

I am quite sensible of the ardent expenses thee must have had in order to forward the plan in contemplation. I hope that thy reward dear friend may be crowned with ever lasting life, etc. I shall endeavor not to enter on a voyage of similar kind until I have advice so to do, for I cannot plead ignorance but see clearly it is against the law of Great Britain, & to violate this good laws of the country where I go I wish not. And to resort to private places is not pleasant to me, neither doth it become the dignity of the subjects. I hear no complaint of the sufficiency of the grant of the settlers' land. I believe they are full satisfied. I have to acknowledge thy kind invitation to take quarters at thy house, feeling myself unworthy to become one of the family, etc.

I much approve of that of employing a vessel from London to Sierra Leone. I think if that was entered in, we should soon be able to man her with navigation from the colony. George Davis, he that I carried from Sierra Leone, has remained with me through the course of the war, has improved in the art of navigation. Could he have a little practice, no doubt in my mind but he would soon be qualified to fill a station on board a ship, etc. I hope thee may not lose sight of the subject of having in the employment as thou hast mentioned, for it ever was my mind & I see nothing that I think would have a tendency of doing so much good for the inhabitants of Sierra Leone as that plan.

I may state to thee that I had the pleasure of being invited to visit the schools with his Excellency the governor. There were 150 boys in the boy school. As far as I was able to judge, they were improving in the school. They tell me [they] are under the inspection of Thomas Hunt,[23] one of the schoolmasters that I carried out from England. He keeps his health very well. I believe is well satisfied to be made use of to fill a station of a schoolmaster, etc.

[23] Thomas Hunt was one of three missionary schoolteachers sent to Sierra Leone by the English Wesleyan Conference in 1811 in response to an urgent request made some five years earlier by the colony's leading Methodist preacher, the Reverend Joseph Brown.

I believe that Governor Macarthy has the good wishes of all the colony, etc.

As to my opinion in rendering the chiefs friendly towards civilization, my opinion may be very erroneous. I think I should recommend this present plan, that of opening roads from tribe to tribe with their consent & establishing factory. The Friendly Society is about to establish one at Port Loko.[24] I think that of making presents to the chiefs only helps to whet their appetites for more, which if these factories were place[d] in different places with such articles as they needed, it would help to enhance them to move industry further. If they can be permitted to get those articles through industry, it would help to make them more industrious & when they get these supplies with enriching the produce of their country for these articles they needed, I think it may gradually wean them from being so strongly influenced with the slave trade, etc. But it is to be lamented to see & hear with what rigor these slave trade is prosecuted. There has been numbers brought in since I have been here, & it's sufficient that far greater number leaves than what is taken.

It is a delicate thing to say much on the character of a person as to H. T. T. I fear that he has a better head than heart. I hope that this kind will be sufficient for thee to be rightly guarded, etc.

As to the practice of dealing in spirits, in my simple opinion it is & ever has been much against the true interest of the inhabitants of Sierra Leone. There is 22 license houses, etc. In answer to these importation of spirits, it is hard to say through what channel it mostly comes. However, I think I may be safe to say the greatest merchant may be the greatest importer.[25] It is so uneven a thing that a vessel or her conductor would as soon think of stopping away from Africa all together as to think of going without spirits. Much of this commodity comes in captured slave vessels. This

[24] Port Loko was a trading center some miles east of Freetown in the colony's interior country. Located on the Loko River, the town was an important commercial depot as early as the sixteenth century, when the Portuguese set up a post there. The natives called the town Os Alagoas, but the Portuguese decided on its present name.

[25] Cuffe is most probably referring to Macaulay and Babington, Ltd. See footnote 27, p. 195.

following is in such a favor, let him come in what part he may, I fear he would be hailed welcome to this coast.

I remit to thy kind care and attention £200 bill after paying the balance of the shipment [of] trade to me, also all other expenses. Pass the other to my credit. Also I forward thee some copies for payment to be remitted or paid to thee. I am at this time short a peek towards America, if it please the Lord to spare me to arrive. I shall endeavor to write thee soon.

My love to thee, thine & all inquiring friends, and [I] am thy affectionate friend

PAUL CUFFE

[Postscript] It's much to be lamented having sold my tobacco to the members of the Friendly Society at one hundred per cent advance from merchandise in America as we differ in opinion what the hundred per cent amounts to. It's agreed by Duncan Campbell[26] and Paul Cuffe to submit it to thy determination. I also enclose to thee the bills at the price which the tobacco was purchased for in America.

I also enclose copy of letters from Michael Macmillian to Macaulay & Babington[27] for 2 tons of wood shipped to their care, which I wish thee to receive the net amount & place also to my credit.

PAUL CUFFE

[p.s.] Brig *Traveller* sailed from Sierra Leone in Africa 1 yr. 4th month 4th 1816.

[26] Duncan Campbell was a Scotsman who was sent to Sierra Leone in 1797 by the Missionary Society, an English nonsectarian Protestant missionary organization. A Presbyterian minister, Campbell for a time worked with the natives in the interior country. But he abandoned the ministry a few months after his wife died in 1798, married a girl from one of the local tribes, and tried his luck with the slave trade. The canny Scot ultimately retreated from the slave trade and moved to Freetown, where he set up a successful mercantile business.

[27] Macaulay and Babington was perhaps the colony's most important import-export establishment. Founded in 1807 by Thomas Gisbourne Babington and Zachary Macaulay, the company prospered for more than twenty years, until local mismanagement wrecked the enterprise.

Left at Sierra Leone schooner *Three Brothers* of Newburyport. Just arrived.

[The British navy] captured and brought to Sierra Leone the schooner *Rebecca* of New York, Francis Hathaway captain. Also there was 3 brigs and 3 schooners taken and condemned. At Sierra Leone in the course of 2 months, these vessels (it was said) was found guilty of carrying on the slave trade. Contrary to the laws of God and man.

p.s. I was informed that Francis Hathaway belonged in Boston. And that John Brown of New York was the owner and supercargo, and the schooner sailed from Charlestown, S. Carolina, was cleared out for Tenneriffe. [The remainder of the ms. is missing.]

Westport, [Mass., n.d., June 1816?]

PETER WILLIAMS, JR.[28]
ESTEEMED FRIEND

Thine of the 2 instant enclosing a letter from Doctor Morris of Boston I have received, thy notes duly observed. I hope these may find thee, thy father, family, and all inquiring friends in health, as these leave me and mine. At this time I am very happy to learn that thou art so well established in this African cause for the great good and improvement of that people. And also to find you have got the institution in Philadelphia willing to wear the yoke of Christian benevolence.

The highest temporal seat in Public office that are held in Sierra Leone by men of color are a printing office. They are Sheriffs' constables, clerks in most of their public offices; they fill the seats

---

[28] One of the free Negro leaders in New York City, Peter Williams, Jr. (1780?–1840), was an enthusiastic supporter of Cuffe's Sierra Leone venture. Williams divided his time between his ministry as an Episcopalian clergyman and the emigration-oriented New York African Institution, which he captained for many years. He preached such a powerful sermon at a memorial service for Cuffe in New York in October, 1817, that it subsequently was published as *A discourse delivered on the death of Capt. Paul Cuffee, before the New York African Institution, in the African Methodist Episcopal Zion church.* . . . His sixteen-page pamphlet has become a valuable source of information for Cuffe biographers. Ironically, by 1830 Williams had become a severe critic of African colonization.

of juror 10 to 2. They also make a court of Request to try causes for debts not exceeding £2-40. Also a weekly Court to try uncivil people, etc. They have no banks. NB: I have no doubt, but other stations will open when these people become qualified to fill them. No other institution of people of color in the inhabited states but yours in New York and Philadelphia are engaged for the benefit of Africa, etc. The Friendly Society in Sierra Leone consisted of 30 members, but when I left they were about to be incorporated. Some supposed it would lessen their number.

I am glad to find that the rice mill have not escaped thy mind. I also hope thee will endeavor to find a man who will erect a saw mill and work her. Also, a man who understands repairing watches. I shall wish to be informed if there should be any vessel sailing to Africa as I should wish to have as much information concerning the mill, etc., as thee was in possession of at that time. I send enclosed to thee the copy of Perry Lockes'[29] acknowledgment to the All Wise Being for His preserving goodness which I thought mistake[nly] though I gave thee before. I do not think it best to publish it. I have sent the original to Boston; they can do as they think best.

I am thy assured friend
PAUL CUFFE

p.s. Tell my friend I think that sailmaker's business would be small, as Paul Cuffe waving [it] away. If he is to render any aid toward the commercial business purposes for the African Institution to enter into, sooner the better.

[Undated, unsigned, not in Cuffe's handwriting]

Minutes of Paul Cuffe's opinions—the most advantageous means of encouragement to be received towards civilization of Africa. That the popularity of the colony of Sierra Leone be

[29] Perry Lockes was one of Cuffe's thirty-eight Sierra Leone volunteers. A skilled blacksmith, Lockes prospered in his adopted country and became an important leader in the Freetown business and religious communities. See also Cuffe's letter to William Allen, April 1, 1816, p. 192.

encouraged, and in order to render them aid and assistance very sound is that there should be some families of good character should be encouraged to remove from America and settle at Sierra Leone in order to become farmers. And to lend them aid in such useful institutions as they are capable of; and in order for this accommodation, it appear to me there should be an intercourse kept open between America and Sierra Leone. That through that channel some people might find their way to Africa. And for their accommodation and reception when arrived, I think proper that a house be built that they have some place of refuge or shelter. I think one thousand pounds might be needed for the beginning of the benevolent proposition.

Westport 14 June 1816

ESTEEMED FRIEND JOHN R. TEILE[30]

Thine of the 21st February last came safe to hand, contents noted. Thy of the first date I also duly received. But I was on the point of sailing for Africa and no immediate conveyance offering, therefore, an answer was omitted. I hope thou will not impute it for the want of good will nor yet to willful negligence.

I am in health, hoping these may find thee enjoying the same blessing.

As I am not in the West India trade, therefore, thee cannot expect any business from me. But rest assured all the business I can send to thee in recommending your house I shall endeavor to lose no opportunity. And you have my best wishes for your welfare and advancement in trade, etc.

I hope that your colony may obtain her independence and live in peace and harmony among yourselves and all mankind. One thing I sincerely hope that your authority will utterly abolish all slavery under its dominions and grant liberty to every of its citizens which is due to every subject of an independent state, etc.

[30] Teile evidently was a Santo Domingo merchant who had business engagements with Cuffe in the days when the Westporter made periodic trading voyages to the Caribbean.

[31] See footnote 19, pp. 97–98.

My friend Stephen Grellet[31] visits Santo Domingo on a religious visit, he being a minister of good esteem in the religious Society of Friends commonly called Quakers—and is accompanied by one, a member of the same Society in New York. Any services you can render them will be kindly received by them and gratefully acknowledged by your assured friend and well-wisher

PAUL CUFFE

Westport 14 June 1816

ESTEEMED FRIEND PETER WILLIAMS, JR.

I arrived home in safety after a passage of 56 days and found them [my family] all well. I wish thee to send the minutes of Perry Lockes to me when thou hast got through with it.

I received a letter from John James [32] of Philadelphia saying it would be good for me to come to Philadelphia to clear up many unfavorable reports that was spread among the people of color concerning the Sierra Leone mission. And [he] states further that several had come forward with a wish to emigrate to Sierra Leone. As the Institution of New York are in possession of every needful information concerning Africa, they can give every information that they may require. I imagine the certificate from Africa, together with the Governor's letter of acknowledgment being made public, will give every information necessary.

My love to thy grandparents, etc. Tell thy father that my wife would have gladly wished to have had it in her power to have taken care of him in her house so he would have run no great risk to have come with me to Westport.

I am thy assured friend,

PAUL CUFFE

Andover, July 10, 1816

DEAR SIR,

I have lately returned from a second tour round the United States. I think soon of going into our Western and Southern

[32] See footnote 7, p. 78.

country again. I should be much gratified to see you before I leave this place. I have kept steadily in view since I saw you last the contemplated measures for the benefit of the people of color, no establishment has as yet been entered upon. I think, however, the prospect is becoming more favorable. I should like to have some further communication with you on the general subject relative to what can be done in this country in aid of our object. And likewise to know more fully your views relative to your contemplated mission to Sierra Leone—the information in your letter directed to Mr. Lord is very interesting. Still it should be pleasing to consult with you relative to this subject.

A number of the Brethren of the Theological seminary[33] in this place take a very decided interest in favor of your proposed plan. They have already done much by presenting your view and encouraging your exertions in their statements in the *Weekly Messenger*[34] printed in Boston. The facts which they have stated are to be found in 7 different papers commencing July 1st 1814 and ending September 2nd of the same year. I much wish you might be favored of the fact referred to above. I think some important advantages would result to the interest in which you are engaged should you visit this place. The young men here favor a personal acquaintance with you, would take greater interest in the object before us, they will more or less of them be settled in important positions of our country and hereafter no doubt greatly aid your benevolent views. I think as circumstances are you should certainly visit this place in the course of the present season. You know not how great an interest you will secure in your favor. Do consider this subject. If you could come on here in 6 or 4 days from the date of this letter, I should hope to see you myself. It is most likely I shall not remain in this place but a short time.

I will mention one circumstance which I connect is highly

[33] Andover, Massachusetts, Theological Seminary.

[34] The Boston *Weekly Messenger*, July 1, p. 4; July 15, p. 4; July 22, p. 2; August 5, p. 4; August 12, p. 4; August 26, p. 4; September 2, 1814. Several of these anonymously written essays were long, turgid and portentous disquisitions on the responsibilities of white Christians to bring the Truth to uninformed degenerate black Africa—an early version of the white man's burden. The remaining essays offered a lengthy pietist account of Cuffe's career and his adventures in Sierra Leone.

interesting to your Brethren, the people of color. I have been lately informed that Mr. Paul the Baptist preacher in Boston not long time since was visited by a gentleman who was taken with at his house and died under his roof. This gentleman previous to his death made his will and gave his estate to Mr. Paul, amounting to 150,000 dollars. I am told Mr. Paul has gone to England to obtain the property. From this circumstance I conclude the gentleman noticed above was an Englishman. Should Mr. Paul receive the amount noticed then he should, I should presume, appropriate at least a part of it to the benefit of people of color in some way. I hope you will find it convenient, or if not perfectly convenient, to visit this place soon.

Yours affectionately
SAMUEL MILLS[35]

Remember me to your family

Westport 6 August 1816

ESTEEMED FRIEND SAMUEL J. MILLS

Thine of the 15th & 22[36] ultimo I have received, contents noted, & am one who rejoice to see good institutions established for the information & reformation of our fellow creatures. [I]

---

[35] Samuel Mills was evidently a man of mediocre intelligence who compensated for his paucity of talent with an almost superhuman energy. The son of a Congregational clergyman with a missionary bent, young Mills had studied at Williams, Yale, and Andover Theological Seminary. He and most of his classmates prepared for missionary work, and several were among the first American missionaries to serve in Burma, Ceylon, and the Indian subcontinent. Mills was ordained in 1815 and plunged immediately into a variety of benevolent activities in the frontier American West and in Eastern cities. Convinced that there was no place in American society for free Negroes, the good clergyman became interested early in his career in large-scale Negro relocation schemes. Mills and Professor Ebenezer Burgess went to Sierra Leone in late 1817 on a "mission of inquiry" for the American Colonization Society. On the return voyage home Mills contracted a fever and on June 16, 1818, he was buried at sea. See Gardiner Spring, *Memoirs of the Rev. Samuel J. Mills, passim;* Staudenraus, *The African Colonization Movement,* pp. 37–47.

[36] I have been unable to locate these letters.

believe in that great day of account it will not be asked what denomination we made or profession to be of, but they who have done good and worked righteousness will be rewarded with a crown of everlasting life.

I feel to encourage the preparation of the young men of color fit for usefulness. It will be a convincing prop to those who show to them in utter abhorrence that they are not capable of mental endowments, etc. I am sorry to be oblige[d] to say on account of the prejudice[37] is so prevalent in this part of the Union on color that here would be no probability of getting a school at all under a colored teacher. I will endeavor to inquire of them at Newport, R. I., etc. If any encouragement, shall inform you accordingly. I think such characters as has been named would be very useful in Africa. The Governor of Sierra Leone inquired particular of me for a schoolmaster of color.

I learn by the public paper that the Southern slave holders are much alarmed on account of the Africans rising. I have thought it would have been prudent for them to have early seen to this in order to prevent this evil, but it appears that they have made use of the very means to bring this destruction among them, (viz.) firstly, taking those people from their native land and making slaves of them; secondly, the cooperating & having children by them, all which is abomination in the sight of God. But as light is breaking forth, it is hopeful that some good might be done, and the people of both sect[s] be preserved.

It appears more are willing to manumit their slaves if they could do it on safe ground. Some has excused themselves for want of law,[38] others for want of means to support them after they was set

---

[37] Cuffe's reference to prejudice is a rare confession, indeed. As we have seen, he generally masked his feelings in public, especially to white people. Consequently, Cuffe's admission that southeastern New England harbored considerable race prejudice suggests that the Westporter personally experienced its severe sting in recent days. It is possible, of course, that a new wave of racism in the area acted as the persuasive force in convincing him that blacks had little future in the United States and should seek, therefore, to relocate in Africa.

[38] For many slaveholders the "excuse" was valid. Southern states after the American Revolution made it increasingly difficult, if not impossible, for private manumission of slaves. South Carolina and Georgia were in the forefront of the movement to restrict manumission. Virginia, the key Southern state, adopted restrictive legislation in 1806 that successfully

at liberty. If those could not be colonized by themselves whither in this country or Africa, or in both, then let their planters give them their plantation on a day until such time that they might be qualified to be their own caretaker, & hope that something may be done which will prevent all insurrection & bloodshed.

I do not expect to send a vessel to Africa this ensuing winter. When I was last in Africa, I was some disappointed in not having a special license from the British government. My correspondent, Wm. Allen in London, a member of the London African Institution, wrote me to come to London and engage with them, and that [I should assist them] when a communication between England and Africa [opened], but it would be leaving part of the Cuffe family in America. I have informed him my wishes was for the good of that people unanswerably. And if we could open a circular route from Africa to England and to America, and in case this should [could] become, I feel disposed to be made use of in any way that it appeared most advantageous. I have not had any reactions from the African Institution in London.

Have instructed several African youths in the way which thee mention, some of which have been very serviceable, and some have gone back among their own tribes and degenerated back into their own old habits. This one thing make against the usefulness of youth in his native tribe, (viz.) their own custom is that the youth shall be in subjection to the elders. Should they offer any thing different from their native habits, they are immediately checked, etc. But not withstanding all this, I think it to be a good thing too, to improve some of the youths of Africa. And when the right time comes, and the way opens, I hope always to be ready to forward any views that you may have in contemplation for the improvement of the human race.

Had I known of thy being in New York when I was there, I should have been unwilling to leave it without seeing of thee. I have just received a letter from Samuel C. Aikins,[39] Andover, and

---

quelled any meaningful efforts toward large-scale voluntary emancipation. See the discussion in Jordan, *White Over Black*, pp. 123–24, 347–48, 574–78; and Franklin, *From Slavery to Freedom*, p. 217.

[39] Samuel C. Aikins, an ardent antislavery crusader, was a Professor of Theology at the Andover Theological Seminary.

I do not know but it may be right for me to visit Andover shortly.

There was a society established in Sierrra Leone, 1812, by the name of the Friendly Society, for the purpose of corresponding with the African Institution in London. There was also a connection of traffic opened between the 2 corresponding societies in order to encourage the African settler with a good market for their produce. They began with £70. When I was there the Friendly Society was worth £1,200 Sterling to themselves. I beg not to have my weakness or foolishness exposed to public view to my ridicule or the detriment of the good work that we trust are on its wheel.

Farewell,
PAUL CUFFE

COPY
[Enclosed in the letter to Mills]

Colony of Sierra Leone, 25th March. **Mr.** Perry Lockes, you are hereby summoned and required to appear at the ensuing General Session of the Peace which will be held at the Court Hall in Freetown on Wednesday, the tenth day of April, at the hour of ten in the forenoon, there to serve as a grand juror. Herein fail not at your peril.

W. D. GRANT
Sheriff

This Perry Lockes was one of the passengers that I carried out. He made great complaint to me to be so called upon. I told him he complained in America because he was deprived of these liberties, and then murmured because he was thus called upon—go & fill thy seat and do as well as thou cans't—I mention this that others may see they have equal rights in Africa.

P.C.

The people that I carried to Africa as settlers were well received, and had land granted to them from the British government. When I left them they were in high spirits, except that situation of citation. They at Sierra Leone much wanted a good millwright. A sawmill is much wanted, also a rice mill for cleaning rice. I wish thee to make inquire: whether there could be such a man found, and, likewise what would be the probable cost of a rice mill; a watch repairer would meet with good encouragement.

P. CUFFE

Westport 7 August 1816

DEAR FRIEND SAMUEL C. AIKINS

Thine of the 23 ult. are at hand. Contents noted, etc.

I think myself happy to think thee will consent to stoop so low as to correspond with one, who are so unworthy of thy notion as I am. So that I may be more serviceable and more faithful in doing good towards my fellow creatures, and meriting the favor and prayers of my fellowmen, amen to the approachful day, when the Lion and Lamb shall lay down together.

I have great consolation in my journeys to Africa, yet I do not feel that the whole object is obtained. My object were that a road may be opened between America and Africa, and between England and Africa, and kept open so that a correspondence could be kept up in order to see what assistance could be rendered to their assistance from time to time. And for to assist in this business there hath been institutions formed in New York and Philadelphia. But they are to state that they have not got much growth.

If this circular route could be kept open, I think it would help to breaken the slave trade, for this traffic are too much carried on by the American citizens under cloak of other nations. And until this is put a stop to, it will be hard to obtain a general manumission. It is reported that there are more than 200 sail of vessels cleared from Havana for the coast of Africa last year, 1815. Cannot anything be done to kill this clandestine traffic? The 2 month I was in Sierra Leone there was 6 vessels brought in who was taken in that abominable traffic. One of the six was under American colors, the others under Spanish colors, no doubt, under disguise.

I observe from the public papers that the Southern people are under great apprehension of insurrection. They no doubt are employed in providing the best means to prevent [slaves from] rising as they apprehend, but at the same time, they are preparing instruments for their own execution. Why not provide means to effectually abolish the slave trade and then free their slaves and colonize them citizens in America or in Africa or in both places; or free them and give them their plantation to work on a day until such a time that they are capable of managing for themselves? I merely make these propositions to look at it in these perilous times as it appears it calls loud for some timely consideration to be taken in view. I received a letter from S. J. Mills, 22 ult., saying that your Society were exerting themselves for the benefit of the African nation. May God prosper the great work in their hands.

Wm. Allen, a member of the African Institution in London, on whom I correspond with, invited me to come from Africa to London and join them in keeping open a communications between England and Sierra Leone. But my object was to keep the road open from America as well as England, otherwise it would be leaving part of the family behind. I have received no answer from Wm. and I cannot be concerned in another journey to Africa until some further provisions are made.

The last voyage I was out I obtained no special license, but was permitted [to land] on sufferance. However, I was respectfully treated, and my passengers well received and had land granted them to work to their satisfaction. I do not expect to go to Africa this winter unless things work more favorable than I expect. I wish to obtain a good millwright. There is a sawmill much wanting in that country, also a rice mill (for cleaning of rice). If thee in corresponding with thy friends to the South can make inquire what a rice mill for cleaning rice would finally cost, also whether there could be one obtained to go who understands erecting such a mill?

I believe if there could be mercantile correspondence opened between the African race in America and Africa, it would have a good tendency to keep open this communication and bring them acquainted with each other, and would be employing their children. And if a religious character wished to visit that country they could obtain a passage, and the information got through this channel might be help to discourage the slave trade. Should I receive any information of importance, I shall endeavor to inform thee accordingly. It would be very pleasant to me to visit you at Andover this fall.

I am your ever well wishing friend til death, Amen

PAUL CUFFE

Westport 10 August 1816

ESTEEMED FRIEND WILLIAM HARRIS[40]

Thine of ye 30th of June to Alexander Howard I have is now before me, and may inform thee that the prospects are unfavorable to go to Africa this ensuing fall on account of particular arrangements to be made with the London African Institution on the British government for the reception and accommodation of those who may undertake to emigrate to that country. All those who go to that country must be sensible that they will want and need a whole year's provision to last them until they can raise a crop. If mechanic could be had such as millwrights, a sawmill, rice mill, is much wanted, and a watch repairer would meet with good encouragement.

I think another year our new settlers would be able to give us more satisfactory account. I am quite sensible that country is a good country. It is a good country and just such country as we the people of color stands in need of. Experience is the best of schoolmasters. In my small experience I have seen some countries exceedingly well situated, by [but] badly managed which rendered the inhabitants miserable. I recommend for us to wait with patience until deliverance comes, and in the meantime to use all good economy to improve our morals both in state and society.

I have no doubt but there would be great openings for us were we but capable of self government. Before we can strive to this we must depart from that monster, I mean intemperance. Examine yourselves, your families. Are you clean? If not, set about this work immediately and clear your houses of keeping company with

---

[40] William Harris was apparently a free Negro who wrote to an Alexander Howard for information on prospects for emigration. Howard's letter to Cuffe is not in the Cuffe papers.

him and do not admit him in your houses in any other shape than a mere medicine.

I formerly keep his company, but for many years I have forsaken him and I find great consolation thereby.

My dear friend, do not be offended with me for I mention this in sincere love for your prosperity, both temporal and spiritual.

I am your assured friend til death.

PAUL CUFFE

Westport 10 August 1816

ESTEEMED FRIEND JED^h MORSE[41]

Thine of the 27 July via New York I have duly read and may inform thee that the prospect for me to go out to Africa this fall is unfavorable. When I went out before, there was not such provisions made for receiving my passengers as I could wish—all which made the load fall very heavy on me. I had to supply these people at my own expense with provisions until they could provide for themselves by raising a crop. And I was not provided for with a license to protect me while in the colony of Sierra Leone.

I am now in further correspondence with my friend Wm. Allen of London on the subject. When suitable provisions and further arrangements can be made, I shall be ready and willing through the permission of God to serve my brethren in any way which may attend to their advancement. I recommend to the people of color in Boston not to flatter themselves with too great prospect of the appearance of new things, but after one or two years progress of the new settlers they then will be able to form a more correct idea. And in the meantime they to use all good economy for to improve their morals both in state and society.

As for my own opinion, I am convinced that this is the country in which this people might rise to be a people if they could be experienced for self government and leave that monstrous evil of

41 The "father of American geography" as well as being the father of Samuel F. B. Morse, the inventor of the telegraph, Jedidiah Morse was an outstanding spokesman for the antislavery movement in the early nineteenth century.

intemperance behind. We feel the want of men mechanics, (viz.) a millwright to construct & raise a sawmill, also a rice mill. Likewise a watch repairer would meet with good encouragement. If on inquiry thee should get information of such a character, I should wish to be informed. Should thou know of any vessel sailing to Africa I should take it kind if thou would have the goodness to inform me. Should wish to write by the first conveyance.

I beg to be excused for taking the liberty of troubling of thee with the perusal of Peter Williams, Jr., letter. He is a man of color and is Secretary to the New York African Institution. He also fills a station as one of the clergy in a congregation held under the profession of the Episcopal Church. He is not ordained, but I believe gives good satisfaction. I also send herein a said Perry Lockes' acknowledgment to our All Wise Creator for His Goodness. His request is to have it published, as thee may observe on the back of it. Thee can act as thee think most prudent with it. Should thou publish it, thee will leave out as much of P. Cuffe praise as thee thinks best. Many people's feelings are hurt at my being repraised, and as I wish to do no hurt, it would be pleasant to me that my name was less repraised or sounded with a small (i).

Perry Lockes was summoned as a grand juror; the summons was sent in a letter to some of the colored brethren in Boston.

I am thy assured friend

PAUL CUFFE

Westport 8th mo 14 1816

DEAR FRIEND JAMES WISE[42]

I arrived at New York on the 29th of the 5 month after a passage of 54 days, all well, for which I desire to be truly ever thankful. I found market extremely dull for my cargo of wood. I

[42] James Wise was a leading figure in Freetown society. A Nova Scotian émigré, he became government printer for Sierra Leone, publishing *The Sierra Leone Gazette,* the colony's semiofficial newspaper. Wise was impressed with Cuffe's plans, joined the Friendly Society, and served for a time as the Society's secretary.

have never been able to make sale of it yet even at the first cost. But [it] is in store in New York on expense and no prospect of sale. Your squills I could not sell at any price whatever. They told me that they had been in habit of buying them all dried. I have brought them home and dried them, but they had some perished. I have got them dry, but have not made sale of them. Had I entered them at the office at thy invoice, they may have brought thee in debt very considerably, as the duty was 30 pr.

The apothecaries sell the best of dried squills at 75/$ or 3/8 by the retail a pound weight. Palm oil & ivory I cannot exactly say their prices, but think they may see so as to clear themselves. Our factories have stopped and have become so well stocked that shares that have sold at $500 has been sold for $5, and even some has been offered as a gift. This is some that have not instruments, but are in the rear. Tobacco $20 to 25 per barrel, has been as high [as] the first quality at $30 per barrel. Flour $11 per bbl; corn at $1.50/ 100 lbs pr bushel; mess pork $25 to 28, prime No. 1, $21; beef, No. 1, $11 to 12, mess, $14; per lb soap at 12 cents; per pound candles sperm, 50 cents, tallow 18 cents; per pound cheese 12½ cts; pr pound butter 25 cents pr lb; eggs 15 cts pr dozen.

I hear *Great Heart* is bound from New York for Africa, by which conveyance I shall embrace by my correspondence in New York. I desire him to furnish thee with account current which will be more satisfactory. My corresponding friend in New York is Peter Wm., Jr., Secretary to our African Institution, which was formed of the men of color for the aid and benefit of the sons of Africa. I shall recommend for them to open the correspondence with the Friendly Society in Sierra Leone which I hope you will answer.

I have had no letter from William Allen since I returned. I do not see that I can visit Sierra Leone until I have some further agreement through the London African Institution with the British government, etc. I do not think there may any prospect of my being out until another year. I hope thee will be able to send and encourage to be sent all the encouragements that were to be remitted to Wm. Allen in London this ensuing fall for me, and those that were only to be paid to thee I wish thee to remit the same to Wm. Allen in London for me; and those that do not fulfill their contracts, I wish thou to call on them by law.

I hope that the Friendly Society have been incorporation as a body, and I hope the new settlers that I have landed are getting on smart, both spiritual and temporal. I also hope that the factory at Port Bagos[43] are going on in a thriving and flourishing state. Give my love to all inquiring friends.

I am thy enthroned friend

PAUL CUFFE

I wish to be informed whether the slave trade increase or decrease. We hear of war & fighting towards Cape Coast.[44]

New Bedford 14 August 1816

GOVERNOR C. MACARTHY

From the gratitude I owe to thee for thy very friendly care and attention to me while at Sierra Leone has often brought thee in my remembrance with desire that thy days may be long, and every blessing of heaven may attend thee here and hereafter forever.

I have not had a line from my friend William Allen since I returned, and as it is of the utmost importance that I should have some agreement through the African Institution with the British government before I visit Sierra Leone, I think I shall not be out until another year. I have many applications to carry out settlers, but I recommend to them to wait see what fruit thou bring forth that has already gone out. I hope thou has been able to obtain of the British government the amount of supplies that I rendered to

[43] Port Bagos was the ancient name for the town of Robaga. Located slightly inland where the Rokel River and Port Loko Creek met, Robaga was an important trading center for the Koya Temne tribesmen of Sierra Leone.

[44] Cape Coast is a leading commercial center in present-day Ghana. The town was a major British administrative headquarters in the late eighteenth century.

the settlers. If so, wilt thou be so kind as to settle the same with my friend James Wise for him to remit to Wm. Allen of London, etc.

At Lat. 26 W and Long. 74 West the little schooner *Princess Charlotte* was upset and all lost but six. The Abolishing Society in New York informed me that there was 237 vessels cleared from Havana for the coast of Africa [in] 1815. Wilt thou be pleased to give my home an account, and to the African Institution, of all the vessels and citizens of the United States of America, or to the Abolishing Society in Philadelphia, so as to have them dealt with according to the laws of their country? All kinds of commercial business is very dull in the United States and provisions [are] high.

I am thy ever well wishing friend

PAUL CUFFE

Westport 14 August 1816

DEAR FRIEND SAMUEL THORP[E][45]

I arrived at New York on the 29 of the 5th month after a passage of 54 days. All well as this leaves me at this time.

As it is necessary that I should have some agreement with the British government, I do not think that I can be out until another year. I have many applications to carry out more settlers. My camwood are still unsold. I have not had any offer for it. Squills are worse than nothing in a green state for they must pay duty, and when that is done they will sell for anything; the apothecaries sell them all dried at by the retail at 3-9 pr pound.

I shall endeavor to send the American price current for thy better guidance. I perceive that many vessels are cleared from the Havana for Africa; & wish all vessels that are condemned at Sierra Leone that appear to be American property and American citizens

[45] Samuel Thorpe was a Jamaica Maroon who succeeded in two professions. He was both a prominent Freetown trader and a popular Methodist preacher. In 1827 the Reverend Samuel Thorpe achieved some notoriety in Freetown in the case of *Barnard v. Thorpe*. He was found guilty of having committed adultery with his neighbor's wife.

that information may be given, with vouchers, so that these might be taken hold of by law, etc.

I am thy real friend

PAUL CUFFE

Westport 14 August 1816

ESTEEMED FRIEND PETER WILLIAMS, JR.

I send to thy care and particular attention a package of letters for Sierra Leone to be forwarded by the first good opportunity. I hear that there is a Captain Hart who belongs at New Bedford who sails in the employ of Peter Remson & Co., South Street, New York.

My dear friend, I wish thee to obtain 3 of your latest prices current, directed as follows (one to Cpt. George Nichol,[46] Sierra Leone, and one to James Wise,[47] Secretary to the Friendly Society at Sierra Leone). And [I] wish thee also to address the Governor with a few lines, at the same time excusing thyself in behalf of your Society by stating to him that it was from seeing a letter given to Paul Cuffe, March 21, 1811, which show the great interest that he took in the advancements and well being of our color, &, etc. Also, if thee think well of it, send the Governor one of your Society's papers, (direct [to] His Excellency), Governor C. Macarthy for information of the American property found in carrying on the slave trade. I wish thee to inquire out this vessel soon, as he expect to sail soon. Give my love to thy father and mother and the rest of thy family, also to [my] Sister Freelove.

I am thy assured friend

PAUL CUFFE

---

[46] See footnote 21, p. 121.
[47] See footnote 42, p. 209.

Westport 14 August 1816

RESPECTED FRIENDS OF THE FRIENDLY SOCIETY
[OF SIERRA LEONE]

I desire to be thankful for having the privilege [of] addressing of you in health at this time, hoping these may meet you enjoying the same blessing.

I hope ere this reach you that you will be incorporated into a respectable body. I desire that you may feel yourselves bound by the principles of Truth and the Joys of nature to stand fast as a Society and grow strong, that peace and harmony may dwell among you so that you may become a people [of] respectability both in the sight of man and before God, and more and more known among the nations of the earth.

I had 54 days passage to New York where I was gladly received there. The African Institution made particular inquiry into all the transactions of note that had happened, and intend to open a correspondence with the Friendly Society in Sierra Leone, all which I hope may take place. The Abolishing Society in New York [noted] that 237 sails of vessels cleared for Africa 1815. I hope that your society will feel entrusted in giving early information of all the American vessels and American citizens with good voice so that they might be dealt with as the law points out. And feel to make use of every means right and just in sight of God to suppress the slave trade.

In Lat^d 26 North and Longitude 75 West the schooner *Princess Charlotte*[48] was upset in a squall and all lost but 6. There was 22, the whole crew [was lost]. God will not always suffer the wicked to go unpunished. Was the 2 girls that was missing ever found?

I am your ever well wishing friend until death, etc.

PAUL CUFFE

P.S. I hope the Society will be able to make the remittance to Wm. Allen for me this ensuing fall.

[48] The repeated reference in his correspondence to the loss of this slave ship suggests the depth of his concern over the continued illicit slave trade with all its attendant horrors. Yet at the same time the tragedy offered Cuffe some solace. He appeared to see in *Princess Charlotte*'s destruction the avenging hand of a just Lord.

Westport 8th mo 14, 1816

AFFECTIONATE FRIEND JOHN KIZZELL[49]

I hope these may find thee in health as they leave me at this time. I had 54 days passage to New York; arrived all well. I have many applications for settlers to remove from America to Africa. But as it is very necessary that I should have some provisions made by the British government, I shall not be able to get things ripe until another year.

In the meantime should it appear that there could be no more view at Sierra Leone, could not there be a settlement made at some other place or port with prudence and equal safety? I only mention this for thee to consider upon as it appears that there are motions of insurrection in the Southern states. I imagine that many will be glad to find some place where they could send them for the peace and tranquility of the world.

Our camwood are unsold. It will not sell even at the first cost. Squills are worth nothing in their green state. They are retailed after dried at 3/9ᵈ per pound.

I am thy assured friend

PAUL CUFFE

Westport 14 August 1816

ESTEEMED FRIEND ANTONA SURVANA[50]

After informing thee that I am well; hoping these may meet thee enjoying the same blessing; I had 54 days passage to New York. All arrived well; found times dull. My cargo is not yet sold; have had no offer for it. Tobacco has been worth $30 per 1000 [lbs].

I made a mistake when I made out your account current of $30, the balance due on in account. Thee may see it ought to be $269, and thee only give me due bill for $239. Therefore there is $30 more due. In thy looking [at] the stated account that I gave thee, if thee should be sensible of the error, thou will be pleased to give

---

[49] See footnote 18, p. 120.
[50] Anthony Survance. See Cuffe's letter to William Allen of 1 April 1816.

me an order on Absalom Jones[51] for the $30 which will be the balance due me and will then come payable by Absalom Jones.

I have had great many applications to take more settlers to Africa, but I shall not be out this fall. There are 237 slave vessels cleared from Havana for the coast of Africa in the year 1815. All the information that thee can possible give the American government so as to have her citizens dealt with according to law. Give my love to Elisabeth and all inquiring friends.

I am thy assured friend

PAUL CUFFE

Westport 14 August 1816

DEAR FRIEND SAMUEL R. FISHER[52]

Thine of 2 June, I have received some time since. I hope these may meet thee and thine in health as these have me and mine at this time, for which I desire to be humble.

I have many applications to take more settlers to Africa, but I recommend to them to wait and hear what returns we may have from our other Brethren that last went out. And as it is proper that I should have some further understanding with the British Government before I pursue a similar voyage, and that will take time, therefore, I have no expectations that a voyage can be undertaken until another year and another season. And the cargo that I brought lays in New York unsold, which renders me unable to undertake such a voyage, not knowing when it will sell.

I particular noticed thy ardent desire for the well being of the African race. It appears to me that there never [was] a time when it calls louder for something to be done for the African nation besides violence to suppress insurrection.

When I arrived at Sierra Leone I meet no letter from Wm. Allen of London, and when it come, no license accompanied it, which

[51] See footnote 14, p. 153.

[52] Samuel R. Fisher was a white Philadelphia Quaker merchant. He, along with John James and Alexander Wilson, had business dealings with Cuffe over the years. As with so many Philadelphia Quaker merchants, Fisher supported actively most of the Society of Friends' antislavery enterprises of the early nineteenth century.

made much against the trade part of my voyage. Although the Governor show me no little kindness, the passengers were well received, and I was permitted to land provisions on my own expense to supply their present wants, I had to remove with my vessel and that part of my cargo that could not be landed in the colony. And my flour I was oblige to sell to them at $12 pr. bbl. and take wood at $100 per ton, which if I could have been permitted to land it, it would [have] sold for $ sixteen per bbl. & received pay in wood at $80 per ton.

From the above circumstances, I cannot undertake another voyage to Sierra Leone until I have some further agreement with the British Government. Thus thou may see that my trading on sufferance in Africa and the cargo I brought not selling, and my not having no pay from any other quarter but what I received from four passengers that I took from the Westward, all which makes the load fall heavy on me. However, I have peace in my own mind and make no doubt but I shall be safely carried through.

I feel somewhat at a loss what steps can or may be taken for the further relief of my African Brethren. Whilst I was writing this letter, two of them came from Boston to seek a passage to Africa.

I have had some correspondence with the Society, who seem to take an interest in ameliorating the condition of the Africans.[53] I have suggested to them whither they could be colonized in some part of the United States or in Africa, or for their owners to give them work on a day until they become capable of being their own caretakers. This is in case of a general manumission, etc.

I have forwarded my accounts current with Antona[54] to James Forten, and it appear that there is $30 more due me. I should think it right then I have Antona['s] due bill, for if they consistently with principles of truth hold, it for me to receive it, etc.

Should thee be called upon, I wish thee to assist in getting the balance due me from Gered's Bank.

I am in great love & esteem thy assured friend

PAUL CUFFE

---

[53] Cuffe appears to be referring to his correspondence with Samuel Mills and Samuel C. Aikins. The American Colonization Society did not get under way until early 1817.

[54] Anthony Survance.

Westport 14 August 1816

DEAR FRIEND PERRY LOCKES

After my affectionate love to thee and thine in health as these
leave me and mine, for whose blessing I desire ever to be thankful
to the Father of all our mercies. I had a passage of 54 days from
Sierra Leone to New York, where we arrived all well on the 29th
of the 5th mo. We found markets very dull and stored my
camwood; and it is still laying, an expense, unsold. It will not bring
the first cost, all which makes me against the voyage.

I had to put all your letters into the post office in New York
before I could be permitted to enter the vessel. I have written
letters to Boston to take on [no] more passengers from Boston to
Sierra Leone until some further arrangements with the British
government. I received letters from Jedidiah Morse and William
Harris, but my reply to them was that there must be some agreement with the London African Institution or the British government, before I can take any more, in order to make some provision
for receiving those passengers and also to provide license for the
Traveller. I fancy all this will not be brought about in time to come
to Sierra Leone until another year.

I have not had no letters from London, rather from the African
Institution. The small notions that you all send to your friends in
Boston I have not as yet had an opportunity to send, but shall
embrace the first opportunity. Tell thy wife that I shall not send
the trunk by this conveyance, but shall take good care of it and
send or bring it by the first safe conveyance. Thee must give my
love to all inquiring friends, and please accept it thyself. And tell
them I hope to see them again if it pleaseth the Lord, but if we
should not be favored to meet here, I hope we may be favored to
meet in the Kingdom of Heaven, never to be separated.

I hope thee may be favored to get on with thy friends in religion
in its pure state of virtue, & wish thee to encourage George Davis
and others of my creditors to send my pay agreeable to the tenor
of their obligations that James Wise holds. And he will see the
sums are forwarded to my friend William Allen in London. They
write me that there are families wants to come to Sierra Leone
from Boston, and a considerable number in New York, but I have

advised them to wait another year and hear further from you to learn how you made out for livelihood.

I am thy assured friend

PAUL CUFFE

Westport 14 August 1816

DR. FRIEND JAMES FORTEN

I hope these may meet thee and thine in health as they leave me and mine for our preservations of our well being, & they're to be ever truly humbled to the Father of Mercies. I wish thee to make particular inquiry of the constitution and cost of a rice mill and a man who understands erecting and managing a sawmill. And if any one was found that would be willing to become settlers in that part of the world on reasonable conditions, they would meet with encouragements.

I do not expect to go to Africa this year as it is necesssary that I should have some further understanding with the British Government before I go again, which will take time.

I think it is time some steps were taken to prevent insurrections without using violence.

I herewith enclose the account current with Anthony Survance showing a mistake in our settlement, or rather an omission, which if our friend Absalom [Jones] consistently allow it, I shall be to receive it, believing it to be justly true. I have written to Anthony on the subject. My particular love and good will to thee and thy family.

Please remember me to the Society and all inquiring friends. I am thy ever well wishing friend till death

PAUL CUFFE

Westport 8th mo 14 1816

RESPECTED FRIEND EDWARD COOKE

We arrived on the 29 of the 5 month after a passage of 54 days to New York. All well. Thy mother and the rest of thy brothers and sisters are all well & have payed thy mother's debts for one year from the 5 mo last. If thee renders her any assistance by that time it will be a great kindness and save the land. If not, the land must be sold. If thee should make any remittance to Wm. Allen for me by next Christmas, I think it would be all for the best. And in that case I shall request Wm. Allen to remit back again to James Wise for thee to turn, and with additional gain soon return it to Wm. Allen again, and so on, until we get a sum big enough to cancel the debt. I hope to hear from thee soon, and remain thy esteemed friend

PAUL CUFFE

My dear friend Edward Cooke, if I could know that thee had given up the use of strong drink, I should feel rejoiced, and would render thee such aid that thee could soon become a man of property.

PAUL CUFFE

Westport 30 August 1816

ESTEEMED FRIEND PETER WILLIAMS, JR.

In consequence of what thee mentioned, (viz.) that we the people of color might establish a mercantile line of business from the United States to Africa, etc., should this still be your mind and you propose to carry it into effect this fall, we have no time to lose. After consulting thyself and friends, please to inform me your resolution. As, also the price of prime tobacco, soap, candles, as also what size vessel would be most advantageous, and such circumstances as may occur. To the view of your mind

I rest thy assured friend (in health)

PAUL CUFFE

Westport 30 August 1816

ESTEEMED FRIEND PELEG HOWLAND[55]

The 111 billets camwood left with thee on my account by Abner Gifford, I wish thee to sell as it is, in the stick, if thee can obtain

[55] Peleg Howland was a New York merchant importer. Cuffe had enjoyed a mutually profitable business relationship with Howland over the years.

the fair New York price. I am unwilling to go to any additional expense in getting it ground unless there are sure sale for it when ground. Should there be an opening for the sale of a few tons more, I have it at Westport, and can forward it on first notice. I also have [a] number tons at New York in the care of Hicks, Jenkens, & Co.

I am thy assured friend

PAUL CUFFE

Westport ye 7 September 1816

ESTEEMED FRIEND THOMAS FOY OF PROVIDENCE [R.I.]

Thine of the 23 ult. came to hand inquiring for a passage to Africa this present fall. Unless I receive some further instruction from the London African Institution concerning receiving such people as may go, and making such provisions for them as may be necessary when arriving there, [I do not expect to go to Africa this season]. But those who are able, I would recommend for them to provide for themselves, as the Irish people do when they come to this country.

As to thy getting a living without a trade, the country are like other countries. It calls for care & attention to industry. The country certainly is a good country to live in. If thee go to that part of the world thee must set thy face against all slave trade, for that trade is ruinous to that country and is contrary to all Christian institution[s].

I have no knowledge who thou art, but I presume thou are some person of color, and that part of the world call for character to fill stations of respectability in the legislature. If we are to state the cost in passage to Africa, it is $100 a person to be found. It would have been proper for thee to have stated thy age & no. in [your] family, and the probable value of thy property. Also, the occupation thee had in prospect to follow for living, etc.

I am thy assured friend

PAUL CUFFE

ESTEEMED FRIEND JAMES WISE

As thou art one of the main spokes in the great wheel in which the Friendly Society are upheld, and I earnestly entreat thee to stand firm for her support, for if she falls and come[s] to naught, it will be a deadly blow to Africa. I am a well-wisher to her prosperity, and could I be the means of her firm establishment, I think I should consent to be made use of in any way which might be for her advancement. I instruct thee to endeavor that she, the Friendly Society, may not give up her commercial pursuits, for that is the great outlet to her national advancement among the historic nations, etc. I foresee this to be the means of improving both your country and nation.

15 September 1816   PAUL CUFFE

Westport 20 September 1816

DEAR FRIEND STEPHEN GOULD

I have to ask the favor of thee to forward the enclosed package. If any opportunity, from Newport; if no opportunity, please to return the package to me by the first convenient opportunity.

I further enclose 2 letters for thy perusal and advice. Or, any remark that will or may attend to throw any light on the subject, will be kindly received by thy assured friend

PAUL CUFFE

A thought has passed my mind whether the American government, at some future day when the liberation of slavery become more general, would not be prevailed upon to settle a colony in Africa, where this people could be colonized in from time to time, as occasion may require.

P.C.

Westport 19 October 1816

ESTEEMED FRIEND PEASON FREEMAN

Thine of the 27th ult. favored by D. Shilling came safe to me by the second hand.

I was pleased that thou was so kind as to assist Mary in letting her friends hear from her in her long silence in a remote part of the world. After my love to my dear friend Mary, hoping these may find her in health as these leave me and mine.

At this time Mary's brother Michael Wainer is removed by death, [one] year ago in the 7th mo[nth] last. He left his third wife a widow. She was the widow of Joseph White. Her maiden name was Mary Amos. She has two daughters by her former husband, and one boy by Michael. His sons Thomas, Gardner and Michael are all gone into the country. Gardner has gone to Cayuga; Thomas and Michael has gone to Oneida [to reside] among the natives [the Oneida Indians].

Paul and John Wainer still remain in the neighborhood. They owns them a small vessel in company with David Cuffe, Jr. They follow the coasting business and are steady young men. Paul and John both have families. David remains single [and] makes his home with his father, and is steady.

As to my family, I have married three of my oldest daughters (viz.), Naomi, Mary, Ruth. Naomi and her husband has both since been removed by death. They left two girls, one aged ten and the other eight years old. They are fine girls. They live with me. They have pretty good school learning for girls of their age. Their mother have been dead six and seven years. Their father for two years last 7 month [July]. He left about $4,000 worth of property. I have thought whether it might not be addition to the girls to be put away [their father's property] to get their education, etc.

I landed thirty-eight settlers in Africa. I have lately received information by letter that three of them are removed by death. Thus, we see no age, nation, or complection in whatever part of the world are exempt from death's summons. My desire is that we may all be wise and be prepared for that great change, that we may rejoice over hell, death, and the grave.

Mary's son Mathew is married and lives on Gayhead, but I rather think at present he is at sea. Mary's sister Sarah is well and enjoys religion to the peace of her own mind by her daily conversation with her Redeemer. She appears in the ministry and sends her love to her sister Mary, longing to hear that she has met with a change from nature to grace.

As to Mary's land, it still lays under the same restriction as all other Indian land: entailed to that tribe's subject to be improved by themselves. Therefore she can improve this land at any time by settling on it, and not otherwise. But she may be informed that the habits of the people are much the same as when she was acquainted there. The land and its situation truly is good. But the habits of that people are such that it renders them miserable.

This I hope may suffice for the present. I am thy much esteemed friend

PAUL CUFFE

ESTEEMED AND MUCH RESPECTED FRIEND PEASON FREEMAN

I am very happy of having the privilege of corresponding with thee by written communication, and should be much more so to have personal communication with thee, but at present cannot give much encouragement until thee can come and see me, all which would be very gratifying to me.

I trust that God has heard the cries of the afflicted and oppressed, and in His good time will rise to our deliverance. There are great exertions made among the nations for the liberation of the enslaved Africans, and if we are faithful on our part I believe the Lord God of Hosts will not be wanting on His part.

These are the impression of the mind of one who wishes well (I trust) to all mankind. Farewell.

PAUL CUFFE

Westport 20 October 1816

ESTEEMED FRIENDS SIMON AND SUSANAH JACKSON

I embrace this opportunity to inform you that I am in health & hope these may meet thee enjoying the like blessing, for which I desire to be thankful to the Father of Divine Mercies.

Isaac Gifford, one of my neighbors, is the bearer of this letter. And by the same conveyance I send thee one barrel of apples which I request you to accept from me as a small present in token of fine regard, etc.

I was much disappointed in not seeing thee in New York last year, but if we never meet whilst here, I hope we may meet in the Kingdom of Heaven when we shall finish our course here below.

In my voyages to Africa I find that country to be a good country for rice, but they have no advantageous means of cleaning it. I wish to introduce in Africa a rice mill for cleaning rice. And as I have no knowledge of a rice mill, I wish to apply to thee for information as thee lives in a country where they raise rice. I wish to be informed what may be the cost of such a machine and whether there could be a man engaged who would be willing to go to Africa and take charge of the buildings, and what would be his conditions. Also, whether there could be any people of color with you who could wish to emigrate to Africa in order to settle in that country in order to assist in cultivation of that country and people.

In my last visit to Africa I carried 9 families who settled at Sierra Leone. They received land granted to them by the British government, each family as much as they needed, as also a lot in the city for a house lot. I expect to receive some further communciations from the London African Institution and should there be any additional encouragements, I shall endeavor to inform thee accordingly. And also, should thee in inquiry find anything that may bring any light to the contemplated subject, I would thank thee for the earliest informations.

Give my love to your brother Richard Hoilston & to Elias C. Miller, as to all inquiring friends. As also to all Christian people.

I do not expect to be concerned in visiting Africa this year.

I am thy assured & ever well-wishing friend

PAUL CUFFE

PS

There are great exertions made among the nations for the liberation of the enslaved Africans, and I trust that their reward will be crowned with a reward of ever-lasting life. May the Lord of Hosts hear the cries of the oppressed and arouse the churches to their Christian duty to liberate the enslaved Africans.

Amen

Westport 20 October 1816

ESTEEMED FRIEND ISAAC GIFFORD

Will receive one barrel of apples marked Simon Jackson. Thee will deliver the barrel of apples to Simon Jackson or his wife Susanah, he or they paying freight for the same. In case they are not to be found, thee will dispose of the apples to the best advantage on my account, etc.

Also I wish thee to get all the information that thee can of a rice mill for cleaning of rice, what one may cost, & also whether a man can be obtained in Savannah that is qualified to erect such a machine [and] who [is] willing [in] another year to go to Africa & become a settler there, what may his conditions be, etc.———— Further, so far as it may be consistent with thy business and safe for thy self, I want inquiry made for people of color to go to Africa, free people of good known character.

I wish thee a safe voyage, a prosperous return with happy sight to thy friends.

PAUL CUFFE

Watch Word

By experience I have ever found when I attended to my business I seldom suffered loss. I have ever found it to be good to make choice of good companions. I have ever found it not to be profitable for me to sit long after dining & make a steady habit of wine and other liquors. These very people who adopt those practices, when they see a sober steady man, they will put business in his way. The surest way to conquer strong drink is to make no use of it. We are born to die and must die.

Amen   PC

———————————

Westport 19 December 1816

DEAR FRIEND WILLIAM ALLEN

Thy long silence and my necessity returns my attention to inform thee that I received a letter from John T. Barry, dated 20

July, acknowledging the receipt of a bill of £200. Since which I have drawn on thee in favor of Wm. Rotch, Jr., for £140, which I have no doubt thee will honor.

Duncan Campbell is one of the members of our Friendly Society at Sierra Leone. Therefore have taken his promissory note, with only his pledging his honor that he would place the amount in thy hands in 8 months after date, as also did several others, (viz.) John Ledam; Morgan V.; Stephen Gabbidon[56] gave one for £164:6ˢ6ᵈ; Anthony and George Davis one for £77:7ˢ9ᵈ payable the first of the 10th mo to be placed in thy hands so that I may draw on thee for the amount by the 1st of the 10 mo last past. Also left with J. wife for sale and remittance 15 boxes sperm candles, £77:45ˢ:00; 8 barrels of pitch at 50/pr bbl, £20:0:00. I shall not draw until I have received advice from thee. Should they be so honest as to remit the amount to thee according to the time agreed to, I hope thee will place the money so that I can receive usury [interest] until [I] drew. For ere these reaches thee, I hope the above may be all remitted in thy care.

I here enclose the Governor's letter which may show my probable expectations of being repaid for the supplies that I furnished the settlers that I carried out. Their bill was made out for one year, but I furnished with £159:08ˢ:3ᵈ or $703.96. Could I be favored to receive the above statement, it would be relief to me at this time.

My dear friend bear with me in making few more remarks. I was at very considerable expense in furnishing the settlers on the voyage out to Africa, & all the aid I had rendered to me was only $120 for the 6 families from Boston. My insurance was $480; my returned cargo of camwood lieth in New York unsold at this time. Portage bill was about $1,000. From these statements, which I think are correct, thee may think would be very acceptable, I here enclose a statement of my outstanding debt at Sierra Leone, and wish thee to inform them that it was expected they would meet

---

[56] Stephen Gabbidon was a young and ambitious Jamaican Maroon. He had a burning ambition to achieve success in business and politics, and to a degree succeeded in both. Gabbidon became one of Sierra Leone's leading importers (often placing orders in London for goods worth £2000 or more), and in 1822 the governor appointed him Freetown's sheriff.

their contracts. I likewise enclose the count current between me and the Sierra Leone Friendly Society in order wherein that thee may see wherein they object in paying me the balance. The reason I have stated heretofore. I consider my demand to be just. However, if they feel obstinate, I shall give up my claim rather than to proceed in a hostile way.

The last account I received from the new settlers in Sierra Leone there were 3 deaths among them, (viz.) a man, woman & child, and I was informed by the same that they had received 13 of the African natives in membership with them who came forth by way of baptism. I feel anxious to keep open a correspondence with that country.

The Institution[s][57] that hath been formed in America among the African race are not so living or so lively as I could wish, either for want of spirit or propriety. I much regret that the British Government cannot be prevailed with to grant the foreign Africans free trade at Sierra Leone. I have thought good would grow out of it. I have thought rather than the little seed that hath been planted at Sierra Leone should perish, I, if favored with life, would consent to bestock some further labor. If the way cannot be opened from the United States, and it was thought best, I would come to England the next season, and join with the body there. I had no wish to leave my family.

If it is recommended to one to see England, would it be best for me to come in my own vessel? If so, what cargo could I bring that would pay its way? I have only some of my weak ideas, and shall submit the whole to your superior judgement.

I am thy assured friend

PAUL CUFFE

PS

It is general time of health in our part of the globe. Our much esteemed friend Wm. Rotch and family are all well, as age doth permit of. We have experienced a very cold summer past; we had frost every month in the summer; on the 25 of September we had 3

[57] Cuffe is referring to the African Institutions he helped establish in Philadelphia, New York and Baltimore when he returned from his first voyage to Sierra Leone.

frosts, very hard frost following after one other which killed almost every green vegetable. Our Indian corn was much injured; many fields was not harvested, but rotted on the stalk. I think it may be stated at not more than half crop. And hay came in about the same proportion; our wheat, barley, oats, etc., come in good. But I believe if we use little good economy we shall have enough to carry us through.

My wife united with me in love to thee & wife

PAUL CUFFE

I desire to be remembered to Cornelius[58] as well as all inquiring friends, and I hope he continues sturdy.

Westport 26 December 1816

DEAR COUSIN THOMAS WAINER

Thine of the 18th pr post & ye 25 by Michael come safe; found us all in health, for which I desire to be thankful. As to thy things, there was no lead to be found, & but one sheet of copper. As to the wagon, Michael thought she had better not be sold. They said rigging heard no market at present. J. Cory[59] has had some of thy blocks, deadeyes, etc. The old scow layed where the high winds and tides carried her. Thy canoe is unsold and is unsaleable. As to thy boxes of glass, they are in my store, but it is very unsaleable time to sell them now as all such articles are very low. I shall attend to the sale of the scow the first opportunity, as also the canoe. But in the case thee wishes to have all things sold, give positive order & I will vender thy things. I hope we all may put our trust in kind Providence, & I believe we shall be provided for. Our crops are cut very short here, particular hay & corn.

All that I could get in Sierra Leone for thee was a letter [of credit] and one brass compass which is worth $8. I am always glad to have good friends, and the way to keep them is not to have [to depend] too much on them for living. I know the seasons has

---

[58] Cornelius Hanbury. See footnote 7, p. 91.
[59] J. Cory was a white New Bedford merchant who over the years engaged in a number of joint commercial ventures with Paul Cuffe.

been hard, yet it appears that country, although we have had so much of its fertility set forth, hath not furnished thy family with the supplies of life. Without living on thy money when thy money is gone, thy family large, & thee growing old, what is to be done in such a case? See to this before it is too late: Look about thyself, awake to industry, deal honestly, live frugally, & limit, rather, prohibit thyself from all unnecessary expenses.

I am a member of the society that are combined for the purpose of discouraging intemperance. Therefore, I take the liberty of inquiring of thee whether thou makes use of intoxicating liquoring? So, my candid advice to thee is to take up a firm resolution & leave off making of any kind of use of it unless for sickness. Confine thyself at home, understanding all business must be attended to, but don't go after strange flesh. Love, merely walk humbly, and fear God. Observe the above advice & I believe thee will get [a]long well & be comfortable here and be happy hereafter.

I do not think that thee will get enough to pay thee for going to Sierra Leone unless thee carry something to trade with to get something. Thy Uncle John situation are no more favorable at this time than when thee went away, & as to Buffington account, I cannot see but for want thereof, thee must take thee body. If thee should think it best to return with thy family, our doors nor hearts are not shut against you but should be glad to see you, if it is best for you to return again.

Dear cousin bear with me: we should rejoice with you unspeakable if we could have the evidence of truth that thee had meet with a change from Nature to grace. I believe when a true reformation takes place in each of our hearts we could all rejoice together and sing praises to the Most High. When thy conscience checks thee, thee in that case has no occasion than to ask whether it is right to proceed, for thy conscience has smote thee. Thus, my dear cousin, thou has my advice freely & fully agreeable to the tenor of thy letter, & I hope thee will not take it unkind. These are the sentiments of thy aged uncle who are fast facing toward the grave, one who wishes well to thee & I

sincerely hope to all mankind,

PAUL CUFFE

[The following is printed.]

TO THE
HONORABLE THE LEGISLATURE OF NEW JERSEY

The memorial and Petition of the subscribers, inhabitants of New Jersey, showeth: That they have viewed with great interest and concern the present condition and future prospects of the free people of color in this and our sister states. While the love of liberty, and the feeling of humanity have produced the emancipation of a great number of these people, and are gradually effecting the freedom of the rest; it is with much regret that your Petitioners observe the degraded situation in which those who have been freed from slavery remain; and from a variety of considerations will probably remain while they continue among the whites.

To enable them to rise to that condition to which they are entitled by the laws of God and nature, it appears desirable, and even necessary, to separate them from their former masters, and place them in some favorable situation by themselves, perhaps in Africa, the land of their fathers. It is therefore respectfully requested of the legislature to instruct by resolution or otherwise, the Senators and Representatives from the State of New Jersey, to lay before the Congress at their next meeting, as a subject of consideration, the expediency of forming a colony on the coast of Africa, or elsewhere, where such of the people of color as are now free, or may hereafter set free, may with their own consent be removed: And your petitioners will, as in duty bound, ever pray.

[The following is in longhand.]

To Capt. Paul Cuffee [sic]

Laboring with many others in the cause of the people of color in the United States and particularly at present in the cause of those who are now free, I desire for myself and others every information on subjects which are or may be hereafter connected with their happiness. Affected with their unhappy situation even after they have been set free, and fearing that their situation may become more and more degraded, most thinking persons are beginning to turn their thoughts to the subject contained in the petition and memorial contained in this paper. Many indulge a hope that could the more virtuous and industrious of our free people of color be removed to the coast of Africa, with their own consent, to carry with them their arts, their industry, and above all, their knowledge of Christianity and the fear of God, great and lasting benefits would arise to the people who might remove thither and to *Africa itself*. Knowing that you have been at Sierra Leona and must be well acquainted with the state and prospects of the colony, we beg of you such information as you may be able to give on the following points and heads—

1. What is the present population of the settlement at Sierra Leona, and what its prospects of happiness and growth
2. What is the nature of the soil and what the advantages for settlement on the coast of Africa from Sierra Leona to the equator
3. Are there any navigable rivers in the country called Guinea, or any positions where a good harbor might be formed along that coast
4. In the region above alluded to, are there any European regular settlements, or does it contain any slave factories
5. Whether in your opinion is there any other situation in Africa where the contemplated settlement or settlements could be formed with greater advantage than in the district mentioned above. The great desire of those whose minds are impressed with this subject

is to give an opportunity to the free people of color to rise to their proper level, and at the same time to provide a powerful means of putting an end to the slave trade, and sending civilization and Christianity to Africa. My residence is at Basking Ridge, New Jersey, but I am now at this place in behalf of friends attending to the subject in a small degree. You will oblige the cause of humanity as well as myself by paying as early and as full attention as possible to this subject. I expect not to be here longer than the twenty-eight of this month, and therefore should any circumstance prevent your answering so as to reach this place by that time, you will please to write to me at my own residence.

Direct here to Robert Finley, at Elias B. Coldwell

Yours

ROBERT FINLEY[60]

Washington City
December 5, 1816

City of Washington, December 26, 1816

CAPT. PAUL CUFFE, SIR, I send on to you a paper containing an account of a late meeting held in this city for the purpose of considering the expediency of attempting to *colonize more or less of the free people of color*[61] now in the United States. You will learn from the paper that the prospect is in favor that something will soon be done in this way.

I believe that a gentleman of this city has written to you[62] for information of which you are possessed with respect to the west coast of Africa. If you have discovered in any of your voyages to Africa a proper place for a colony or for the commencement of such an establishment, be so good as to communicate the information speedily. Any information you can give to aid the contemplated plan will be gladly received.

I should not be surprised if the general government during this present session were to direct a vessel to be dispatched with the proper persons to the coast of Africa for the purpose of making discoveries. When would be the proper season for entering on such a voyage? How long would the vessel probably be absent from this country? Should such an effort be made, most likely the vessel would sail to England on her way out.

[60] The Reverend Robert Finley of Basking Ridge, New Jersey, was the driving force behind the formation of the American Colonization Society in 1817. It was Finley and his pamphlet, *Thoughts On Colonization,* that led to the founding of the Society in Washington. A dynamic Presbyterian clergyman, well connected by marriage, Finley believed that Negroes could not achieve self-realization in a mixed society. Negroes were capable of great accomplishments, but only in an all-black land. Hence, according to Finley, mass emigration to Africa was essential both for the black and the white race.

[61] Italics in the original manuscript.

[62] Robert Finley. See his letter of December 5, 1816.

I hope you will immediately communicate whatever facts you may be possessed of which you think would aid the contemplated plan. Should you write to me, direct [the letter] to this place.

I send on at this time a small pamphlet[63] on the subject of colonizing free people of color.

> I am your friend
> SAML. J. MILLS

If the General Government were to request you to go out for the purpose of exploring in your own vessel would [you] engage in this service, if offered proper support?

Westport 6 January 1817

RESPECTED FRIEND SAMUEL J. MILLS

Thine of the 26 ult. I have received with the paper of the day, but the pamphlet spoken of in the later part of thy letter I did not receive. The other letter spoken of in thine was so directed that I received thine first.

I observe from the paper, the ardent engagement of the body of that meeting. I hope they will be guided by wisdom's best means. The cause I believe to be good, but the amount of the object is so large that I have not been able to enumerate the amount thereof. But as far as my weak abilities would admit of, I have endeavored to make use of a unit, thinking that to be a place for me to enter any in the great object in contemplation, and to advance as wisdom points out the way. But when many obstructions was thrown in the way by government as well as individuals, I was almost brought to a halt, and to say, can I be right?

But the subject has so lived with me that I last month wrote to William Allen, one of the members of the Royal African Institution in London, on the subject. I also sent him a pamphlet of the establishment that I received from your establishment in New York, etc.

The population of Sierra Leone 1811 was about 2000 and

63 Robert Finley's *Thoughts On Colonization* (Washington, 1816).

about 1000 of the suburbs. Since that time they have not been numbered, but the colony according to my judgement from 1811 to 1815 had much improved. The soil for cultivation in the Colony of Sierra Leone are not flattering, but very advantageously situated for a town, and ship navigation.

The course of Africa abounds with rivers. The great river Gambia, according to the best information given to me, are extreme fertile, as also the island Buno[64] at the mouth of this river. But they are said to be some sickly to the northern constitution. There is a river about 50 leagues south of Cape Sierra Leone called Shaboro [Sherbro], good navigation and soil very fertile according to information given to me by a citizen of Sierra Leone. The man has ever been extreme earnest that a settlement should be established at that place, with those people that may come from America. He is a man of good character, not so much given to liquor as the general run of that people.

These may do for small settlement or small beginning, but were there a willingness for a pretty general removal of this people, and the south part of Africa (viz.), the Cape of Good Hope, if it could be obtained, I think it looks most favorable. However, I only mention the subject and leave all to the judgement of my superiors. There is the great river course which layeth near the equator, and its power propellation and fertility of the land, I hope will not always be neglected.

I must approve of a vessel being sent as thou hast mentioned. Should one be sent, I take the liberty of naming Peter Williams, Jr., Secretary to the African Institution in New York, to be in my opinion to be a suitable man to make one of the number for such a plan. There is a similar institution established in Philadelphia,

[64] The mouth of the Gambia River is located some four hundred miles north of Freetown. Englishmen were attracted to the area as early as the 1770's. In the 1780's a few humanitarian utopians urged the English government to establish convict colonies along the Gambia now that the American colonies were no longer open for the dumping of English criminals. A few such colonies were attempted, but most met with complete failure. Nevertheless, the Gambia River continued to intrigue British Africanists. They saw the region as one of unusual fertility, and the Gambia River as one of the principal arteries for penetration into the African interior and its fabled wealth. For further information, see Philip D. Curtin, *The Image of Africa*, pp. 89–95.

James Forten is the Corresponding Secretary. I wish these institutions to be brought as much into action as would be best. By that means the colored population of these large cities would be more awakened than from an individual & a stranger, and thereby be prevailed on for their own good, etc.

I observe what I have experienced. 1815 I carried out to Africa 9 families, containing 38 in number, and 1816 I have had so many applications for taking more that I believe I could have had the greater part out of Boston. I should think if a vessel were to arrive on the coast about Christmas would be a good season, as the dry season at that time have commenced, which is generally preferred. As to the length of the voyage, it would depend on the extent of the discoveries. I think from 12 to 18 months, more, especially, if the voyage were to extend as far as the Cape[65] and the Tristan Islands.[66]

My vessel at this time is about to sail for North Carolina and from there to St. Domingo. Is expected to return in ye 6th mo. I have not calculated on going out myself (not for a certainty), but all my voyages I hope may be in behalf of forwarding the great cause of contemplation. It will be a consolation to my mind, to be made use of in any way, which may forward the plan, so far as is advisable by my friends.

I am thy assured friend

PAUL CUFFE

Westport 8 January 1817

ESTEEMED FRIEND JAMES FORTEN

I desire to be thankful for the privilege of informing thee of our being generally in health, hoping these may meet with thee & thine enjoying the same blessing, for which I desire ever to be trust thankful unto the Father of all our Mercies.

[65] The Cape of Good Hope.
[66] The Tristan da Cunha Islands are a group of volcanic islands in the South Atlantic approximately 1,500 miles due west of the Cape of Good Hope. The islands were a British possession.

I have lately received a letter from a gentleman in the city of Washington[67] announcing to me the concern that rests at the seat of government for the welfare of the people of color. They mention to me whether I will join them in going to England and Africa to seek a place where the people of color might be colonized. With a number of propositions & question I have answered him thereto, informing [him] at the same time of the African Institution in Philadelphia, New York, etc., in order that a correspondence might be opened with them in which they may become useful to their fellow citizens.

Give my love to the members of the African Institution and tell them I wish them a joyful New Year, hoping they have all their energies renewedly engaged to celebrate the year in behalf of the African race and to the honor and glory of God, Amen.

Paul Wainer & owners of the sloop *Resolution* have requested me to inform thee that they are bound to North Carolina and are so short of funds that it is very inconvenient for them to pay thee for their mainsail according to expectation; but were willing to allow interest, and I will pledge my word for the payment of the debt. Should the money be wanted immediately, please to inform me, and the amount shall be forwarded by thy assured friend.

PAUL CUFFE

PS

Give my love to Charlotte & the children & tell them I often see them in a contemplate view. Dear James thou art often the companion of my mind. In much love I subscribe myself your affectionate and ever well-wishing friend.

PAUL CUFFE

Westport 8 January 1817

RESPECTED FRIEND ROBERT FINLEY

Thine of the 5th of December I have duly received, but not in time to answer thee at Washington.

[67] See Robert Finley's December 5, 1816, letter to Cuffe, pp. 231–33.

I observe from the printed petition[68] in thy letter the great and laborious task you are engaged in, and my desires are that you may be guided by wisdom's best means. I stand as it were in a low place, and am not able to see far; but blessed be God who hath created all things, and for His own Glory they are & were created. He is able to make use of instruments in such a way as He pleases, and may I be resigned to His holy Will.

The population of Sierra Leone[69] 1811 was about 2,000 and about a 1,000 [lived in the] suburbs, etc. Since that time they have not been numbered, but I think the colony from 1811 to 1815 hath much improved. They are entitled to every privilege of free-born citizens, and fill stations in their courts. The soil in the colony of Sierra Leone for cultivation are not flattering, but are very advantageously situated for a town and a good ship harbor.

The course of Africa abounds with rivers. The great river Gambia lieth about 350 miles N.W. of Sierra Leone. I have had the river of Sherbro much recommended by John Cowell, a citizen of Sierra Leone.

These may be for small beginnings, but were there a willingness for a pretty general removal of the people of color, and the South part of Africa (viz.) the Cape of Good Hope, could be obtained, I think it looks most favorable. There are the great river Congo which lieth near the Equator. It is said she has very extensive population, and land fertile.

If there were a spot fixed on the coast of Africa, and another in the United States of America, would it not answer the best purpose to draw off the colored citizen? I think it would be a good plan that a vessel and suitable persons [be commissioned] to discover what place would be most advantageous to colonize these people.

Answer to thy 4th question: Sierra Leone are (as far as I have been informed) the only British colony on the coast of Africa. There are many trade factories on the coast. In our ardent labors for the liberation of the African race, I hope we may not be unmindful to make use of every wise and prudent means to more effectually put a stop to the citizens of the United States being concerned in carrying the slave trade—either by requesting the

[68] See p. 231.
[69] Cuffe means Freetown proper.

Governor at Sierra Leone to obtain our citizens and deliver them to our Government, as prisoners taken in a clandestine trade, or furnish our Government with such evidences or vouchers as would enable her to provide against them, agreeable to the tenor of the law of the United States. [The remainder of the letter is missing].

Westport 16 January 1817

ESTEEMED FRIEND JAMY BRINE [JAMES BRIAN][70]

Rest assured that my long silence of not giving thee a short history of my late voyage to Africa was not for want of love and good will: I have to toil for the support of my family & have many applications of inquiry which requires immediate answer. And I being no scholar, all causes me to employ many a hour when sleep would be comfortable to my body. Yet I wish to attend to my duty without murmuring.

I arrived at Sierra Leone after a passage of 56 days, 38 passengers all in good health. A canoe was sent to me in the offer from a merchant: what brig is this? where from? where bound to? and what cargo? I answered him with few lines to the governor for his permission to anchor. The wind and tide being in, we were soon in and was boarded by the Custom House boat. He informed [me] no American was permitted to anchor in their waters, but he would permit me to anchor until 9 o'clock next morning.

It being 7 Day towards sunset, I directed the vessel to stand off, & repaired on shore. It being 7 Day evening, the governor was gone to his country seat, but when I returned on board I found the governor's permission to anchor. I was much disappointed in not having no license from the British government. The governor told me he was willing to give me every indulgence, but could not give me anything that would secure me from a seizure of a man-of-war which he looked for every day. However, I lay 2 months & 1 day. No men-of-war arrived, & I received no injury.

---

[70] James Brian was a Wilmington, Delaware, Quaker merchant. A longtime Cuffe business associate, Brian was also most interested in Negro emigration.

My settlers, in viewing the shore from the vessel, & towards evening, appeared to be dissatisfied; but on landing the next morning and going to Meeting, they expressed great satisfaction. Until few days previous to my leaving them the port, I was in at one of their houses, when the man appeared to be murmuring. On inquiry I found that he had a summons to attend the Court as one of the Grand Jury. I told him it appeared he was dissatisfied at not being equal; & with being equal, go & do as well as he knew, would be all as was required of him. They had each family a town lot & 50 acres of land to farm on 2 miles from town. Since I left I received letters from them informing of the death of one man and woman & one child, & that they had received 13 of the natives into their order by way of ordinance of baptism.

The Little Society, when I first visited Africa called the Friendly Society, still exist. When they open a correspondence with the London African Institution, Wm. [Allen] remitted, rather, advance them a small sum of £70 Sterling. And by their careful conduct, by making shipment, the Society had made themselves worth £1200 Sterling, and at [the] time [I left, were] erecting a factory at the head of navigation in that river, which I conceive would be very advantageous to themselves & a good step to bring the native in friendly connection with the colony. As they [the natives] may get supplies from the factories without calling on the slave ships, but not to deal in slaves, but to discourse, [this contact may] discourage that traffic and make them self-respectable among their fellow citizens, the Europeans, so as to overcome and do away [with] that prejudice that has so long prevailed in the world.

I received letters whilst at Sierra Leone to return by way of London, and there to join them [the African Institution] in the improvements of Africa by way of Sierra Leone. But I considered that part of the great family of Africa [that] was in our region and ought not to be neglected. I since have had a number of propositions from different characters whether anything could be done. I answer nothing; nothing of much amount can be effected by an individual or private bodies, until the government removes the obstruction which hath hitherto been thrown in the way.

I observe from the national intelligence that the cause of the people of color have very weighty concerned many of the eminent weighty characters near to the seat of government. And [this concern] it is to be hoped may find its way to the general government. I learn by a pamphlet sent me from New York that thee in grand society hath established a school there for the purpose for instructing the African youths in order that they may be prepared for teacher & preacher to their own nation. I thought that was saying great deal, but if any good may be done let no obstructions take place. For they that are not against are on our side.

It is in contemplation of colonizing the free blacks [that] Africa has been suggested, and a colony in the United States has also been spoken of, but I have taken the liberty to propose two colonies: one in Africa and another in the United States, as it is not at all likely all may be prevailed on to emigrate to Africa. But before we wreck our understanding too much, liberate those already in bondage.

Would it not be wise in our government to endeavor more effectually to abolish the existing slave trade by directing the government at Sierra Leone to furnish the government of the United States with such evidences as would enable her to deal with her citizens as the law points out? Or, to detain the American citizens when taken in slave vessels trading contrary to law of the United States, and send them home criminals, to be tried by their own government laws, etc.

However, I wish not to say more than becomes me; neither do I wish for my zeal to lead me before wisdom['s] best guide. I observed in the papers when I arrived from Africa a schooner upset at sea and had seventeen lost & six of the crew taken up by a vessel from B. [Bahama] Island bound to the West Indies. One who was saved was stated in the paper belong to Taunton, Mass. This schooner sailed from Sierra Leone whilst I was there. The night before she sailed, 2 African girls kidnapped was discovered by another. Alarm was made. The Governor sent a file of soldiers on board, detain[ing] her until next morning. A search was made; no discovery; she was let go. But the girls was not found whilst I stayed, which was several weeks.

PAUL CUFFE

Westport 16 January 1817

ESTEEMED FRIEND WM. GIBBONS

Although I am not perfectly acquainted with thee, yet thy language are familiar and thy engagements sincere; my spirit feels to travel with such engaged minds.

In 1811 the number of the colony were about 2,000. 1816 the number was estimated to be about 3,000. There are about 20 Europeans, exclusive of the castle,[71] who acts as managers of the colony, & some few as merchants. These few Europeans hath pretty much the control of the colony. Yet the people of color are entitled to every privilege of a free-born subjects. They sit in their courts as jurors, 10 to 2 Europeans. They act as constable and sheriffs. Yet it cannot be said that they are equal, for the prejudice of tradition is perceptible. But I believe much lieth at their door. When they become capable of self government, much of this evil will be overcome.

There appears a good understanding to exist between the colonist and the natives. The natives visit the colony pretty much every day with their canoes brimming [with] cattle, sheep, hogs, fowl, rice, ivory, & all kinds of the fruit of their land. Thou may have observed that of 90 of the African children had had the ordinance of baptism administered to them, but I have been informed since I left Sierra Leone that 18 of the native Africans came forward and received the ordinance of baptism. The professed society are the Church of England, the Baptist, the Methodist, and interceding their devotions, and strictly attended to. But all their ceremonies it doth not have the happy effect so as to make them a moral people.

The slumbering world seemeth awakened, and making many inquiries where the people of color may be colonized were a general manumission to take place. As it [is] unlikely that all will be prevailed on to remove to Africa, suppose they were to establish the colony in Africa & another in America to colonize the people of color?

All new settlements has much to encounter with. Sierra Leone

71 English soldiers garrisoned in a fort in Freetown for the protection of the colony.

has meet with many disaster. She has been twice seriously attacked by the natives. Great destruction once by the French; and insurrections with herself; her store ships once caught on fire & burned up with all the colony's [food]; but after all this disasters, I think it may be said she is gaining ground.

I am thy assured friend

PAUL CUFFE

Philad. January 25th 1817

ESTEEMED FRIEND [PAUL CUFFE]

Permit me to inform you that I received your friendly letter by post informing me of you and [your] family['s] good state of health through the blessing of Divine Providence.

In my last letter to you I mention my intention of writing you again very shortly on account of Anthony Servance's property, the sale of which I expected would have taken place in the course of a day or two. But to our utter disappointment we could not get a single bid for it. Indeed, I am very much afraid that the ground rent[72] will eat up the whole of the property. The amount in May next will be 170 dollars. We have had but one offer for it, and that was 50 dollars clear of all encumbrances, and I believe we shall be forced to take it, which, I am very sorry, will come far short of the claim you have against him.

The African Institution met at the Rev. R[ichard] Allen's[73] the very night your letter came to hand. I read that part to them that wished them a happy New Year, for which they desired me to return you many thanks. I must now mention to you that the whole

---

[72] Warehouse charges.

[73] Richard Allen was a prominent Philadelphia Negro. Active in a number of Negro amelioration projects, this one-time slave established the Philadelphia Bethel Church in 1794. Five years later Bishop Francis Asbury of the Methodist Church ordained Allen as a deacon. Later on he became an elder in the church. By the turn of the century Allen's church became known as the Bethel African Methodist Episcopal Church (the A.M.E.) and branches were started throughout the Northeastern states. When the branches united in one organization in 1816 as the African Methodist Episcopal Church, Allen's creation became the leading Negro Methodist group in the United States.

continent seems to be agitated concerning the colonizing the people of color. You mention to me in your letter that a gentleman from Washington had written to you on the subject for your opinion. I suppose it must have been the Rev. Robert Finley from the state of New Jersey. He convened us together the other night at the Rev. A[bsalom] Jones on this interesting subject. He mentioned his intention of writing you.

Indeed, the people of color here was very much frightened. At first they were afraid that all the free people would be compelled to go, particularly [those] in the southern states. We had a large meeting of males at the Rev. R. Allen's church the other evening. Three thousand at least attended, and there was not one soul that was in favor of going to Africa. They think that the slaveholders wants to get rid of them so as to make their property more secure.

However, it appears to me that if the Father of all Mercies is in this interesting subject (for it appeared that they all think that something must and ought to be done, but do not know where nor how to begin), the way will be made straight and clear. We, however, have agreed to remain silent, as the people here, both white and color, are decided against the measure. My opinion is that they will never become a people until they come out from amongst the white people. But as the majority is decidedly against me, I am determined to remain silent,[74] except as to my opinion which I freely give when asked.

I must now inform you of an imposter which is going the rounds of this state calling himself John Cuffe, and said he is your son. He was taken up in York County, Pennsylvania, and lodged in jail, from which he wrote John James begging him to send a description of him so that he might be liberated. I have got the letter before me. John James brought the letter to me so that I might write you. He desires to be kindly remembered with all his family to you. I was intending to have given you some extracts from the letter, but having come across a publication of him in full I will enclose it to

[74] Forten did remain silent, indeed. He was so discreet in not revealing his inner feelings toward Negro relocation that until recently historians were convinced that this most important Negro leader consistently opposed emigration. Forten subsequently did lose interest in emigration, but his disillusionment came long after Cuffe's death and the abortive failure of the Sierra Leone experiment. See also discussion on pp. 67–69.

you. The signature of the letter is John Cuffe, son of the old & esteemed Capt'n Cuffe. We know you had no son of that name.

You will please give my love to your nephews and tell them any arrangements you make will be satisfactory to me. Charlotte has been very ill with the sore throat, but thank to God she has quite recovered, but longs to see you all. [She] thought during her indisposition [that] could she but have seen you, it would have made her well. All the family join me in love to you all.

I remain very affectionately yours unalterably

JAMES FORTEN

I shall be glad to hear from you very shortly and your opinion of the colony.

[Newspaper clipping]   *York, Penn. Jan. 16 [1817]*

PAUL CUFFE—An African, pretending to be the son of the celebrated Paul Cuffe, came here about 8 or 10 days ago. He was received as Paul Cuffe, in this place, and entertained by members of the society of friends. He said, he was on his way to Congress, for the purpose of soliciting aid in a project he had on foot, to colonize Sierra Leon, or the Lion Country, on the west coast of Africa, and had been the first man that put a yoke on a pair of oxen in Sierra Leon.

He tarried in this place several days, and though he is an artful fellow, he told in the course of conversation upon the Sierra Leon project, some inconsistent stories. He said, for instance; that he would lay a memorial before Congress embracing a view of his Sierra business. One of the friends advised him to have a sufficient number of copies to supply all the members. This he said was already done and he had them along with him. On being pressed to show one of them, he could not make it appear that he told a strait story. This gave rise to suspicion that he was not a REAL Cuffe of the Cape Cod breed. He proceeded from this place to Baltimore—letters were sent from here giving intelligence of the suspiciousness of his character.

The letters were read to him at Baltimore, upon which, he came back to this place to clear up his character. He appears not to have done it to the satisfaction of the friends here, as they took him before a magistrate and had him committed to the care of Robert Wilson. On his examination it appeared that he could neither read nor write but at the same time exhibited proof of a keenness of intellect seldom met with in persons of his colour. The real celebrated Paul Cuffe resides in the state of Massachusetts in the vicinity of Cape Cod, or entrance of Boston Bay.

Westport, 23 January 1817

Respected Friend James Forten

It's rather out of necessity, than vice or virtue, that constrains me at present thus to address thee, but I long in love.

Some few months ago a colored man came to New Bedford, called on my son-in-law, saying that he was Richard Allen's son in Philadelphia, and was a minister of the gospel, and was recommended to him by his father-in-law Paul Cuffe, and his name was R. Holston Allen. He even went into the pulpit with the minister, and had settings with the colored people. But I am sorry to say from constraint that he was a great scoundrel, and his name varied as but suited his calling. He lastly went by the name of Samuel Bailey.

He left New Bedford, went to Boston, and with false letters of recommendation from William Rotch, Jr., sometime stating to be brother-in-law to P. Cuffe and lived in New York. He succeeded in getting $900 worth of goods packed and ordered for New York. The merchant was thoughtful enough to write to Wm. Rotch, and [thus] saved his goods.

The villain by this time arrived [once more] in the neighborhood of New Bedford. Wm. Rotch took him, but he made his escape from the officer. He next appeared in New York with false letters of credit to the amount of $10,000. He was had before the authorities and acquitted on condition of his leaving the state immediately.

He went to Albany, got into the employ of Ira Potter, stayed nearly one month, got a suit of plain clothes. [He] stole notes here valued at $200. He arrived at York in Pennsylvania. There he was Paul Cuffe going to Congress. After staying at Joseph Jessup three nights and two days, attended first day's Meeting, Joseph grew suspicious of him. He rode off on the 11th instant.

Jesse Talbot of Baltimore wrote me a letter saying this hypocritical man was in Baltimore and there had really made use of my name, being bound to Congress with memorials of plans in civilizing Africa, etc. Jesse Talbot being an acquaintance of mine, on hearing this rumor, sends for the man, and after awhile he came. And on examination he was P. Cuffe, Jr., and then was a son-in-law to P. Cuffe. So his twist show him to be a villain, and a great one.

I have written to them at Baltimore, and I hope by the time this reaches thee that he may be other ways employed. Should he make his appearance in Philadelphia, please to stop his mad dream. I hope all my friends will be very cautious of such imposters. Thus thou hast the unpleasant short history of the villain as far as I have any knowledge.

NB Beware of wolves in sheeps clothing are the advice of thy affectionate and ever well-wishing friend

PAUL CUFFE

Give my love to my old friend John James and all inquiring friends, and accept it thyself and [your] wife.

I am about sending the *Traveller* to St. Domingo to George Christopher, and think I shall send him a plow.

Please to inform Samuel R. Fisher and such other of my friends as thee thinks well of [of the false Paul Cuffe] in order to put a full stop to his mad dream.

Westport 28 February 1817

ESTEEMED FRIEND SAMUEL R. FISHER[75]

Having a convenient opportunity to write thee by my neighbor Prince Wing, he accompany Amos Pease of Vermont on a reli-

[75] See footnote 52, p. 216.

gious visit. Remembering the kindness, care and attention of thee and thy house, I believe I may say I was a stranger, & ye took me in, naked, and ye clothed me, imprisoned, and ye ministered unto me, etc. (I am sensible of what I have wrote). I hope these may meet thee and thine in perfect health.

My wife hath been confined to the house through the cold season of the year. About 4 weeks ago I was seized with a very ill-turn. I was taken at 4 o'clock, and at 12 o'clock at night I was relieved. The symptoms are past describing, only it was as much as human nature was capable of enduring. But kind Providence hath returned me to my usual health. May I be truly humbled for my preservation. May we often call to remembrance that we have no certain continuing city here, but above all things may we seek one to come whose builder is God: that when we put off this body of mortality we may be clothed with the spirit of immortality: that we may be prepared and favored to experience that glorious Resurrection with our Lord and Savior Jesus Christ. In the bonds of love and friendship, of everlasting peace, farewell saith my soul.

PAUL CUFFE

Dear Friend I feel freedom to inform thee that the subject that hath claimed the attention of so many of the citizens of the United States, that of becoming advocates for the improvement of the degraded situation of the African race, hath not vanished, nor, I hope, in any wise diminished in the view of my mind. But on the account of the government's impeding the way, and my funds being small, it render me incapable of doing any further at present than to keep up a correspondence with those engaged in that service, (which) they have become very numerous.

The Presbyterian Synod hath established a society at New York–New Jersey for educating the African race in order, they say, to make teacher and preacher of their own race. If they can do anything that good may grow out of it, Amen to it. I have received letters from some at Washington by which it appears that they are at work at the seat of government. I further perceive that the African Institution in Philadelphia seems to be alarmed at the movements of the time, but my desire to these are to be quiet and trust in God. If we, the African race, are faithful I believe that God will not be wanting on his part.

Give my kind love to thy wife & children, to Josephy Clark & all inquiring friends. Tell thy wife the overshoes that she got for me have become so comfortable that I cannot well do without them. I have them shod with leather and make great use of them.

I am thy assured and ever well-wishing friend

PAUL CUFFE

Westport 1 March 1817

DEAR FRIEND JAMES FORTEN

Thine of the 25th of January I received, together with the account of that false Paul Cuffe. He had the impertinence to write to me, after he was put in prison, as my son John Cuffe. I answered his letter to let him know that I knew nothing of him, but hoped that he might not be permitted to go out again to deceive the nations until the thousand years should expire. I have heard nothing from him since.

Anthony Survance property are coming in light to what was expected. However we must take what we can get. I was glad to be informed that the African Institution were in spirit of assembling themselves together, although they seemed to be little alarmed at the movement of being colonized in a free state. Don't be uneasy, but be quiet and trust in God who hath done all things well.

I have been asked the question again & again concerning colonizing the free people of color, but it is quite useless to give thee my opinion on the subject when works speaks louder than words. As I have been engaged in that service, I have pointed out the Cape of Good Hope. However, I should rather prefer of a voyage to that part or place where it should be recommended for that purpose. However, it certainly would be best to obtain a peaceable and quiet possession in whatever part of the globe we might pitch. I have suggested of settling 2 colonies, 1 in the United States and the other in Africa.

If the free people of color would exert themselves more & more in industry and honesty it would be a great help towards the liberating those who still remain in bondage. May the Father of all Mercies and the God of Peace to influence the hearts of the sons and daughters of the race of Africa that they may stretch forth their arms to God and unite in celebrating His name with high praises of thanksgiving. That would be pleased to relieve them from the binding chain of slavery and lead them forth by the way that they may become the faithful followers of the true and living God.

My wife hath been confined to the house through the cold season of the year. About 4 weeks ago I was seized with a very severe turn, indeed. I was [away] from home. The attack lasted from 4 in the afternoon until 12 at night. I underwent as much [pain] as human nature was capable of enduring. May we be prepared for sudden death and the day of the Lord's visitation.

My wife & family unites with me in love to thee and thine through time, amen.

PAUL CUFFE

Philadelphia, March 4th 1817

ESTEEMED FRIEND [PAUL CUFFE]

I am induced to trouble you with these few lines, solely to inquire of you concerning a certain colored man, who calls himself Cuffe Johnson, and said that he had sailed with you when young, that he left you and shipped on board of a brig bound from Boston, to Charleston, called the *Swan,* Capt'n. Yeabe. The said Capt'n. Y. took him to [New] Orleans, and there sold him as a slave.

He appears to be about twenty years of age, and about five feet two or three inches in height, very black. I think by his dialect that he is an African by birth. He desired me to inform you that he had a mole or scar on his left breast, which he used to show you when he sailed for you, which was about twelve years ago. He further stated that his free papers was recorded in New Bedford.

Now sir, if you have any knowledge of such a person or boy sailing with you at any time, I will thank you to write me by the return post as he is with his master here at present, but we do not know how long he may continue here. I am certain if you can find out any of his friends you will. Charlotte and the children join me in love to you all.

I remain very affectionately yours

JAMES FORTEN

———————————

P.S. This comes in great haste.[76]

Washington City, March 12, 1817

My worthy friend, your letter 2nd mo 6th inst. has been received. I thank you for the information which it contains. I send on to you a pamphlet giving an account of exertions lately made to colonize free people of color. From the pamphlet you will learn the present state of affairs. The committee to whom the memorial of the Colonization Society was referred did not report until late in the session, and there was so much business before Congress that they did not get upon the report. The subject will no doubt be revived early the next session and will have a fair hearing.

I think on the whole it is fortunate that the discussion of this important question is deferred until the next session. It will give the friends of colonization efforts an opportunity to collect information and present facts calculated to aid their design. For the meantime the friends of Africa and our own country [can gather information] which has a favorable bearing on the general subject, and forward it to the Secretary of the Colonization [Society] residing in this city. Perhaps we can aid in the formation of auxiliary colonization societies in different places either among the whites or the people of color.

You will perceive by the report of the committee to whom the memorial was referred that they propose that Congress should request the Executive to apply to the English government for land to permit people of color to go to the Sierra Leone colony. What do you think would be the result if this application should be made in due form? In my opinion the English government would

[76] I was unable to locate Cuffe's reply, if he made one.

not admit people of color from the United States into their colony
without imposing some restrictions as to their numbers and you
should know how it was when Mr. King made the application at
the request of Mr. Jefferson. It is true the state of the colony has
since that time altered much for the better. But still I think that
comparatively but few could be accommodated at the colony.
Would the English admit a free trade with the colony?

A number of the Board of Managers of the Coln. Society think
that with the aid of President Monroe the enquiries suggested by
the committee may be answered during the present year. We can
address our ministers abroad on this subject and thus ascertain the
course to be pursued. So in this case the way would be prepared
for the next Congress to dispatch a vessel with the proper persons
to make discoveries and to fix upon the place for the colony. The
Board of Managers have thought of employing an agent to go to
Sierra Leone and perhaps to other places on the coast of Africa
this summer or fall. They wish for a more particular history of
Sierra Leone and for further information relative to the coast.
Should they send out an agent he would most likely go to England
in going out or returning. His object in going to England would be
in part to become acquainted with some of the members of the
African Institution and to obtain their reports and likewise to
excite an interest in the liberal public in that country in favor of
the object. What should you think of such a measure? Your two
voyages to Africa have been of great service in preparing the
public mind to an attempt to colonize your colored brethren and
probably much is depending on your future assistance with respect
to the success of efforts of this kind. I hope you will hold yourself
in a state of readiness to aid any great efforts which may hereafter
be made.

Whenever the subject of colonization shall be discovered by
Congress some will object that the free people of color will not go
to Africa again, that it will cost too much to transport them and to
afford them the necessary protection. Again it will be said that
many of these people are very useful and are wanted in this country. We should be prepared to meet objections as far as possible
and trust in God for the success of our efforts. We live in an
eventful day when great things are doing for the purpose of diffus-

ing knowledge and improving the condition of the poor and needy. In such a day as this we ought to expect great things and we ought to attempt great things. In your last letter you mention the Cape of Good Hope as being perhaps a good place for a colony. I doubt whether it could be obtained from the English without giving a very large sum. And much of the country is very poor around the settlement. Would not Sherbro answer better or some place further down the coast? But this point can be determined only by a better acquaintance with the coast.

I have stated some enquiries in my letter which I wish you to answer as far as you can. I will repeat the enquiries again and add a few more.

1. In what manner would a request from our government for liberty to send free people of color to Sierra Leone be received by the British government?
2. Should the request be granted, would these Americans have equal privileges to trade in the colony?
3. Should an effort be made to explore the West Coast of Africa to find a place for a colony? Now grant as some ought to be employed, would one vessel be sufficient and what number of men would be required?
4. As a preparatory step to foster greater exertions, would it be best to have an agent go to Africa and to England during the succeeding summer and return—or to either of these places?
5. How should we answer those who say that people of color will not go to Africa if a place is provided?
6. Would those persons who are ready to go to Sierra Leone be ready to aid in establishing a new colony in another place?
7. What was the expense of carrying out those persons who went to Africa with you and how was the expense defrayed?

Be so good as to add anything you think interesting.

I hope you will write to me soon. Direct your letter to this place. Your sincere friend

SAMUEL J. MILLS

I have obtained between 6 and 700 dollars for the African school. In the course of the post session [of Congress] I have become acquainted with Mr. Elisha Tyson[77] of Baltimore. He is much pleased with the exertions which have been lately made to colonize people of color as are the Friends generally.

Westport 8 July 1817

AUNT FREELOVE [CUFFE]

I improve this opportunity to write unto thee to inform thee that Uncle Paul received the things that thee sent him on the 26th ult., which was very acceptable, and the letter, which was more so.

Uncle Paul has greatly recovered again. His fever has left him. He is mostly free from pain but very weak. He has a moderate appetite, as much as is necessary according to his strength. He eats a little pork and it revives him. Everything that he has eaten has set extremely well with him. He take[s] no apothecary medicine except physic. He has been so very sick that he together with us did not expect to continue long. I verily thought that he would not live from one day to another for many days together. But through the goodness of God he has recovered wonderfully in about six or seven days. He sets up in the chair one hour or one hour and half three or four times in a day. For two days we have walked him across the room many times.

We feel much encouraged about him if nothing else should turn against him. But he is now attended with weakness in one of his hips. I fear that the fever is about to settle there. He has been attended with dreadful sweats, when at the same time his feet up to his knees would be in a cold chill. But now he is attended but little with these difficulties. Sister Cynthia nurses him. . . .

Wrote by request of Uncle Paul

So I remain thy cousin

DAVID CUFFE, JR.

---

[77] See footnote 10, p. 151.

Philadelphia July 14, 1817

CAPTAIN PAUL CUFFE, SIR, I received your friendly letter of the 4 mo. 23rd at the City of Washington, on my return from Virginia to this place. I thank you for the information which it contained. During my trip through Virginia I have found many ardent friends of the colonization plan, and many of them are actuated by the purest motives. They hope that the best interests of the people of this country will be promoted and also the best interests of the free people of color as well as the inhabitants of the African continent should the colony be established in Africa. It is the general wish that the place for the colony may be on the West Coast of Africa.

With respect to the disposition of the free people of color on the subject of going to Africa it is becoming more favorable. I am confident that this is the fact with the best informed of these people.

The person who wrote to you from the African Institution in this place giving our account of the meeting which was held here by the people of color and of their unanimous disposition not to go to Africa could not have been highly informed.[78] The general meeting chose a committee to give their sentiments on the subject of going to Africa. Robert Finley had a conference with eleven of the committee. He explained to them the purity of the motives which actuated many of those persons who were forward in forming the American Colonization Society. After a discussion of the subject, they gave a unanimous expression of their perfect conviction that benevolence to them and the land of their fathers guided the movements that were made at Washington, and that the hand of God was securely moving this business. They acknowledged the desirableness of being separated from the whites.

Of the eleven members of the committee present eight gave their opinions in favor of an establishment in Africa. They thought it the situation where they should have the fairest prospect of becoming a great and independent people. The decision of this committee makes known to us how the free people of color will decide on this subject when they rightly understand our object. Friend Paul, if

[78] See James Forten to Cuffe, Philadelphia, January 25, 1817, pp. 243–45.

this effort to colonize the free people of color in Africa is of God (as I believe it to be), it will prosper. But it must be done by human instrument; the days of miracles are past, the friends of this effort must pursue undeviatingly that course which we think Divine Providence marks out for them. I hope [once] proper places can be found and obtained for these people to settle on the coast of Africa they will go to them. I think it is highly desirable in the present stage of the business that you should go to Africa to Sierra Leone this fall with as many of these people as you can carry. It matters little whether those that go at this time go from Boston or south of that place. It is, I conceive, of infinite importance in order to keep awake the public feeling on this subject that more or less should go out. Perhaps should you offer to go out a greater proportion might go out as candidates than did when you went before who would be able to defray their own expenses. Perhaps were you to make known your object you might have the aid of some of your Eastern Friends or others favorable to the measure. But while you have so generously commenced this mighty effort do not value further sacrifices in order to effect it in order to bring the tone of public feeling to its proper point. We may have enemies in commencing this object, but later generations will do our memories justice. But far more than all posterity can give, we shall have approving consciences and the approbation of the God of heaven. We have reason to believe since God has the hearts of all men in his hands, that the liberal public will soon come to our aid, state legislatures, the general government will render their assistance.

I do not suppose that should the general government send out a vessel to explore the coast of Africa that it would go so far south as the Cape of Good Hope and the Tristan Islands. Probably some place or places would be selected between the Sierra Leone colony and the mouth of the Congo.

The Board of Managers of the American Colonization Society wish to have me go to Sierra Leone and to obtain all the information I can relative to a suitable place on the African coast for a colony. They wish me to go immediately. I shall most likely comply with this request if they shall be able to raise money to bear my expenses. They wish this step to be taken this season to forward this information to Congress during the next session. They think the government would be most likely to send out a national vessel to explore the coast of Africa should they secure favorable information from an agent who had been there. One of the managers of the Colonization Society lately received a letter from Mr. Clarkson (England) encouraging them to send out agents to pursue the proper territory and make the necessary purchases. Or rather he advised that the United States government should do this. I think your going to Sierra Leone with a cargo of these people would be directly constituted to induce the government to act in aid of our object. Thy going might have a like tendency—at least it would be keeping the subject before the minds of the public.

The auxiliary convention of the State of Maryland was formed at Baltimore last week, at least a constitution for such a society was adopted at a very respectable meeting of the citizens. Mr. Ward, a man of color of that place informed me that the most informed people of color in the city were thinking seriously of going to Africa. I hope you write me immediately on receiving this letter. Mr. Clarkson mentioned Sherbro, the place you refer to in your letter as the best place he knew of for a colony. He referred the Board of Managers to you for information.

With respect to obtaining a place in our new country to where those people may be settled at least more or less of them, the prospect is not at present favorable. Neither the general government or state legislatures as far as I can learn approve of such a measure. But still this plan will be kept in view; at the same time I think we should look principally to Africa until Providence opens a door elsewhere. Should I go to Africa soon I shall most likely go by way of England and expect to arrive on the coast country in December.

Your sincere friend

SAMUEL J. MILLS

Philad. July 25th 1817

DEAR AND ESTEEMED FRIEND [PAUL CUFFE]

This will inform you that your favor of 9 July came safe to hand, and I am extremely sorry to find by it that you have been dangerously ill. I likewise find that it has pleased the Almighty God, to remove from this transitory world your loving and affectionate Sister, permit me to console with you in your great loss. Still, I know that you are sensible that your loss is her gain.

I am very happy to inform you that we have at present in our city an African Prince, the grandson of King Lurker, from the coast, about 50 leagues south of Sierra Leone. He is about 8 years of age, sent from the coast to Havanna, and from there to the Abolition Society for his education. He is now in charge of Robert Douglas. He was ten days at my house. He is a fine smart promising boy. I am in hopes that his education here may be of beneficial service to the cause. It may have the tendency of opening a correspondence between King Lurker and the Society, which may result in something advantageous to the community, and that the Almighty may make him the instrument in doing great good. I will thank you to inform your nephew, Paul Wainer, that I received the amount of his note from Messrs. T. & T. Rotch, with many thanks. They wanted to pay the interest but I would not receive any more than the amnt. of the note.

The African Institution is very much concerned about the will of Samuel Giste, but they do not know what can be done with them, the blacks, at present. But I hope and pray that the time is not far distant when there will be an asylum for those poor souls to take their rest.

Charlotte is very much concerned about your not being able to write your last letter. She thinks you must be very ill indeed. John Ruthy & Rachel James all spent last third day evening with us, and all their conversation was mostly concerning you. They all desired me to remember them very particularly in my first letters to you. I will thank you should you receive any information from the African Institution of London, to please advise us of the same should you think it proper.

Permit Charlotte & myself to return you many thanks for your good wishes for us and the prosperity of our children. You must now permit us to reciprocate the same to you and yours. The members of the African Institution desires very particularly to be remembered to you, Mr. [Absalom] Jones and Mr. [Richard]

Allen, likewise. Charlotte joins me in love to you, your wife and all the family.

I remain very affectionately yours

JAMES FORTEN

Westport, September 10, 1817

DEAR SIR [James Forten]

Your favour of the 25th of July came safe to hand. My father being ill at that time was not able to answer it and since his removal I have undertaken it in his stead though an entire stranger to you.

It has pleased Almighty God to remove from this transitorial world my affectionate and venerable father after a long and severe sickness of about fourteen weeks confined to the house and most of the time to his bed. Three weeks before his departure, he was able to walk from one room to the other which gave us hopes of a speedy recovery, but howsoonever our joy turned into mourning—his indisposition again made rapid progress. We then called in an eminent physician from Rhode Island who gave great encouragement, thinking he would soon raise him, but he would always be a weakly man.

He wished the physician not to encourage, but said the Lord's will, not mine, be done. He refused his medicine, saying it was not in the power of medicine to remove the disorder, but should it please the Almighty to raise him up once more to His own honor and glory, He would do it, and said, Thy will, not mine, be done. He bore his indisposition with great fortitude and resignation in full confidence of being rewarded in an after state.

He has not been well one day since last February. Of his illness at that time, perhaps he apprised you. Since then [he] has constantly complained of his stomach and great weakness. In the morning of 27 August, he appeared to be perfectly resigned and took a solemn leave of his wife and family and near connections, and bid us a long and eternal farewell and seemed to be like a morning without a cloud. Between the hours of nine and ten, one of his old friends coming in, he spoke in a wonderful manner, saying there were many amongst us who were making high professions that had never arrived to that simplicity comparable to an infant state. Then said not many days hence you shall see the glory of God appear, adding, I do know that my works have gone beforehand to judgment.

Being asked if he would not take a little nourishment, answered, by no means, but let me pass quietly away. About six o'clock in the evening he said, I can no longer strive against nature. All is well. And said to his sister-in-law, Jane, who was attending on him, Feed my sheep and my lambs. Then, calling for some water that came from the boiling spring, he drank it through a quill. After drinking two glasses, he was strong enough to hold the tumbler and drink freely of seven glasses. From that time, he revived and partook of some nourishment which he had not done for several days.

We see the Lord is able to kill and to make alive, blessed be the name of the Lord. He described to us in a wonderful manner his view of the celestial city, saying the streets were paved with transparent glass and pearls, comparing it to apples of gold in pictures of silver, saying he longed to be gone to join with Moses and the lamb in the Eternal Song. Then his voice failed him. He had much to say to his family and friends, but his strength would not permit it. His weakness was so great that at times he was a little deranged toward the last, and the day before his departure he was very restless, often wishing to be moved. There is no doubt it is well with him and that our loss is his eternal gain. It is very gloomy since his departure. The plains that knew him shall know him no more.

I presume you will excuse the liberty I have taken in writing to you. My education has been a limited one, and I am not accustomed to writing to strangers.

My Mother sends her love to you, your wife and children, and respects to all our friends. Give my love to your wife and John James' family, particularly to his wife. Tell her I should have written, but time will not permit it. And acknowledge the present she sent by the hand of my worthy father. Hoping at some future day to visit your region should health and strength permit of it.

Paper will not permit of further additions. Must therefore stop the course of my pen after bidding you adieu.

Affectionately
RHODA CUFFE

Westport 12 September 1817

JOHN CUFFE TO FREELOVE CUFFE

Here is some accounts of the doings and sayings of our honored and much beloved brother Paul Cuffe.

The 27th of August A.D. 1817 between the hours of 8 and 9 in the morning then he took a solemn leave of his family, wife, children, grandchildren, brothers, sisters and others. Shaking hands with all, showing fellowship and friendship, bid all farewell. It was as broken a time as was most ever known amongst us and seemed too long to be unloaded to go to dwell well with angels and with the souls of just men and women in the heavens above to receive the rewards of the righteous. Between the hours of 9 and 10 one of his neighbors coming in, [Paul] said to him, friends, and others, making great professions, had kindly grown up to the stature of an infant, then said that "my works are gone to judgment aforehand." That I do know then, he said, "not many days hence you shall see the glory of God." 6 o'clock in the evening he said "all is well," and then said "feed my lambs and sheep also." And [he] said much more, but being so weak and spoke so low I could not understand so as to take the true sound.

And he also said to us all not to hold on upon him, but to give him up and let him go. I with my friends had lain very low with earnest prayers to God and his Christ that he might be restored to health again. With my tears strewn to the ground until then seeing his agon[ies], pangs and distress, I yielded up, say as St. Paul's friends did, the will of the Lord be done.

He still kept failing from day to day. Some days [he] took no nourishment at all in, nor medicine, except cold water, until first day morning at 2 o'clock in the morning 7 September A.D. 1817, then brother Paul Cuffe departed this life.

This is solemn news that will not soon be forgotten with lament not from the teeth outward but from the heart with tears in very deep.

I may say that I wept much. He died in the 59 years of his age, after three months sickness. He appeared to bear it with patience through the whole and was sensible to the last moments, and was sensible that the close drew near, and said to the nurse that he was little more than a dead man. [He said to the nurse] "let me pass quietly away," waving his hand to his attendant that would have fanned him. So he fell asleep in Jesus and is gone home to glory, where wicked men in, nor devils cannot afflict. He was a loving husband, tender father, and a kind neighbor and a faithful friend.

The time appointed [for the funeral] and [we] all met together under a great solemnity, on the second day of the week, the second hour in the afternoon. And after waiting in great silence, testimonies then being borne by friends, he was borne to the grave and decently buried. A large crowd of people of all societies [attended the rites]. I do not remember as I ever were at so large a concourse of people to any funeral before. He was buried in Friends Burying Ground, at the South Meeting House in Westport.

MS. MEMORANDUM OF RUTH CUFFE

Fall River, [Mass.] February the 12, 1851.

As nigh as I can remember, it was fifty-three years ago that I was to work at my brother-in-law's Gardener Wainer in Westport, the east side of the river, and my sister wanted me to go at the store at Russells Mills in Dartmouth and buy her some things out of the store. She told me to go to Captain Hull's store and do my trading for she had all their trading done at his store. And I went for her and when I got there, there was several men at his store. And Mr. Hull told me to take a seat and set down and wait a little while til he had waited upon them men and then he would wait upon me.

And as soon as they was gone out of the store, he asked me what my name was. I told him that my name was Ruth Cuffe. He asked me what my father's name was. I told him that my father's name was David Cuffe. Then Mr. Hull told me that my grandfather Cuffe was a slave man to his father. He told me that his father bought my grandfather Cuffe so that he should have his freedom, and his father set down the day of the month and date of the year that he bought him in and how many dollars he gave for him. And when grandfather Cuffe had worked out long enough to pay for himself, then his master Hull freed him. He gave him good wages so that he should be a free man. And as soon as he had worked long enough to pay for himself, his master gave him his freedom.

The day before he freed him, he went to a squire and had a paper wrote to give Cuffe his freedom and the next morning the squire come to Mr. Hull's and carried the paper with him. And he got there just as they was a going to set down to breakfast. And they all set down and Cuffe with them. And after had done breakfast, then the squire told Cuffe to leave his seat for he wanted to talk with him. The squire then asked him if he did want to be a free man and be his own man. He said that he wanted to be free but he had no money to buy himself and he wanted his master Hull not to sell him to no one, and when he made his will to give his children his property to fix it so that his children never should sell him for he was afraid that he would be sent away to the western gulf and put on the plantation. His master Hull told him that never should be.

The squire told Cuffe that he would be a free man in a few minutes. He then took the paper out of his pocket and read it to Cuffe. The squire told Mr. Hull to write his name on the paper, and he did. And then he told Mr. Hull's wife to write her name on the same paper and she did. Then the squire read the paper over again to Cuffe and told him he then was a free man, his own man, and he must go from there that same day. Then Cuffe cried and bedewed himself with tears. He said that he did not know what to do, and where to go he knew not, for he had no home and no money. He said that they had ought to let him known of it two or three weeks ago, then it would not been so hard to him. For then it was a rainy day, and where to go he knew not. The squire told him that he must certainly go from there that day, for that would show that he was his own free man and gone from there.

The squire told him that he would hire him and give him good wages. And he hired him right away. And his master Hull, that was, hired him the next month and gave him good wages. The squire then gave Cuffe his paper that he wrote and told him to put it into his own chest and lock it up there and take the key of his chest and put it in his pocket and keep it himself.

Then his master Hull, that had been, gave Cuffe good advice while the squire was there. He told him to live a steady life and take good care of his money that he was going to work for and save it so as to get him a home sometime or other. So Cuffe took two suits of his every day cloth with him and went away from there that same day.

This, Captain Hull told me at the time I was in his store, and, he said, about the time my grandfather Cuffe had his freedom Ruth Moses came up from Harwich. And after awhile my grandfather married her. She came into Dartmouth and worked there till she married.

And Captain Hull told me that the Slocums would not have my grandfather Cuffe's children to go by the names of Slocum. So they called them by their father's name, Cuffe. I was about seven years old when we had to go by the name of Cuffe. I remember it well.

RUTH CUFFE, *doctoress*
[midwife?]

Addenda

As nigh as I can remember, it is about fifty-five years ago that my sister, Cynthia, went to Captain Hull's house on a visit at Russells

Mills, and he told her that his father was the last master that her grandfather Cuffe had. He told her that he bought so as to free him and he did free him, for slaves was then sold at a low price for there was much talk that slaves was to all be freed. But some of them was sent away to the West Indies and sold to be put on the plantations. And he told my sister that the Slocums altered the name of Slocum of her grandfather's children and called them Cuffe after their father's name.

So I cannot write no more about it. And whether Captain Hull had been a seafaring man or not, I cannot tell, or whether he had been a Captain of a company on the land, I do not know. Captain Hull told me that he was old enough then to remember all that was done and said at the time my grandfather was freed the same day at the time he sat by and see'd his father and mother write their names on the paper to free Cuffe. All of this I wrote with my own hand.

RUTH CUFFE
doctoress

A

BRIEF ACCOUNT

OF THE

SETTLEMENT AND PRESENT SITUATION

OF

THE COLONY

OF

SIERRA LEONE,

IN AFRICA;

As communicated by Paul Cuffe. (A man of colour)
To his friend in New York: Also, An ex-
planation of the object of his visit,
and some advice to the people of
colour in the United States.

TO WHICH IS SUBJOINED

An address to the people of colour, from the Convention of Delegates from the Aboli-
tion Societies in the U. States.

NEW-YORK:
PRINTED BY SAMUEL WOOD,
No. 357, Pearl-Street,

1 8 1 2.

A Brief Account, &c.

Having been informed that there was a settlement of people of colour at Sierra Leone under the immediate guardianship of a civilized power, I have for these many years past felt a lively interest in their behalf, wishing that that inhabitants of the colony might become established in the truth, and thereby be instrumental in its promotion amongst our African brethren. It was these sentiments that first influenced me to visit my friends in this colony, and instead of repenting, I have cause to rejoice in having found many who are inclined to listen and attend to the precepts of our holy religion. Nevertheless, I am convinced that further help will be requisite to establish them in the true and vital spirit of devotion; for although there are many who are very particular in their attendance of public worship, yet I am apprehensive that the true substance is too much overlooked; and by thus mistaking the form for the substance, that their religious exercise is rendered rather a burden than a pleasure. It is not however my object to extend these observations at present. I merely wish to convey a brief account of the situation of the colony as I found it, hoping the information may prove serviceable and interesting to some of my friends in the United States.

Sierra Leone is a country on the west coast of Africa. Its situation is inviting, and its soil generally very productive. A river of the same name passes through the country, and the land for a great extent on each side is peculiarly fertile, and with the climate well calculated for the cultivation of West-India and other tropical productions. In the year 1791 an act passed the British parliament incorporating a company called the Sierra Leone Company, whose object was to settle and and cultivate these lands, and open a trade with other countries in the products of the soil. The first settlers amounted to about 200 white persons, and a number of free blacks or people of colour from North America; and their experiments in sugar, cotton, &c. soon convinced them that they would be abundantly rewarded for their labour. The promising appearance of the settlement soon attracted the attention of the neighbouring chiefs, who with their subjects generally, became very friendly. The colony is now considerably increased, and continues to be in a flourishing situation. The population at present as taken by order of Governor Columbine in the 4th mo. 1811, is as follows [p. 268]:

Besides which there are 601 Crue Men, so called from their being natives of a part called Crue Country, from which they have emigrated since the establishment of this colony.

These people have not yet been enrolled in the list of citizens, but are generally hired by the inhabitants as labourers. The disposition

	[Males]	[Females]	[Children]
Europeans, ...	22	4	2
Nova-Scotians, ...	188	295	499
Maroons, ...	165	195	447
Africans, ...	20	43	37
	395	537	985
			537
			395

Making together, ...   1917

prevails very generally to encourage new settlers who may come amongst them either for the purpose of cultivating the land, or engaging in commercial enterprise. A petition, of which the following is an outline was lately presented to his excellency governor Columbine, and signed by several of the most respectable inhabitants, viz.

1st.   That encouragement may be given to all our brethren, who may come from the British colonies or from America, in order to become farmers, or to assist us in the cultivation of our land.

2d.   That encouragement may be given to our foreign brethren who have vessels for the purpose, to establish commerce in Sierra Leone.

3d.   That those who may undertake to establish the Whale Fishery in the colony may be encouraged to persevere in that useful and laudable enterprise.

There are at this time 7 or 8 schools established throughout the colony. One of these is for the instruction of grown persons, and the others contain together about 230 children, who are instructed in all the necessary branches of education.

The inhabitants have likewise six places of public worship, which are generally well attended. Their times for meeting on the sabbath are at 5 and 10 o'clock in the morning, and at 2 and 6 o'clock in the evening. Also, the week through, many of their meetings are attended at 5 in the morning and 6 in the evening. There was also a society formed here some time since for the further promotion of the christian religion. I have met with one of their epistles, which I shall insert at the close of my communication.

An institution was formed on the 1st of the 12th mo. last for the relief of the poor and disabled. It is now regularly held [it meets] on the 1st second day in every month, at which time proper persons are appointed to take charge of those under the care of the institution. A general meeting is held once every six months. Every one can judge of the happy effect of such institutions as these in improving the dispositions and softening the manners of our native brethren.

The colonists have instituted 5 courts, consisting, first of the Court of Quarter Sessions, which is held four times in the course of the year. The governor always presides as judge, and is attended by a justice of the peace, sheriff's clerk, messengers of the bailiff and constables. The pettit jury consists of 12 men selected from the Europeans, Nova-Scotians, and Maroons.

2d. Mayor's Court. This formerly sat on the 5th day of every week; but the time for holding it has since been prolonged to every three months.

3d. The Court of Requests which is held on the 7th day of every week. The power of this court is confined to the trial of debts not exceeding two pounds. 12 men are selected for this purpose, and four of the number transact the business of a sitting.

4th. The Police Court, which is likewise held on the 7th day of every week, and is constituted of the same number of persons as the court of requests. Their business is confined to the trial of persons for disorderly conduct.

5th. The Court of Vice Admiralty, which is held as occasion may require.

The inhabitants are governed entirely by the British law, and are generally peaceable and willing to abide by the decisions of their civil magistrates. Governor Columbine lately issued a proclamation in which he offers the protection of these laws to any slave who may arrive in the colony with the consent of his or her owners, and leaves them at liberty to remain or go elsewhere, as they may think proper.

On the 18th of the 3d month, I travelled in amongst the natives of Africa. The first tribe I met with was called the Bullone Tribe. Their king, whose name is George, appeared to be very friendly. He could speak but very little English himself, but had a young man with him by the name of Peter Wilson, who had received his education in England, and appeared to be a man of very good information. This tribe, from what I could gather have adopted the mode of circumcision, and seem to acknowledge by words, the existence of a Deity. So accustomed are they to wars and slavery that I apprehend it would be a difficult task to convince them of the impropriety of these pernicious practices. I gave the king a Testament [a Christian Bible] and several other books, and let him know by the interpreter the useful records contained in these books, and the great fountain they pointed unto.

The Mendingo Tribe professes Mahometanism. I became acquainted with two men of this tribe who were apparently men of considerable learning; indeed this tribe generally, appeared to be a people of some education. Their learning appeared to be the Arabic. They do not allow spirituous liquors to be made use of in this tribe.

They have declined the practice of selling their own tribe, but notwithstanding this, they continue to sell those of other tribes, and thought it hard that the traffic in slaves should be abolished, as they were made poor in consequence thereof. As they themselves were not willing to submit to the bonds of slavery, I endeavoured to hold this out as a light to convince them of their error. But the prejudice of education had taken too firm hold of their minds to admit of much effect from reason on this subject.

ADDRESS.
To my scattered brethren and fellow countrymen at Sierra Leone.

Grace be unto you and peace be multiplied from God our Father, and from the Lord Jesus Christ, who hath begotten a lively hope in remembrance of you; and for which I desire ever to be humbled, world without end.   Amen.

DEARLY BELOVED FRIENDS AND FELLOW COUNTRYMEN,

I earnestly recommend to you the propriety of assembling yourselves together for the purpose of worshipping the Lord your God. God is a spirit, and they that worship him acceptably must worship him in spirit and in truth; in so doing you will find a living hope which will be as an anchor to the soul and a support under afflictions. In this hope, may Ethiopia stretch out her hand unto God. Come, my African brethren and fellow countrymen, let us walk together in the light of the Lord—That pure light which bringeth salvation into the world, hath appeared unto all men to profit withall. I would recommend unto all the saints, and elders, and sober people of the colony, that you adopt the mode of meeting together once every month in order to consult with each other for your mutual good. But above all things, let your meetings be owned of the Lord, for he hath told us that "where two or three are gathered together in his name, there he would be in the midst of them." And I would recommend that you keep a record of your proceedings at those meetings in order that they may be left for the benefit of the young and rising generation. In these meetings let it be your care to promote all good and laudable institutions, and by so doing you will increase both your temporal and spiritual welfare. That the Prince of Peace may be your preserver, is the sincere desire of one who wishes well to all mankind.

PAUL CUFFE.

The following advice, though detached from the foregoing address, appears to be intended to accompany it.

ADVICE.

First. That sobriety and steadfastness, with all faithfulness, be recommended that so professors may be good examples in all things; doing justly, loving mercy, and walking humbly.

Secondly. That early care be extended towards the youth, whilst their minds are young and tender, that so they may be redeemed from the corruptions of the world—such as nature is prone to—not swearing, following bad company and drinking of spirituous liquors. That they may be kept out of idleness, and encouraged to be industrious, for this is good to cultivate the mind, and may you be good examples therein yourselves.

Thirdly. May servants be encouraged to discharge their duty with faithfulness; may they be brought up to industry; may their minds be cultivated for the reception of the good seed, which is promised to all that will seek after it. I want that we should be faithful in all things, that so we may become a people, giving satisfaction to those, who have borne the heat and burden of the day, in liberating us from a state of slavery. I must leave you in the hands of him who is able to preserve you through time, and to crown you with that blessing that is prepared for all those who are faithful unto death.

Farewell, PAUL CUFFE

Copy of an epistle from the society of Sierra Leone, in Africa, to the saints and faithful brethren in Christ.

Grace be unto you and peace from God our Father and from the Lord Jesus Christ.

We desire to humble ourselves with that thankful acknowledgment to the Father and fountain of all mercies for the liberty and freedom we enjoy, and our prayer to God is that our brethren who live in distant lands and are held in bondage, and groan under the galling chain of slavery, that they may be liberated, and enjoy the liberty which God has granted unto all his faithful saints. Dearly beloved brethren in the Lord, may the power and peace of God rule in all your hearts, for we feel from an awful experience the distresses that many of our African brethren groan under. Therefore we feel our minds engaged to desire all the saints and professors in Christ, to diligently consider our cause, and to put our cause to the christian query, whether it is agreeable to the testimony of Jesus Christ for one professor to make merchandise of another. We desire that this may be made manifest to all professors of all christian denominations who have not abolished the holding of slaves.

We salute you, beloved brethren, in the Lord with sincere desire, that the work of regeneration may be more and more experienced. It would be a consolation to us to hear from the saints in distant lands; and we could receive all who are disposed to come to us with open arms.

Our dearly beloved Brethren, we also salute in the love of God, to be obedient unto your masters with prayers lifted up to God, in whom we would recommend you to confide, who is just as able in these days to deliver you from the yoke of oppression, as he hath in time past brought your fore-fathers out of the Egyptian bondage. Finally, brethren, may the power and peace of God rest in all your hearts. Grace be unto you and peace from God our Father and from the Lord Jesus Christ. Amen.

Signed by John Gordon, preacher, Warrick Francis, James Reed, Joseph Brown, Moses Wilkinson, Larsus Jones, John Ellis, Adam Jones, George Clarke, Peter Frances, George Carrell, Edward Willboughly, Thomas Richardson, senr., Eli Achim, John Stevenson, James Wise.

To the free Africans and other free people of colour
in the United States.

The convention of deputies from the abolition societies in the United States, assembled at Philadelphia, have undertaken to address you upon subjects highly interesting to your prosperity.

They wish to see you act worthily of the rank you have acquired as freemen, and thereby to do credit to yourselves, and to justify the friends and advocates of your colour in the eyes of the world.

As the result of our united reflections, we have concluded to call your attention to the following articles of advice. We trust, they are dictated by the purest regard for your welfare, for we view you as Friends and brethren.

In the first place, We earnestly recommend to you, a regular attention to the important duty of public worship; by which means you will evince gratitude to your Creator, and, at the same time, promote knowledge, union, friendship, and proper conduct amongst yourselves.

Secondly, We advise such of you, as have not been taught reading, writing, and the first principles of arithmetic, to acquire them as early as possible. Carefully attend to the instruction of your children in the same simple and useful branches of education. Cause them, likewise, early and frequently to read the holy Scriptures; they contain, among other great discoveries, the precious record the original equality of mankind, and of the obligations of universal justice and benevolence, which are derived from the relation of the human race to each other in a common Father.

Thirdly, Teach your children useful trades, or to labour with their hands in cultivating the earth. These employments are favourable to health and virtue. In the choice of masters, who are to instruct them in the above branches of business, prefer those who will work with them; by this means they will acquire habits of industry, and be better preserved from vice, than if they worked alone, or under the eye of persons less interested in their welfare. In forming contracts, for yourselves or children, with masters, it may be useful to consult such persons as are capable of giving you the best advice, who are known to be your friends, in order to prevent advantages being taken of your ignorance of the laws and customs of our country.

Fourthly, Be diligent in your respective callings, and faithful in all the relations you bear in society, whether as husbands, wives, fathers, children or hired servants. Be just in all your dealings. Be simple in your dress and furniture, and frugal in your family expenses. Thus you will act like christians as well as freemen, and, by these means, you will provide for the distresses and wants of sickness and old age.

Fifthly, Refrain from the use of spirituous liquors; the experience of many thousands of the citizens of the United States has proved, that those liquors are not necessary to lessen the fatigue of labour, nor to obviate the extremes of heat or cold; much less are they necessary to add to the innocent pleasures of society.

Sixthly, Avoid frolicking, and amusements that lead to expense and idleness; they beget habits of dissipation and vice, and thus expose you to deserved reproach amongst your white neighbours.

Seventhly, We wish to impress upon your minds the moral and religious necessity of having your marriages legally performed; also to have exact registers preserved of all the births and deaths which occur in your respective families.

Eighthly, Endeavour to lay up as much as possible of your earnings for the benefit of your children, in case you should die before they are able to maintain themselves—your money will be safest and most beneficial when laid out in lots, houses, and small farms.

Ninthly, We recommend to you, at all times and upon all occasions, to behave yourselves to all persons in a civil and respectful manner, by which you may prevent contention, and remove every just occasion of complaint. We beseech you to reflect it is by your good conduct alone, that you can refute the objections which have been made against you as rational and moral creatures, and remove many of the difficulties, which have occurred in the general emancipation of such of your brethren as are yet in bondage.

With hearts anxious for your welfare, we commend you to the guidance and protection of that Being who is able to keep you from all evil, and who is the common Father and friend of the whole family of mankind.

By order and on the behalf of the convention,

THEODORE FOSTER, *President*

Attest. THOMAS P. COPE, *Secretary*
Philadelphia, January 6th, 1796

Select Bibliography

Adams, Henry, *The Life of Albert Gallatin*. New York, 1943.

Alexander, William, *Memoir of Captain Paul Cuffee, A Man of Colour: To Which Is Subjoined The Epistle of the Society of Sierra Leone, In Africa, &c.* York, England, 1812.

Annals of the Congress of the United States, 13th Congress, 1st and 2nd Sessions.

Anonymous, ed., *A Narrative of The Early Life, Travels, and Gospel Labors of Jesse Kersey, Late of Chester County, Pennsylvania.* Philadelphia, 1851.

Anonymous, ed., *Life of William Allen With Selections From His Correspondence,* 2 vols. London, 1846–47.

Aptheker, Herbert, *A Documentary History of The Negro People in The United States,* 2 vols. New York, 1965.

Bainton, Michael, *West Africa City, A Study of Tribal Life in Freetown.* London, 1957.

Booth, Charles. *Zacharay Macaulay: His Part In The Movement For The Abolition of The Slave Trade And of Slavery.* London, 1934.

Borden, Alanson, *Our County and Its People: A Descriptive And Biographical Record of Bristol County Massachusetts.* Boston, 1899.

Briggs, Asa, *Victorian Cities.* New York, 1965.

Brown, Isaac V., *Biography of The Rev. Robert Finley, D.D.* Philadelphia, 1857.

Cadbury, Henry J., "Negro Membership in The Society of Friends," *The Journal of Negro History, XXI* (April, 1936).

Clarkson, Thomas, *An Essay on the Slavery and Commerce of the Human Species.* London, 1786.

————, *The History of the Rise, Progress and Accomplishment of the Abolition of the African Slave Trade by the British Parliament,* 2 vols. London, 1808.

Colton, Calvin, ed., *The Life, Correspondence and Speeches of Henry Clay,* 10 vols. New York, 1857.

Crisp, Stephen, *A Short History of a Long Travel from Babylon to Bethel. Written on the 9th Month, 1691.* London, 1711.

Cuffe, Paul, *A Brief Account of the Settlement and Present Situation* of the Colony of Sierra Leone in Africa as Communicated by Paul Cuffee [sic] (A Man of Colour) to His Friend in New York. New York, 1812.

————, Papers. New Bedford, Massachusetts, Free Public Library.

Curtin, Phillip D., The Image of Africa: British Ideas in Action, 1780–1850. Madison, Wis., 1964.

Donnen, Elizabeth, ed., Documents Illustrative of the History of the Slave Trade in America, 4 vols. Washington, D.C., 1935.

Drake, Thomas E., Quakers and Slavery in America. Gloucester, Mass., 1965 printing.

Elliot, Jonathan, The Debates in The Several State Conventions on The Adaption of the Federal Constitution. Philadelphia, 1901.

Fairfax, Fernando, "Plea for Liberating the Negroes Within the United States," American Museum or Universal Magazine, VIII (December, 1790).

Fitzpatrick, J. C., ed., The Writings of George Washington, 33 vols. Washington, D.C., 1931–1941.

Franklin, John Hope, From Slavery to Freedom, 3d ed. New York, 1967.

Fyfe, Christopher, History of Sierra Leone. London, 1962.

Garrison, William Lloyd, Thoughts on African Colonization, or an Impartial Exhibition of the Doctrines, Principles and Purposes of the American Colonization Society. Boston, 1832.

Greene, Lorenzo J., The Negro in Colonial New England: 1620–1776. Port Washington, N.Y., 1966.

Harris, Sheldon H., "Paul Cuffe's White Apprentice," American Neptune, XXIII (July, 1963).

Hepburn, John, The American Defense of the Christian Golden Rule. n.p., 1714.

Holme, Benjamin, An Epistle to Friends and Tender Minded People in America: Being an Exhortation of Brotherly Love to Them to Prize the Favours and Mercies Which the Lord Has Been Pleased to Extend unto Them. London, 1722.

Howard, Horatio P., A Self-Made Man, Capt. Paul Cuffee [sic]. New Bedford, Mass., 1913.

Hunt, Gaillard, ed., The Writings of James Madison, 10 vols. New York, 1900–1910.

————, "William Thornton and Negro Colonization," Proceedings of the American Antiquarian Society, new series, XXX (1920).

Isaacs, Harold R., The New World of Negro Americans. New York, 1964.

James, C. L. R., The Black Jacobins: Toussaint L'Ouverture and The San Domingo Revolution, 2d ed. New York, 1963.

Jones, Augustine, "William Rotch of Nantucket," American Friend, VIII (1901).

Jordan, Winthrop D., *White Over Black: American Attitudes Toward The Negro, 1550–1812*. Chapel Hill, N.C., 1968.

Klingberg, Frank J., *The Anti-Slavery Movement in England: A Study in English Humanitarianism*. New Haven, 1968.

Kup, A. P., *A History of Sierra Leone 1400–1787*. London, 1961.

Litwack, Leon F., *North of Slavery: The Negro in the Free States, 1790–1860*. Chicago, 1961.

Locke, Mary S., *Anti-Slavery in America: 1619–1809*. Gloucester, Mass., 1965.

Lovejoy, David S., "Samuel Hopkins: Religion, Slavery, and the Revolution," *The New England Quarterly*, XL (June, 1967).

Malone, Dumas, *Jefferson the Virginian*. Boston, 1948.

Mehlinger, Louis R., "The Attitude of the Free Negro Toward African Colonization," *The Journal of Negro History*, I (July, 1916).

Mercury (Liverpool), October 4, 11, 1811.

Metropolitan (Georgetown, Va.), August 23, 26, 1835.

Morgan, George, *The True Patrick Henry*. Philadelphia, 1907.

A Narrative of the Early Life, Travels, and Gospel Labors of Jesse Kersey, Late of Chester County, Pennsylvania. Philadelphia, 1851.

The National Intelligencer, January 11, 1814.

Nell, William C., *The Colored Patriots of the American Revolution*. Boston, 1855.

Niles Weekly Register, 1814–17.

Park, Edward H., *Memoir of the Life and Character of Samuel Hopkins*. Boston, 1854.

Patten, William, *Reminiscences of the Late Reverend Samuel Hopkins, D. D. of Newport, R.I.* Providence, 1843.

Quarles, Benjamin, *The Negro in the American Revolution*. Chapel Hill, N.C., 1961.

Redkey, Edwin S., *Black Exodus: Black Nationalist and Back to Africa Movements, 1890–1910*. New Haven, 1969.

Rhoads, Frances T., *The Friends Meeting House, Fourth and Arch Streets, Philadelphia, A Centennial Celebration*. Philadelphia, 1904.

Ricketson, Daniel, *The History of New Bedford, Bristol County, Massachusetts*. New Bedford, 1858.

Salvador, George, *Paul Cuffe, The Black Yankee, 1759–1817*. New Bedford, 1969.

Second Annual Report of the American Society for Colonizing the Free People of Colour in the United States. Washington, D.C., 1819.

Sherwood, Henry Noble, "Early Negro Deportation Projects," *The Mississippi Valley Historical Review*, II (March, 1916).

———, "The Formation of the American Colonization Society," *The Journal of Negro History*, II (July, 1917).

———, "Paul Cuffe," *The Journal of Negro History*, VIII (April, 1923).

Spring, Gardiner, *Memoir of the Rev. Samuel J. Mills.* New York, 1820.

Standard-Times (New Bedford), November 6, 1961.

Staudenraus, Peter J., *The African Colonization Movement 1816–1865.* New York, 1961.

Sunday Herald (Boston), October 29, 1961, Sec. IV.

Thompson, Mack, *Moses Brown, Reluctant Reformer.* Chapel Hill, N.C., 1962.

The Times (London), August 2, 1811.

Webb, Elizabeth, *A Letter from Elizabeth Webb to Anthony William Boehm with His Answer.* Philadelphia, 1783.

Williams, Peter, Jr., *A Discourse Delivered on the Death of Capt. Paul Cuffee* [sic], *Before the New York African Institution, in the African Methodist Episcopal Zion Church, October 21, 1817.* New York, 1817.

Index

Abolishing Society, 212, 214

Abolition Society, 258

abolitionists, 25, 27, 38, 58, 78fn., 163fn., 272-74; Cuffe's views on, 75; in England, 53, 103fn., 104fn., 105, 107fn., 165

Abrina, H.M.S., 140-41

Achim, Eli, 272

Acoaxet, Westport, 29

Adams, Henry, 58fn.

Africa—colonization projects, 13-14, 41-47, 59, 67-71, 74, 76, 196, 206, 217, 219-44 *passim,* 251-57, *see also* Sierra Leone; Westernization projects, 14, 38-41, 56, 104-5, 112, 176-78, 180, 181, 183, 206, 219-44 *passim*

African Association, 153, 162-63

African Convention, 107

African Institution, Baltimore, 60, 228

African Institution, London, 60, 78fn., 91fn., 93fn., 165, 212, 234, 258; aims, background of, 46, 49, 164, 165; Cuffe's bid for aid from, 47fn., 130, 167-169, 179, 188, 203, 206, 207, 210, 211, 218, 221, 225; help given to Cuffe, 48, 50-51, 61, 103, 175, 184; reception for Cuffe, 53-54, 94fn., 103; support of Sierra Leone, 55, 79fn., 204, 240

African Institution, New York, 60, 196fn., 199, 205, 209, 210, 214, 228, 235, 237

African Institution, Philadelphia, 60, 185fn., 196, 205, 228, 235-37, 248, 249, 255, 258

African Methodist Episcopal Church, 243fn.

"African" school, 152, 154

Aikins, Samuel C., 203, 205, 217fn.

Alexander, William, 52fn.

Allen, Joseph, 103

Allen, R. Holston, 246

Allen, Rev. Richard, 243, 244, 246, 258-59

Allen, William, 103, 127, 130fn., 210-12, 214, 218, 220; biographical data, 46, 90fn.; his concern for Sierra Leone, 46, 55, 95, 96, 175-78, 240; letters from Cuffe, 60, 65fn., 99, 105, 181-82, 187-95, 234; letters to Cuffe, 175-78, 203, 206, 215fn., 216; his encouragement of Cuffe, 48-49, 53, 55, 61-62, 64, 93, 184, 203, 206; meeting with Cuffe 90-91, 94-96, 99, 101; *Life of* (cited), 51fn., 53fn., 54fn., 55fn., 170fn.

Almy, William, 147

Alpha (sloop), 20, 61, 90, 99-101, 168, 182

American Colonization Society, 70-71, 74, 201fn., 217fn., 233fn., 251, 252, 255-57

American Neptune (periodical), 23fn., 77fn.

American Revolution, 18, 19, 42, 116fn., 120fn.

American Society for Colonizing the Free People of Color, 74

Anglican Church, 128, 242

antislavery movement, 27, 154fn.,

We desire to humble ourselves with that thankful acknowledgment to the Father and fountain of all mercies for the liberty and freedom we enjoy, and our prayer to God is that our brethren who live in distant lands and are held in bondage, and groan under the galling chain of slavery, that they may be liberated, and enjoy the liberty which God has granted unto all his faithful saints. Dearly beloved brethren in the Lord, may the power and peace of God rule in all your hearts, for we feel from an awful experience the distresses that many of our African brethren groan under. Therefore we feel our minds engaged to desire all the saints and professors in Christ, to diligently consider our cause, and to put our cause to the christian query, whether it is agreeable to the testimony of Jesus Christ for one professor to make merchandise of another. We desire that this may be made manifest to all professors of all christian denominations who have not abolished the holding of slaves.

We salute you, beloved brethren, in the Lord with sincere desire, that the work of regeneration may be more and more experienced. It would be a consolation to us to hear from the saints in distant lands; and we could receive all who are disposed to come to us with open arms.

Our dearly beloved Brethren, we also salute in the love of God, to be obedient unto your masters with prayers lifted up to God, in whom we would recommend you to confide, who is just as able in these days to deliver you from the yoke of oppression, as he hath in time past brought your fore-fathers out of the Egyptian bondage. Finally, brethren, may the power and peace of God rest in all your hearts. Grace be unto you and peace from God our Father and from the Lord Jesus Christ.   Amen.

Signed by John Gordon, preacher, Warrick Francis, James Reed, Joseph Brown, Moses Wilkinson, Larsus Jones, John Ellis, Adam Jones, George Clarke, Peter Frances, George Carrell, Edward Willboughly, Thomas Richardson, senr., Eli Achim, John Stevenson, James Wise.

To the free Africans and other free people of colour
in the United States.

The convention of deputies from the abolition societies in the United States, assembled at Philadelphia, have undertaken to address you upon subjects highly interesting to your prosperity.

They wish to see you act worthily of the rank you have acquired keep a record of your proceedings at those meetings in order that they may be left for the benefit of the young and rising generation. In these meetings let it be your care to promote all good and laudable institutions, and by so doing you will increase both your temporal and spiritual welfare. That the Prince of Peace may be your preserver, is the sincere desire of one who wishes well to all mankind.

PAUL CUFFE.

The following advice, though detached from the foregoing address, appears to be intended to accompany it.

ADVICE.

First. That sobriety and steadfastness, with all faithfulness, be recommended that so professors may be good examples in all things; doing justly, loving mercy, and walking humbly.

Secondly. That early care be extended towards the youth, whilst their minds are young and tender, that so they may be redeemed from the corruptions of the world—such as nature is prone to—not swearing, following bad company and drinking of spirituous liquors. That they may be kept out of idleness, and encouraged to be industrious, for this is good to cultivate the mind, and may you be good examples therein yourselves.

Thirdly. May servants be encouraged to discharge their duty with faithfulness; may they be brought up to industry; may their minds be cultivated for the reception of the good seed, which is promised to all that will seek after it. I want that we should be faithful in all things, that so we may become a people, giving satisfaction to those, who have borne the heat and burden of the day, in liberating us from a state of slavery. I must leave you in the hands of him who is able to preserve you through time, and to crown you with that blessing that is prepared for all those who are faithful unto death.

Farewell,   PAUL CUFFE

Copy of an epistle from the society of Sierra Leone, in Africa, to the saints and faithful brethren in Christ.

Grace be unto you and peace from God our Father and from the Lord Jesus Christ.